CONCENTRATE Q&A
PUBLIC LAW

CONCENTRATE
Q&A
PUBLIC LAW

Richard Clements

Leader of International Partnerships (Law),
Bristol Law School, University of the West of England

SECOND EDITION

OXFORD
UNIVERSITY PRESS

OXFORD

UNIVERSITY PRESS

Great Clarendon Street, Oxford, OX2 6DP,
United Kingdom

Oxford University Press is a department of the University of Oxford.
It furthers the University's objective of excellence in research, scholarship,
and education by publishing worldwide. Oxford is a registered trade mark of
Oxford University Press in the UK and in certain other countries

First edition 2016

Impression: 1

Published in the United States of America by Oxford University Press
198 Madison Avenue, New York, NY 10016, United States of America

British Library Cataloguing in Publication Data

Data available

Library of Congress Control Number: 2018949479

ISBN 978–0–19–881991–2

Printed in Great Britain by
Ashford Colour Press Ltd, Gosport, Hampshire

Contents

Editor's Acknowledgements

The brand-new Concentrate Q&A series from Oxford University Press has been developed alongside hundreds of students and lecturers from a range of universities across the UK.

I'd like to take this opportunity to thank all those law students who've filled in questionnaires, completed in-depth reviews of sample materials, attended focus groups, and provided us with the insight and feedback we needed to shape a series relevant for today's law students.

I would also like to thank the lecturers the length and breadth of the UK who have given so generously of their time by being heavily involved in our lengthy review process; their inside information gained from experience as teachers and examiners has been vital in the shaping of this new series.

You told us that you wanted a Q&A Book that:

- gives you tips to help you understand exactly what the question is asking;
- offers focused guidance on how to structure your answer and develop your arguments;
- uses clear and simple diagrams to help you see how to structure your answers at a glance;
- highlights key debates and extra points for you to add to your answers to get the highest marks;
- flags common mistakes to avoid when answering questions;
- offers detailed advice on coursework assignments as well as exams;
- provides focused reading suggestions to help you develop in-depth knowledge for when you are looking for the highest marks;
- is accompanied by a great range of online support.

We listened and we have delivered.

We are confident that because they provide exactly what you told us you need the Concentrate Q&As offer you better support and a greater chance for succeeding than any competing series.

We wish you all the best throughout your law course and in your exams and hope that these guides give you the confidence to tackle any question that you encounter, and give you the skills you need to excel during your studies and beyond.

Good luck
Carol Barber, Senior Publishing Editor

This is what you said:

'The content is exceptional; the best Q&A books that I've read.'

Wendy Chinenye Akaigwe, law student, London Metropolitan University

'Since I started using the OUP Q&A guides my grades have dramatically improved.'

Glen Sylvester, law student, Bournemouth University

'A sure-fire way to get a 1st class result.'

Naomi M., law student, Coventry University

'100% would recommend. Makes you feel like you will pass with flying colours.'

Elysia Marie Vaughan, law student, University of Hertfordshire

'Excellent. Very detailed which makes a change from the brief answers in other Q&A books . . . fantastic.'

Frances Easton, law student, University of Birmingham

This is what your lecturers said:

'Much more substantial and less superficial than competitor Q&As. Some guides are rather too simplistic but the OUP guides are much better than the norm.'

Dr Tony Harvey, Principal law lecturer, Liverpool John Moores University

'Cleverly and carefully put together. Every bit as good as one would expect from OUP; you really have cornered the market in the revision guides sector. I am also a huge fan of the OUP Concentrate series and I think that these books sit neatly alongside this.'

Alice Blythe, law lecturer, University of Bolton

'I think Q&A guides are crucial and advise my students to buy early on.'

Loretta Trickett, law lecturer, Nottingham Trent University

'Students often lack experience in writing full answers but seeing suggested answers like this provides them with confidence and structure. I will be recommending this book to my students not just for revision purposes but for the duration of the unit.'

Nick Longworth, law lecturer, Manchester Metropolitan University

Guide to the Book

Every book in the Concentrate Q&A series contains the following features:

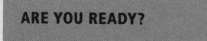
ARE YOU READY?

Are you ready to face the exam? This box at the start of each chapter identifies the key topics and cases that you need to have learned, revised, and understood before tackling the questions in each chapter.

DIAGRAM ANSWER PLANS

Not sure where to begin? Clear diagram answer plans at the start of each question help you see how to structure your answer at a glance, and take you through each point step by step.

KEY DEBATES

Demonstrating your knowledge of the crucial debates is a sure-fire way to impress examiners. These at-a-glance boxes help remind you of the key debates relevant to each topic, which you should discuss in your answers to get the highest marks.

SUGGESTED ANSWER

What makes a great answer great? Our authors show you the thought process behind their own answers, and how you can do the same in your exam. Key sentences are highlighted and advice is given on how to structure your answer well and develop your arguments.

QUESTION

Each question represents a typical essay or problem question so that you know exactly what to expect in your exam.

LOOKING FOR EXTRA MARKS?

Don't settle for a good answer—make it great! This feature gives you extra points to include in the exam if you want to gain more marks and make your answer stand out.

CAUTION!

Don't fall into any traps! This feature points out common mistakes that students make, and which you need to avoid when answering each question.

TAKING THINGS FURTHER

Really push yourself and impress your examiner by going beyond what is expected. Focused further reading suggestions allow you to develop in-depth knowledge of the subject for when you are looking for the highest marks.

Guide to the Online Resources

Every book in the Concentrate Q&A series is supported by additional online materials to aid your study and revision: www.oup.com/uk/qanda/

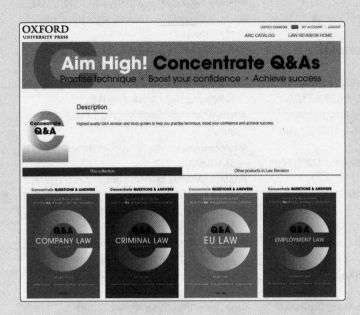

- Extra essay and problem questions.

- Bonus questions to help you practise and refine your technique. Questions are annotated, highlighting key terms and legal issues to help you plan your own answers. An indication of what your answers should cover is also provided.

- Online versions of the diagram answer plans.

- Video guidance on how to put an answer plan together.

- Flashcard glossaries of key terms.

- Audio advice on revision and exam technique from Nigel Foster.

Table of Cases

Table of Statutes

(European Convention on Human Rights Is tabled under Sch 1 of the Human Rights Act 1998)

European Legislation
Primary Legislation

Secondary Legislation
Directives

Other Jurisdictions
United States of America

Introduction

One of the things that makes Public Law different from the other subjects that you study as part of a law degree, is that it is an area where law is intertwined with politics. Public law is different from the other compulsory law subjects in that much of it is not really law at all. Some areas of Public Law are not made up of cases and statutes, but a study of how government and government officials actually do things. So, to understand Public Law properly it helps to have some knowledge of current affairs and politics. Students often think that it is unfair to expect them to know things that are not in the textbook or were not covered in the lecture, but you do need to know about the political background to this subject in order to understand it. You will find your study of Public Law very much easier, and probably more interesting, if you keep up with the current affairs of the UK, even if the UK is not your country. Public Law is a compulsory subject because of the vital importance of having an understanding of the constitution of the country, the laws of which you are studying.

One particular aspect of Public Law is the considerable overlap of topics. In reality no country's constitution operates in conveniently separated boxes. Similarly, your approach should not be to compartmentalize. You must think across topics and make the links in your answers. It will make all the difference to your understanding of and success in the subject. As the UK does not have a 'written constitution', the syllabus is accordingly very wide-ranging. Different Public Law courses will include some different topics, and syllabuses may emphasize different themes, although there is a universal core of content. In this book, we have tried to tackle the most typical topics.

Essay Questions

In answering essay questions, you must try to put forward a clear and structured argument, which leads to a conclusion. You must give reasons for the conclusions that you reach. The **PEA** (Point, Evidence, Analysis) method can be useful. Make each point carefully, back it up with evidence, analyse that evidence, and come to a conclusion. We could take as our example, Question 2 in chapter 2, *'The main purpose of constitutional conventions is to ensure that the legal framework of the Constitution will be operated in accordance with the prevailing constitutional values or principles of the period.' Discuss.* After the introductory paragraph, the answer that I have provided makes the **point** that conventions are not laws. It then examines the **evidence** by giving examples of how conventions interact with laws in the UK constitution. The **analysis** then looks at how the courts have treated conventions and their effect on the law. In the next paragraph, the argument in the essay can progress, by showing that conventions are rules, but not the same kind of rules as laws. The same kind of question can be 'hidden' in what looks like a rather dense and obscure quotation. Do not worry if you have never seen the quotation before or have never heard of the author. If you have studied and understood the subject area, the question should hold no fear. For example, a question like the following might seem intimidating, but in reality it is not hard:

The short explanation of the constitutional conventions is that they provide the flesh which clothes the dry bones of the law; they make the legal constitution work; they keep it in touch with the growth of ideas.

(Sir Ivor Jennings)

Discuss.

It is obviously about constitutional conventions! It indicates that only a small part of the constitution is law, the 'dry bones', because if we only looked at the laws we would get a very misleading impression of the constitution. The 'flesh' is conventions, which can grow and develop and make the constitution work. Give examples. In reality, this is a very similar question to the one that we actually use in chapter 2.

Problem Questions

In answering problem questions, the **IRAC** system can be used. The letters stand for Issue, Relevant Law, Application, and Conclusion. Sometimes this is called the **ILAC** system, which stands for Issue, Law, Analysis, and Conclusion. **IRAC** is better, because it reminds us that the law that we cite must be relevant to the issue raised in the problem, not just vaguely connected to the area of law being considered. We can take as our example, the first question in chapter 8, which is about a public protest. If we look at the second paragraph, we can see that the first legal **issue** raised is that there a number of demonstrators standing on the pavement. This should give you a clue from your studies of Public Order law. Obstruction of the highway is a commonly used offence in this area and this is the **relevant law**. You need to look at and **apply** the case law on this offence to the facts. Compare the facts in our problem to the facts and the legal rulings in the leading cases. Which case fits best? A **conclusion** is reached that it is unlikely that the offence has been committed. Most of the problems in this book raise several legal issues, so it is best to use **IRAC** on each issue as it arises. Do not start your answer by summarizing all the relevant law, and then later applying it to all the legal issues. Deal with legal issues as they arise in the problem, one by one. It is harder to do it this way, but much more impressive to an examiner.

    Whether you are writing an essay or a problem answer it is always best to do a rough plan first, listing the main points that you intend to cover. For a problem question, you might also include a list of the main cases. For an essay, you would need not just cases, but also authors' opinions and examples.

Preparing for Examinations

As with most things in life, it pays to be organized when revising for exams. First make sure that you have a full set of the material given out in the year or semester. This means all the lecture handouts, PowerPoint presentations, and your own notes. Students often forget about the preparation and work that they do for seminars/tutorials. This is very foolish, as lecturers design these sessions to go over the main issues in the course and often work on very similar questions to those that are going to be used in assessments, such as exams. I can never understand students who just forget about all the work that they have done on the course and go straight to a textbook for their revision. We always assess you on what we have tried to teach you during the course.

The college or university where you are studying will have different styles and lengths of examination. Old exam papers will be available, and from those you should be able to see the style of assessment. You might be able to identify a trend, as it is likely that the same important issues in Public Law will be assessed every year. It is unwise, if you want a really good mark, to question spot to the extent of learning a pre-prepared answer to a question before the exam. For example, you might be asked about parliamentary sovereignty, the question last year being about how this was affected by membership of the European Union. This year, however, the question might be about parliamentary sovereignty, disregarding the effect of EU law. Similarly, a question on a subject area might be in essay or problem form, as illustrated in this book. What you need to do is understand a topic, realize what the problem or disputed areas in that topic are, and be prepared to react to what the question is actually asking you to do. Finally, this is a topical subject, so look for examples of constitutional events in the news in the weeks leading up to the examination.

Conclusion

If you have done some work and have some basic knowledge, there is nothing to fear. Public Law is not like mathematics: there is no definitively right or wrong answer. What matters is how you get there: identifying the right topic and issues; finding the relevant law, constitutional examples or opinions; showing that you understand the material well enough to analyse it for its true meaning; and applying it to the question set.

If you are asked for your view, give it, but ensure that it is given in addition to and not instead of substantiated, objective argument. Reform crops up more and more in essay questions. Even if the entire question is devoted to 'what would you do' in reforming the UK constitution or an aspect of it, you must still give an explanation, analysis, and evaluation of what currently happens, then turn to an informed, corroborated argument for (and model of) reform. Having put forward a proper argument supported by evidence, may you then give your own *political* viewpoint? If the terms and nature of the question make it necessary or appropriate, yes. A problem question on public disorder will very likely require strict application of law to facts only, but a discursive essay question on the same topic may well seek your view. If you were asked, for example, to give an opinion upon whether the **Public Order Act 1986** unduly restricted freedom of expression and protest, you may do so, but you must put forward a reasoned argument, supported by relevant and material facts. If you are asked for an opinion on the way in which EU law has affected the traditional doctrine of the sovereignty of the UK Parliament, do not express the view that you hate all things European and that you dislike the way foreigners are taking over this country! Instead, what you should do is show that you are aware of the domestic case law, European Court of Justice case law, and EU treaty law on this subject, and, in a really good answer, that you are aware of why the law has evolved in that way.

2 Constitutions: the nature and sources of the United Kingdom constitution

ARE YOU READY?

The questions in this chapter are all essays. The first is about written and unwritten constitutions, the second about constitutional conventions, the third about the rule of law, the fourth the separation of powers, and finally, the fifth is about federalism. In order to attempt these questions, you need to have covered all of the following topics in your work and your revision:

- understanding what a constitution is and the difference between a written and unwritten constitution;
- understanding what a constitutional convention is and the important role that conventions play in the constitution of the UK;
- understanding the constitutional theory of the rule of law;
- understanding the constitutional theory of the separation of powers;
- understanding the difference between a federal and a unitary state.

KEY DEBATES

Debate: Written Constitution

The UK is one of the very few countries without a written constitution, although more and more of the constitution is being incorporated into Acts of Parliament, so in a sense it is becoming more written. Because there is no written constitution, much of the UK constitution is convention, the accepted way of doing things. Although this allows the government of the country to evolve and adapt to change, it can also lead to a lack of identifiable rules to restrain the behaviour of those in charge.

Debate: Constitutional Theories

The separation of powers is an established constitutional theory, but it only partially applies to the UK constitution. The Rule of Law is the theory most closely associated with the UK, but what does it actually mean and does it have any real role to play in how the constitution actually operates?

Debate: Federal or Unitary State

The UK is regarded as a unitary state, with ultimate power residing in the UK Parliament at Westminster. With increasing demands for more home rule and even independence in Wales and Scotland, is this still true?

QUESTION | 1

A written constitution would make a great improvement to the United Kingdom system of government.

Discuss.

CAUTION!

- First, you have to explain what a constitution is and why every country has one.
- You need to take an example of a written constitution for the purposes of comparison.
- But remember to give adequate consideration to the UK constitution, which is unwritten.
- Remember to define what written/unwritten actually means.

DIAGRAM ANSWER PLAN

> The purpose of a constitution

⬇

> Written constitutions are adopted following independence or revolution

⬇

> A written constitution may state the basic values of a country

⬇

> Written constitutions are a higher source of law, with a special amendment procedure

⬇

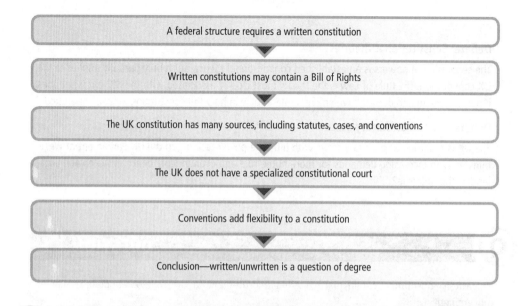

A federal structure requires a written constitution

⬇

Written constitutions may contain a Bill of Rights

⬇

The UK constitution has many sources, including statutes, cases, and conventions

⬇

The UK does not have a specialized constitutional court

Conventions add flexibility to a constitution

⬇

Conclusion—written/unwritten is a question of degree

A **SUGGESTED ANSWER**

Every organized state has a constitution, but it does not necessarily have to be a written one. Even clubs and societies have a constitution, as there have to be some rules and the members need to know who has the power to make decisions or take actions. So what is the purpose of a constitution of a nation state? A constitution grants legitimacy to the state and its government, provides for how the state is to be governed, limits the power of those who govern, and (in a liberal democracy) protects the individual citizen from them. It is there to ensure that those who run the state do not behave in an *arbitrary* manner. They must act according to the rules and procedures and not persecute or oppress the citizen. A constitution provides for these things but, just as importantly, it would also state who has the power to do what. Who can make laws, is there a Head of State, is there a Prime Minister, and who has the real power to decide?[1]

[1] Start by defining what a constitution is.

Nearly every country in the world, apart from the UK, New Zealand, and Israel, has a written constitution. Generally, countries adopt a written constitution when there is a dramatic break with the past and there is a need to make a fresh start with a new system of government. For example, the end of the eighteenth century saw the United States obtaining its independence (from the UK) and the French Revolution overthrowing the rule of King Louis XVI, each country consciously embracing a new beginning with a new, written constitution. In contrast, the UK system of government has changed gradually and there has never been such a drastic break with the past for politicians or the people to want the 'fresh start' of a new, written constitution.[2]

[2] The simple explanation why the UK does not have a written constitution.

The **Constitution of the US 1787** is generally considered a 'classic model' written constitution, starting as it does (the Preamble) with a declaration of values and principles:

We hold these truths to be self-evident, that all men are created equal, that they are endowed by their Creator with certain unalienable Rights, that among these are Life, Liberty and the pursuit of Happiness.

[3]Comparison between a written and the UK's unwritten constitution.

The UK has no such statement. Instead, writers such as Bagehot and Dicey propound our constitutional values.[3]

A written constitution often lays down a special procedure under which the constitution can be changed. For example, **Article V of the US Constitution 1787** stipulates that two-thirds of both Houses of the Congress or two-thirds of the legislatures of the states can propose amendments to the constitution. The proposed amendment then has to be ratified by the legislatures of three-quarters of the states.

[4]Comparison between a written and the UK's unwritten constitution.

In contrast, there is no special procedure to change any part of the UK constitution.[4]

The written constitution of a federal country will tend to set out the federal structure, providing for the powers of the regions (the states of the United States or provinces of Canada, for instance) and the powers of the federal (national) government. The unification of once independent countries to form a new, single, federal state is often the reason for adopting a written constitution and this occurred in the United States, Canada, Australia, Nigeria, Malaysia, and Germany, to give just a few examples. The UK, as the name suggests, is a union of once separate countries, but it is not federal. Instead, the Parliament of the UK, which sits at Westminster, retains full legislative supremacy. It has granted varying degrees of self-government to Scotland, in the **Scotland Acts 1998, 2012, and 2016**, to Northern Ireland in the **Northern Ireland Act 1998** and to Wales in the **Government of Wales Acts of 1998** and **2006**. The UK Parliament can, however, repeal those Acts and regain full powers to govern Scotland, Northern Ireland, and Wales.

[5]Comparison between a written and the UK's unwritten constitution.

There is no written constitution to stop the sovereign Parliament of the UK from doing this.[5]

Many written constitutions contain a list of rights to which the citizen is entitled. Often, as in the United States and Germany, they are constitutionally protected and cannot easily be taken away by the Executive or Legislature. The UK has a **Bill of Rights from 1689**, but that was designed more to reduce the power of the king rather than to grant rights to his subjects. The **Human Rights Act 1998 (HRA 1998)** now gives domestic force to most of the **European Convention on Human Rights 1950 (ECHR)**. **Section 3 HRA 1998**, however, carefully preserves the supremacy of Parliament.

[6] Comparison between a written and the UK's unwritten constitution.

UK courts cannot 'strike down' (judicially review) primary legislation, even if it is incompatible with human rights, and Acts of Parliament can still restrict human rights.[6]

Most written constitutions contain some sort of 'organization chart' of government and explain whether there is a President or Prime Minister, or both, and what their powers are, who has the power to legislate, who appoints the judges, and so on. There is no equivalent in the UK, as the system of government has just evolved over the centuries. The UK Head of State is the monarch, which is a matter of ancient common law, and there is no law that says that there has to be a Prime Minister.[7]

[7] Special feature of the UK's unwritten constitution.

The UK constitution is to be found in many sources. Acts of Parliament are important and many are of constitutional significance, for example the **Act of Settlement 1700** and the **European Communities Act 1972**. More and more of the UK constitution is now found in Acts of Parliament. These can be very important changes, for example the **HRA 1998**, which makes human rights directly enforceable in UK courts for the first time, and the **Constitutional Reform Act 2005 (CRA 2005)**, which strengthens the separation of powers. This indicates that nothing is permanent in the UK constitution; everything may change. For example, the **European Communities Act 1972** is about to be repealed by the European Union (Withdrawal) Bill 2017–19.

Case law also constitutes an important source of the UK constitution. For example, the House of Lords reaffirmed the principle of the supremacy of Parliament in *Pickin v BRB* **[1974] AC 765**, but a few years later had to moderate it, to take account of membership of the European Union, in *Factortame (No. 2)* **[1991] 1 AC 603**. Unlike many of the countries with a written constitution, the UK does not have a distinct Constitutional Court that rules on constitutional issues. The Supreme Court, established under the **CRA 2005**, deals with all types of law not just constitutional issues and lacks the power of the US Supreme Court to, for example, strike down unconstitutional legislation. All legal cases, constitutional or not, go through the same court system in the UK.[8]

[8] Special feature of the UK's unwritten constitution.

Historic documents such as the **Magna Carta 1215** and the **Bill of Rights 1689** are important for establishing constitutional principles—for instance, that the king or Executive does not have unlimited power—but these documents do not have the special, formal legal status of a written constitution.

A lot of the UK constitution is not law at all and consists of constitutional conventions, which were defined by A.V. Dicey in his *Introduction to the Study of the Law of the Constitution* (Macmillan 1885) as, 'understandings, habits or practices' which regulate how members of the government behave. Much of the most important parts of the constitution can be found in convention, such as the

[9] Special feature of the UK's unwritten constitution.

office of Prime Minister, the Cabinet, ministerial responsibility, and how the considerable legal powers of the Queen are exercised by ministers in her name.[9] As constitutional conventions are not law, they are not legally enforceable (***Attorney-General v Jonathan Cape Ltd* [1976] QB 752**), and whilst in one sense they are constant, they may also be said to be constantly changing. That case referred to the well-known convention of collective responsibility, but in January 2016, Prime Minister Cameron suspended it, leaving Cabinet ministers free to campaign for both sides in the EU referendum.

This is supposed to be the major advantage of an unwritten constitution: its flexibility and its ability to evolve. By contrast, it can be difficult to change a written constitution. On the other hand, if everything can change, as it can with the UK constitution, then the protection of individual liberties is less strong. Also, without a written constitution, the citizen, and even the politician, may find it more difficult to discover the true constitutional position.

Some think that Prime Ministers and the governments that they lead have too much power and can take away any right by simply using Parliament to pass an Act or by merely changing a convention. However, even in countries with written constitutions, that document is unlikely to reveal the full constitutional position. For instance, in the United States, the power of the Supreme Court to strike down legislation for 'unconstitutionality' is not found in the written constitution but instead in a case, ***Marbury v Madison* [1803] 1 Cranch 137**.

[10]Written and unwritten constitutions have been compared, but they are not so different.

The difference between a written and an unwritten constitution is not as great as some suppose.[10] It is not possible to write down everything in a document that will be valid for all time. Much of the UK constitution is in Acts of Parliament anyway and that is increasingly the position today. Every country has different constitutional arrangements and those of the UK just reflect its individual history of being one of the oldest unified states in the world.

➕ LOOKING FOR EXTRA MARKS?

■ You might have knowledge of the constitution of another country. Use that knowledge in your answer.

■ More and more of the UK constitution is becoming written—given statutory form. Give examples of this.

■ There are always debates about giving the UK a written constitution. Study those debates.

QUESTION | **2**

The main purpose of constitutional conventions is to ensure that the legal framework of the Constitution will be operated in accordance with the prevailing constitutional values or principles of the period.

*(**Re Amendment of the Constitution of Canada** [1982] 125 DLR (3d) 1)*

Discuss.

CAUTION!

- Be very clear what is law and what is convention.

- 'Convention' can also mean an international treaty. Do not confuse this with a constitutional convention.

- Be sure to put some examples of conventions in your answer.

DIAGRAM ANSWER PLAN

> Conventions are understandings, habits, or practices governing the conduct of ministers

▼

> Conventions are not laws and therefore not enforceable by the courts

▼

> Conventions may contradict the strict legal position

▼

> Identification of a convention

▼

> Conventions distinguished from law

▼

> Conventions are enforced by peer pressure, public opinion, or personal morality

▼

> Conclusion—conventions allow the constitution to change

SUGGESTED ANSWER

In all constitutions, even those that are written, like that of Canada, various practices or ways of doing things that are not strictly provided for in the constitution develop over the years. These practices can harden and become the accepted way of doing things. Then they may be called conventions. In *Re Canada*, although the written Canadian constitution did not require it, it was the convention that the consent of the Canadian provinces be obtained before changes were made to the constitution.[1]

¹If you know about the source of a quotation, use that knowledge.

In the UK, a country without a written constitution, conventions are particularly important. In the late nineteenth century, A.V. Dicey drew attention to the role of conventions in the UK. He believed that most of the UK constitution and many of its most important parts consisted of conventions. This did not mean that there were no rules, merely that a lot of the rules were not laws. As he put it in *Introduction to the Study of the Law of the Constitution* (Macmillan 1885), conventions were 'understandings, habits or practices' or 'constitutional morality' regulating the conduct of ministers and their officials. They were not laws, because the courts could not enforce them.

If one looks only at the legal rules of the constitution, this gives a significantly misleading impression. Legally, the Queen may refuse the Royal Assent to a parliamentary bill. However, by convention she always agrees, taking the advice of Her Majesty's Government. As a matter of law, the Queen chooses the Prime Minister, but by convention it is always the person who can command a majority in the House of Commons. By law the Queen chooses her own ministers, but by convention they are chosen by the Prime Minister.[2]

²Give examples of laws distinguished from conventions.

Conventions are clearly not the law because, as in the earlier examples, they sometimes contradict the strict legal position. The courts take judicial notice of conventions and in considering them, where relevant to the case decision, they may influence that decision, but the courts cannot enforce conventions because they are not law. In *Attorney-General v Jonathan Cape* **[1976] QB 752**, there is an interesting discussion of the various conventions relating to Cabinet secrecy, but the court could not enforce them, only the *law*, breach of confidence.

There are many examples of convention. The office of Prime Minister and the existence of the Cabinet are conventional only. Ministers are accountable to Parliament and responsible for the actions of their civil servants, by convention. Significant parts of the Ministerial Code reflect and flesh out conventional behaviour; although the Code is written down, it is not legally enforceable. Conventionally, Parliament meets every year, though the **Bill of Rights 1689** says only that it should meet 'frequently'.

Conventions do not just affect politicians and the monarch, they apply also to the judges, to councillors, and to all involved in the workings of the constitution. So, for example, it is a convention that judges do not involve themselves in party politics.[3]

[3] You must give plenty of examples of conventions.

One of the difficulties with conventions is identifying one. It can be hard to differentiate between what is convention and what is merely the everyday behaviour of, for example, politicians. Whereas some, such as Dicey, saw conventions as *describing* what happens, others consider conventions to *prescribe* acceptable conduct.[4] In *The Law and the Constitution* (Macmillan 1959), Jennings recommended a three-stage test. First, what are the precedents; how often and how consistently has this practice been observed before? Secondly, did the actors in the precedent believe themselves to be bound by the rule, obliged to follow the precedent? Thirdly, there must be a reason for the rule. In other words, the convention must fit in with the perceived notion of what should be done and how, according to the accepted principles or values of the constitution, such as democracy or ac-countability. This test works well with some of the major conventions, for example the convention that Royal Assent is always given. The precedents are very strong, no monarch having refused since 1708. It seems clear that the present Queen considers herself bound by the convention, having strictly followed the precedent throughout her 60-year reign. The principal reason for the rule is that a hereditary monarch should abide by the wishes of the democratic government; it would be unacceptable for an unelected monarch to interfere. Whilst the convention regulating Royal Assent is a strong, well-established example of the Jennings test, it is not so clear-cut with some others, such as when a minister should resign, and this to some gives rise to doubts about conventions generally.

[4] The key question is whether conventions are *rules.*

Conventions are continually changing. Up until 1902, a Prime Minister could come from the House of Lords or Commons. Since then they have always had to be members of the Commons, the elected chamber. In 2011, the then, Coalition Government accepted that the House of Commons should debate the matter before UK troops were deployed abroad. By 2016, a different, Conservative Government, stated this did not apply as troops might need to be deployed in an emergency. So is there a convention of parliamentary approval or not? Conventions may evolve over time, leading to uncertainty over what is the exact constitu-tional position. For example, in 1975 Prime Minister Wilson suspended the convention of collective responsibility, so that ministers could cam-paign for both 'In' and 'Out' votes in the EU referendum. In 2016, Prime Minister Cameron did the same. Is this an emerging convention or just an attempt to hold a divided party together? Conventions are called rules, but they do not look much like rules. They are often vague. In contrast with laws, there is no body or designated procedure for making a convention. In many cases, despite the efforts of writers like Jennings, it is hard to say whether a convention exists or not.[5]

[5]Conventions do not look much like rules.

Even if existence and breach of convention are established in a given situation, there may still be difficulty in enforcement. In court, if a law is broken a binding penalty can follow. But what if, for example, a minister is revealed to have lied to Parliament in clear breach of convention? Whereas the minister may choose to resign or be forced by the Prime Minister to resign, this is not necessarily the case. Whilst Foreign Secretary Lord Carrington and his ministerial team resigned as a matter of honour in 1982 following the Argentinean invasion of the Falklands, such proactive conduct is rare.[6] If one traces through the many ministerial 'lapses in conduct' of the 1990s and 2000s, many were seen to cling to office and try to ride out the media scrutiny and political pressure, usually supported by the Prime Minster of the time. The major apologists for conventions had their solutions. Dicey states that if a convention were to be broken, it would cause legal problems. His example was that if Parliament did not meet every year the budget could not be authorized, nor could a standing army, both legal necessities. It is hard to see how this could apply to some conventions, for instance ministerial responsibility. Jennings believed that conventions had to be obeyed because 'the system' would break down if they were not, and 'political difficulties' would arise. If the Queen refused her Royal Assent there would be a crisis, as indeed there could be if the Prime Minister tried to govern without a Commons' majority. But there would be no crisis if an unimportant minister declined to resign.[7]

[6]Examples of ministerial resignations are useful for this essay.

[7]Rules can be enforced, but can a convention be enforced?

Re Canada considered the sanctions available. In extreme cases of unconventional behaviour a constitutional superior can dismiss the guilty person. In 1975, the Prime Minister of Australia was dismissed by the Governor-General for trying to govern without an approved budget. Prime Ministers sometimes dismiss erring ministers. The real enforcement, though, is reflected in the quotation in the question. Conventions merely reflect 'the prevailing constitutional values or principles of the period'. This recognizes that conventions change over time. It would now be utterly unacceptable for the Queen actively to rule the UK or for an unelected peer to lead the government. It also means that constitutional 'rules' are not like legal rules. As Dicey suggested, conventions are more like moral rules. Politicians, judges, and others refrain from breaking conventions because they accept the rule in terms of right and wrong behaviour, or perhaps because they fear the disapproval of their peers or the public. As with any moral rule, there are genuine disagreements as to what the rules are, and some rules are considered more important than others. There are strong ('normative') conventions such as those that surround the role of the Queen. These will seldom, if ever, be broken. In contrast, there are weak ('simple') conventions; for example, individual ministerial responsibility, perhaps more honoured in the breach than the observance.[8]

[8] Conventions are rules, but they are not like legal rules.

The UK system, heavily reliant on conventions, is able to accommodate enormous constitutional change without the need for a revolution or new constitution. That the Queen no longer governs is just one example. The weakness is that the evolution of the constitution cannot be halted and government may be tempted by the lack of *legal* restraint to take more power for itself.[9]

[9] Conventions have their advantages and disadvantages.

LOOKING FOR EXTRA MARKS?

- This answer argues that conventions are a good feature of the UK constitution. You could argue the opposite.
- Look into some of the theoretical writing about constitutional conventions.
- Study the media for recent examples, for instance ministerial resignations.

QUESTION | 3

Insofar as Dicey's general statement of the rule of law may be taken to involve the existence in the English constitution of certain principles almost amounting to fundamental laws, his doctrine is logically inconsistent with the legislative supremacy of Parliament.

Discuss.

CAUTION!

- There are many versions of the rule of law theory, but the question asks about the Dicey version.
- The question makes a specific criticism, that this version of the theory conflicts with the supremacy of Parliament.
- Concentrate on the rule of law, not other aspects of the constitution.
- Do not confuse the rule of law with the separation of powers.

DIAGRAM ANSWER PLAN

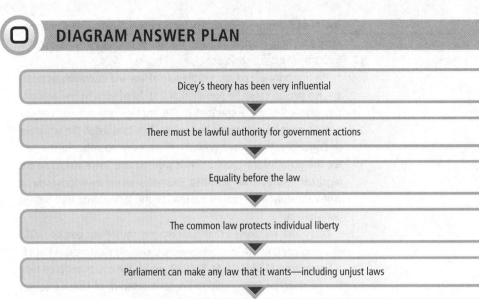

Dicey's theory has been very influential

▼

There must be lawful authority for government actions

▼

Equality before the law

▼

The common law protects individual liberty

▼

Parliament can make any law that it wants—including unjust laws

▼

The judiciary seek to control the impact of unjust laws

▼

Conclusion

SUGGESTED ANSWER

The idea of the rule of law was not invented by Dicey, but he popularized it in the late nineteenth century. His book, *Introduction to the Study of the Law of the Constitution* (Macmillan 1885), can be seen as a strong defence of the English constitution when compared with the constitutions of other countries, particularly those with written constitutions. De Smith states:

His ideas . . . were very influential for two generations; today they no longer warrant detailed analysis.

Constitutional and Administrative Law (Penguin 1998)

It is true that Dicey's ideas went out of fashion for a time, but they have now come back into favour, particularly with senior members of the Judiciary. Indeed, they are now specifically mentioned in sections of the **Constitutional Reform Act 2005.** So, once again, these ideas demand detailed analysis.[1]

[1]Introduction—the rule of law is still important.

It is often said that the UK has an 'unwritten constitution', meaning that it is not codified and much of it has no formal legal status. Dicey argued that far from being a concern, this presented positive advantage. In the UK there was a long tradition of respect for individual liberty and democracy, upheld in the country's constitutional arrangements. In short, it could be called the rule of law. Dicey summarized it under three main principles.[2]

His first principle concerned the rule of law and discretionary powers. No person could be punished or interfered with by the authorities unless the law authorized it. Put another way, all government actions must be authorized by the law. This contrasted the situation in England with a country where there were no rules. In the latter, the government could do as it pleased and there would be no legal controls over its activities. Examples would be imprisonment when someone had broken no law, or the lack of any trial before punishment.

Dicey also considered that governments should not possess wide discretionary powers. These ideas were classically illustrated in *Entick v Carrington* **(1765) 19 St Tr 1030**, where the courts declared that the Secretary of State could not order the search of Entick's house, because there was no law authorizing such searches. The court would not accept arguments of 'state necessity' or that there was one law for government activities and another for ordinary people.

Dicey's second principle has the resounding title of 'equality before the law', namely that the government and its officials should not have any special exemptions or protections from the law. He did not like the French *droit administratif* system, where government activities were dealt with by separate administrative courts. These he considered to be too partial to the government, and inferior to ordinary courts of law.

The final principle concerns individual rights. The English constitution respects personal liberty. There is no need for a bill of rights because civil liberties are respected anyway. The courts protect them in their decisions by developing the common law in a way that respects individual liberty. Parliament legislates on particular problems. In contrast, bills of rights are documents that promise all sorts of rights. These promises are so general and capable of so many meanings that they are meaningless. Also, the bill of rights might not be respected by the government and might be unenforceable.

Dicey's theory is open to many objections, some applicable even when he wrote it.[3] Some might say that his ideas are so vague and wide-ranging that they have no real meaning. Others might say that Dicey's theory is so obvious that it is not worth stating it. Of course, the government must obey the law and the courts enforce it in a modern constitutional system. Dicey misunderstood French administrative courts. They are not biased in favour of the government and they do at least as well, if not better, in controlling the government as the 'English' courts. Separate public law or constitutional courts are the

[4] Public Law published a one-hundredth anniversary edition about Dicey's rule of law.

normal arrangement in continental Europe. E. Barendt ([1985] Public Law 596) argues that Dicey also misunderstood the nature of written constitutions.[4] Although in 1885 bills of rights might just have been pious declarations that no one could enforce, nowadays most countries that have them possess sophisticated enforcement mechanisms.

The main criticism of Dicey's view of the rule of law is that it fails to deal with the supremacy of Parliament, his other favourite theory. The sovereignty (or supremacy) of the UK Parliament means that, at least in theory, it may pass whatever laws it wishes. If Parliament legislates in a way that is contrary to the principles of the rule of law, it is still

[5] This case is a well-known example of Parliament's ability to disregard the rule of law.

the law and there is nothing that the courts can do about it. For example, statutes can effectively annul inconvenient court decisions, as with the **War Damage Act 1965**, which reversed with retrospective effect *Burmah Oil v Lord Advocate* **[1965] AC 75**, where the House of Lords had ordered the government to pay compensation to Burmah Oil for the wartime destruction of its oil installations.[5] Statutes also grant government officials some immunity from legal action, for instance the **Crown Proceedings Act 1947**. Some Acts of Parliament grant the government wide and uncontrolled discretionary powers, such as much of its twenty-first-century counter-terrorism legislation. Dicey claimed that Parliament would restrain the government. Perhaps that was true in 1885, but nowadays a government may effectively control Parliament if it has a Commons majority.

A key element of Dicey's rule of law was that the government must possess clearly defined legal powers to authorize its actions.

[6] Although Dicey is the main focus of this essay, referring to other authors is desirable.

This aspect of the rule of law was emphasized by a later writer, Joseph Raz. The law must be clear and published, so that the citizen knows what is permitted and what is not.[6] Under the UK's unwritten constitution, it is in fact difficult to be precise about the legal powers that government possesses. Prerogative powers can be ill-defined, as in *R v Home Secretary ex parte Northumbria Police Authority* **[1988] 1 All ER 556**, where the court accepted the existence of a prerogative power, to maintain peace in the realm, which had not previously been identified. Also, much of the constitution is convention, not law; for example, the powers of the Prime Minister. As they are not law, the courts cannot control these powers. Indeed, there must be some doubts about whether the courts are always keen to ensure that the government keeps within its legal powers. In *Malone v Metropolitan Police Commissioner* **[1979] Ch 344**, Malone's telephone had been 'tapped' by the police. He claimed that there was no law that authorized telephone tapping. These facts have strong

[7] Did judges still regard the rule of law as an important principle?

similarities to *Entick*. However, in *Malone* the domestic court came to the opposite conclusion: no law forbade telephone tapping by the police, therefore it must be legal.[7]

Perhaps Dicey never intended his rule of law as an accurate description of the 'English' constitution. Perhaps he was just trying to say that this is the way it should be, not the way it actually was. These were the ideals that government, administrators, and judges should endeavour to uphold.

The significant growth in judicial review since the 1980s has subjected ministerial action to the check of the rule of law and has imposed a restraining influence on excess, notably in areas such as counter-terrorism measures. The rule of law has attracted the attention of many senior judges. In *M v Home Office* [1994] 1 AC 377 the House of Lords confirmed the rule of law in its basic meaning.[8] The government must obey the law. It had no immunity from court orders and government ministers could be held liable for contempt.

[8] Judges regard the rule of law as important.

Although Dicey disagreed with the idea of a bill of rights, the **Human Rights Act 1998 (HRA 1998)** has increased interest in, and perhaps the standing of, the rule of law. Many of the Articles of the **European Convention on Human Rights 1950**, now domestically enforceable under **HRA 1998**, embody values similar to those espoused in the rule of law. For example, detention without trial was disapproved of by Dicey and potentially breaches **Articles 5** (liberty of the person) and **6** (fair trial).[9] It was considered by the House of Lords in *A v Home Secretary* [2005] 2 AC 68, which concerned the detention without trial of foreign nationals who were suspected of terrorism. The Lords held that this was contrary to human rights on the narrow ground of unjustifiable racial discrimination: UK nationals were just as likely to be suspected of terrorism. Lord Bingham (at 113) quoted Professor Lauterpacht:

[9] Human rights has similarities to the rule of law.

The claim to equality before the law is in a substantial sense the most fundamental of the rights of man.

Equality before the law was, of course, one of the main elements of Dicey's theory. In the follow-up case, *A v Home Secretary (No. 2)* [2006] 1 All ER 575, the House of Lords rejected the use of evidence obtained by torture, not just because it was forbidden by various international human rights conventions but because it was contrary to the common law traditions of this country. That is just the sort of argument that Dicey would have used.

[10] Conclusion—judges will uphold the rule of law.

Parliament may sometimes fall from its highest standards and pass laws contrary to the rule of law, as seen earlier in some counter-terrorism legislation, but the judges will attempt to uphold the rule of law, as far as possible within the supremacy of Parliament.[10]

+ LOOKING FOR EXTRA MARKS?

■ Although the question requires you to concentrate on Dicey's theory, your conclusion could be comparison with another version of the theory.

■ Judges often talk about the rule of law. Find some other cases.

■ Lord Bingham writes interestingly on the rule of law.

Q QUESTION | 4

Explain what is meant by the 'separation of powers'. To what extent is it an important element in the constitutional arrangements of the UK?

! CAUTION!

■ The United States makes a useful comparison, but you must concentrate on how separation works in the UK.

■ Do not confuse the theory of the separation of powers with the theory of the rule of law.

■ The simplest way to answer this question is to use Montesquieu's version of this theory.

DIAGRAM ANSWER PLAN

The popular version of this theory is by Montesquieu

▼

The constitution of the United States is a good example of separation

▼

The Executive or law-applying function administers and implements the law

▼

The Legislative or law-making function make the law

▼

The Judicial or law-enforcing function interprets, applies, and enforces the law

▼

In the UK, the Executive and Legislature are fused

▼

The Judiciary are separate and independent

▼

Conclusion—the judiciary helps to control executive power

A   SUGGESTED ANSWER

The separation of powers is an ancient and very simple idea: that government power should not be concentrated in the hands of one person or body, otherwise tyranny results. Ancient Greeks, such as Aristotle in his *Politics*, first propounded a version of this theory, but the most famous version is that put forward by Montesquieu in *The Spirit of the Laws* (Cambridge University Press 1748). Montesquieu described three functions of government: the Legislative or law-making function, enacting rules for society; the Executive or law-applying function, covering actions taken to maintain or implement the law, defend the state, conduct external affairs, and administer internal policies; and finally the Judicial or law-enforcing function, which is the determining of civil disputes and the punishing of criminals by deciding issues of fact and applying the law. His view was that:

[1] This quotation is short and easy to remember.

There would be an end to everything, if the same man, or the same body . . . were to exercise those three powers.[1]

This can be interpreted in several ways, but most likely he meant that the three functions should be carried out by separate organs of state and that each organ should only carry out its own function. For instance, the Legislature should not judge and the Executive should not make laws. The Legislative, Executive, and Judicial branches should have equal status so each could control the excessive use of power by another branch.

This theory was adopted and developed by James Madison and incorporated into the **Constitution of the United States 1787**, which still remains a classic example of an attempt to implement the separation of powers. **Article I** declares 'All legislative power herein granted shall be vested in a Congress of the United States', **Article II** that 'The executive power shall be invested in a President of the United States', and **Article III** that 'The judicial power of the United States shall be invested in one Supreme Court and inferior courts as the Congress may from time to time ordain and establish.'[2]

[2] The US Constitution is often used as an example of the separation of powers.

In the United States, the President is not a member of Congress; elections for the Presidency and for Congress are separate. There is also an elaborate system of checks and balances between the three branches of state. For example, under **Article I, Section 7** the President may in effect veto legislation passed by the Congress if at least one-third of either House of Congress agrees with him. The Supreme Court has the power to declare the acts of both the President or Congress unconstitutional and illegal, but this power is not found in the written constitution, but in case law: *Marbury v Madison* **(1803) 1 Cranch 137.**[3]

[3] Separation involves each branch of government checking on the other branches.

The constitution of the UK is nothing like this, in that there is no written constitutional document setting out a formal separation of powers. Historically, the king and his *Curia Regis* embraced all three branches of government. Even today, formally, the Queen still appoints all government ministers and all members of the Judiciary, she summons Parliament and must give the Royal Assent to bills before they become law. The Executive is part of the Legislature in that government ministers must be members of one of the Houses of Parliament.[4]

[4] This is why the Montesquieu's theory cannot work in the UK.

This has led many constitutional commentators to dismiss the relevance of the theory of the separation of powers to the UK constitution. Instead they have concentrated on 'checks and balances', such as ministerial accountability to Parliament. More recently, some writers, such as C. Munro (*Studies in Constitutional Law* (2nd edn, Butterworths 1999)), have tried to reinterpret these 'checks and balances' as a UK version of the separation of powers. Many senior judges have echoed this, as we shall see.

It is argued that although all members of the Executive, government ministers, are also members of the Legislature, these two groups are not identical. There are around 100 government ministers, but they are greatly outnumbered by 'ordinary' members of the Legislature amongst the 650 MPs and 798 peers. The Executive does not have complete control over the Legislature, as even MPs of the governing party do not always do as they are told. The Legislature can also hold the Executive to account by means of debate, oral and written questions, and the system of select committees.[5]

[5] This is sometimes regarded as the UK's version of the separation of powers.

The personnel of the Legislature and the Judiciary are also largely separate. Under **Schedule 1 to the House of Commons Disqualification Act 1975**, judges cannot be members of the House of Commons; and the **Constitutional Reform Act 2005 (CRA 2005)** ended the judicial function of the House of Lords, replacing it with a new, separate UK Supreme Court in 2009.[6]

[6] The **CRA 2005** strengthens the separation of powers in the UK.

The office of Lord Chancellor, once a classical illustration of fusion of power, has been reformed by the **CRA 2005** so as to enhance judicial independence and separation of powers between the Judiciary and Legislature. The Lord Chancellor is still a Cabinet minister but no longer a judge, head of the Judiciary or 'Speaker' of the legislative

House of Lords. It is no longer the convention that the Lord Chancellor need have any legal experience or qualification. Although the current Lord Chancellor, David Gauke, is a solicitor, he is the first legally qualified Minister of Justice since 2012. The Prime Minister used to appoint judges, but under the **CRA 2005** judges are now selected by a Judicial Appointments Commission; the Lord Chancellor must appoint on the recommendation of the Commission, although he does not have to accept their first choice.

The Legislature cannot tell the Judiciary how to decide a case and in order to protect judicial independence it is extremely hard for the Legislature to dismiss a judge from office. Under **s 133 CRA 2005**, judges of the High Court and above hold office 'during good behaviour' but may be removed on an address by both Houses of Parliament. Thus a judge cannot be removed because a politician does not like her decision in a case.

The courts accept the supremacy of Parliament, that Parliament can make any law that it wants, but insist that they have the right to interpret its meaning. As Lord Diplock put it in **Duport Steel v Sirs [1980] 1 All ER 529** at 541:

It cannot be too strongly emphasised that the British constitution, though largely unwritten, is firmly based on the separation of powers: Parliament makes the laws, the judiciary interprets them.

The Judiciary are strong upholders of the separation of powers, as for instance in **R v Secretary of State for the Home Department ex parte Fire Brigades Unions [1995] 2 AC 513**, where the Law Lords refused to allow the Executive to ignore the legislative will of Parliament. As Lord Mustill explained, Parliament, the Executive, and the courts each have their distinctive roles. Parliament can make any law that it wants, the Executive governs according to those laws and the courts interpret those laws and see that they are obeyed.[7] Similarly, in **R (Miller) v Secretary of State for Exiting the European Union [2017] UKSC 5**, the Supreme Court insisted that leaving the EU required legislation from Parliament, as the **European Communities Act 1972** would have to be repealed, removing some rights of UK residents.

Despite these arguments that there is a form of the separation of powers operating in the UK constitution, it has to be reiterated that this is not a formal separation as suggested by Montesquieu or as found in the United States. Since the **Human Rights Act 1998** came into force in 2000 this has caused problems. **Article 6** provides the right to a fair trial, including a hearing 'by an independent and impartial tribunal established by law'. This led the House of Lords to rule in **R (Anderson) v Home Secretary [2003] 1 AC 837** that the Home

[7] Judges are independent and separate in the UK.

Secretary should not play a part in setting the minimum custodial tariff to be served by a murderer as this was an aspect of sentencing, a job for the Judiciary and not the Executive.

Section 3 CRA 2005 gives the first statutory guarantee of judicial independence. The Lord Chancellor and other ministers of the Crown 'must uphold the continued independence of the Judiciary' and 'must not seek to influence particular judicial decisions through any special access to the Judiciary'. So it can be seen that the UK is becoming more concerned about the lack of a formal separation of powers in its constitution and has taken significant steps in recent times to enhance it, especially judicial independence. A full separation of powers looks unlikely, however, as this would be a radical departure from the tradition of parliamentary democracy: the Legislature would have to be separate from the Executive, precipitating a totally different way of electing a government, selecting a Prime Minister, and holding government to account. Such radical change does not seem likely.[8]

[8] The separation of powers cannot be complete in the UK.

LOOKING FOR EXTRA MARKS?

- If you have knowledge of the separation of powers in the constitution of another country, use that knowledge.
- Try to consider other versions of the separation of powers theory.
- Look for other cases where separation of powers is discussed.

QUESTION | 5

The United Kingdom is becoming a more federal country.

Discuss.

CAUTION!

- The UK is not usually thought of as a federal state, but think about what 'federal' means.
- Be clear on the structure of the UK, but do not get bogged down in detail.
- You can agree or disagree with the statement, but give your reasons, backed up with knowledge of the UK constitution.

DIAGRAM ANSWER PLAN

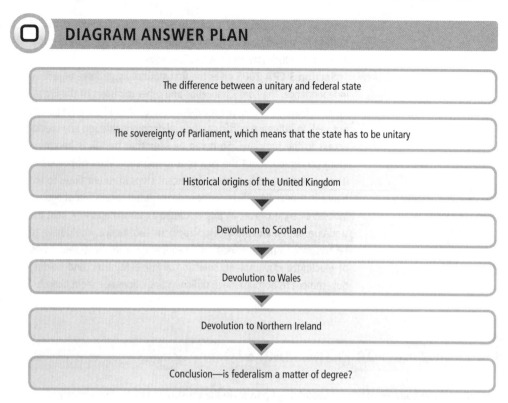

The difference between a unitary and federal state

The sovereignty of Parliament, which means that the state has to be unitary

Historical origins of the United Kingdom

Devolution to Scotland

Devolution to Wales

Devolution to Northern Ireland

Conclusion—is federalism a matter of degree?

A) SUGGESTED ANSWER

It is usually assumed, without too much discussion, that the United Kingdom is a unitary state. Like many other basic ideas in the UK constitution it can be traced back to the nineteenth-century writings of A.V. Dicey, where he stated in his *Introduction to the Study of the Law of Constitution* (1885) that:

Unitarianism, in short, means the concentration of the strength of the State in the hands of one visible sovereign power be that Parliament or Czar.

By contrast:

Federalism means the distribution of the force of the State among a number of co-ordinate bodies each originating in and controlled by the constitution.

[1] What we mean by 'federalism' has to be defined.

Crudely then, unitarianism means a concentration of power at the centre, whilst federalism means a distribution of power between the central authority and, say, regional governments.[1] Some would be satisfied with this rough-and-ready distinction, but Dicey is saying that there is more to it than that. The sovereignty of Parliament meant that the UK had to be a unitary state, because Parliament did not share its supreme legislative authority with any other person or body.

[2] According to Dicey, the supremacy of Parliament makes federalism impossible in the UK.

Conversely, in a federal state, supreme authority would lie in a written constitutional document, which would divide power between the central authority and the regions, provinces, states or whatever they might be called.[2] It is therefore necessary to consider the structure of the UK to establish whether any divisions of authority between different governmental spheres may be identified.

[3] Despite this, the UK did not adopt a federal structure.

The structure of the UK is not as uniform as is sometimes supposed, because it is a union of several countries that were once separate.[3] Wales was conquered by England in the Middle Ages, but the two countries were not formally united until an Act of Parliament in 1536. The same legal system operates in both England and Wales, but some of the administration of government was devolved to Wales as long ago as 1964 with the establishment of the Welsh Office, headed by the Secretary of State for Wales, a minister in the Westminster government.

Scotland was never conquered by England, but instead the two countries voluntarily united. From 1603 they were ruled by the same king and by the **Treaty of Union 1707**, the two countries merged to form Great Britain. Their two separate parliaments became one, but, in the Treaty, care was taken to preserve some distinctly different Scottish institutions. Private law, the courts, the church, and universities were all protected from change by the new Parliament of Great Britain. As with Wales, some of the administration of government was restored to Scotland with the establishment of a Scottish Office and a Secretary of State for Scotland in 1928.

[4] The different countries of the UK have different histories.

Ireland presents a far more complicated picture.[4] The kings of England had been trying to conquer and subdue that country since the twelfth century. In 1800 there was an attempt to emulate the 1707 union of England and Scotland. The **Union with Ireland Act 1800** formed the United Kingdom of Great Britain and Ireland and established one Parliament for the new country. This arrangement did not prove as enduring as the union of England and Scotland, because of the growth of a 'Home Rule' movement in nineteenth-century Ireland, which turned into demands for outright independence in the early twentieth century. The southern part of Ireland broke away in 1920 to form an independent country, the Republic of Ireland.

Northern Ireland remained part of the United Kingdom and under the **Government of Ireland Act 1920** had its own Parliament, Prime Minister, Cabinet, and civil service. This Parliament, however, only had limited subordinate powers to legislate, no power to raise taxes, and it was clear that the Westminster Parliament retained supremacy. Due to the upsurge of nationalist feeling in the late 1960s and 1970s, this Unionist-dominated 'Stormont Parliament' was suspended in 1972 and never restored. 'Direct rule' from the UK Parliament replaced it.

Because of an increase in support for nationalist political parties in Scotland and Wales, the Labour Government of 1978 tried to begin a process called 'devolution'. Scotland and Wales would be granted more powers of self-government, but the Westminster Parliament would retain sovereignty. The Labour Government tried to implement this for Scotland and Wales in 1978, but there was insufficient support expressed in the referendums held in each country.

When the Labour Party returned to power in 1997, they resumed the process of devolution. In the **Scotland Act 1998**, a Scottish Parliament, elected by the voters of Scotland, was re-established with full legislative power, except for those matters specifically reserved to the Westminster Parliament. A Scottish government has been established, with ministers and its own 'First Minister'. Indeed, the **Scotland Act** could almost be regarded as a kind of 'written constitution' for Scotland, for it defines many things that are left to convention in the Westminster arrangements. It specifies how the First Minister is to be chosen and requires 'special majorities' of two-thirds, to do things like call an early general election or dismiss a Scottish judge.

[5] Choose examples to support your argument.

The powers of the Scottish Parliament were extended in the **Scotland Act 2012** and included the power to vary the basic rate of income tax by up to 3 per cent and to determine spending priorities.[5]

Since 1998, the Scottish Parliament has grown in influence. Under the 'Sewel Convention', the UK government agreed that it would not legislate on matters devolved to Scotland, unless the Scottish Parliament consents. In 2011, the Scottish Nationalist Party gained control of the Scottish Parliament and decided to seek their long-term aim of independence for Scotland. A referendum on Scottish independence was held on 18 September 2014, but the electorate voted 'No' to independence by a majority of 55 per cent to 45 per cent. The support for independence was greater than expected, so the UK government responded by agreeing to grant more powers of self-government to Scotland.

[6] Important evidence for the growing power of Scotland's government.

The **Scotland Act 2016** gives more power over tax, welfare, and the oil and gas industries and turns the Sewel Convention into law.[6] The Act declares that the Scottish Parliament and Scottish government are permanent parts of the UK's constitutional arrangements and that the UK will not normally legislate in devolved areas without the consent of the Scottish Parliament. The Act does, however, claim ultimate supremacy for the UK Parliament. This was confirmed by *R (Miller) v Secretary of State for Exiting the European Union* **[2017] UKSC 5**. The Parliament of the UK could authorize leaving the EU, without the agreement of the devolved legislatures of Scotland and Northern Ireland.

Under the **Government of Wales Act 1998**, Wales was given an elected Assembly. The Assembly only has the power to enact delegated legislation, although it too has the equivalent of a First Minister and a government, which is accountable to the Assembly. The powers of the Welsh Assembly were extended by the **Government of Wales Act 2006**, allowing the Assembly to legislate on more areas. There is also the possibility of the Welsh Assembly gaining full legislative powers, if the people of Wales agree in a referendum. Yet the 2006 Act clearly states that the UK Parliament retains the ultimate power to legislate for Wales. The Silk Commission reported in 2015 and suggested that more power should be devolved to Wales, along the lines of the **Scotland Act 2016**, including the Sewel Convention being given legal force.[7]

[7] More evidence to support the argument.

The **Northern Ireland Act 1998** restored devolved government to that country and established an elected Assembly with legislative powers. However, it has considerably less power than the Scottish Parliament, as it is unable to legislate on a number of matters reserved or excepted to the Westminster Parliament. Unlike the **Scotland Act**, the **Northern Ireland Act** makes clear that it does not affect the power of the UK Parliament to make laws for Northern Ireland on any subject. There is a Northern Irish government, however, with ministers accountable to the Assembly. As in the Scotland and Wales Acts, there are provisions distinctly resembling a 'written constitution'. For instance, 'special majorities' are required to elect the First Minister and Deputy First Minister. Because of disagreements between the nationalist Sinn Fein and the loyalist Unionist parties, the Westminster Parliament resumed control in 2000, restoring devolved government in 2006. In Northern Ireland the current priority is to make the existing devolution arrangements work for both the nationalist and unionist parties, rather than to extend self-government.

So has the UK become a federal state? According to Dicey, a federal state would need a written constitution to guarantee that the autonomy granted to Northern Ireland, Scotland, and Wales could not legally be removed again by the Westminster Parliament. It has been argued (earlier) that Scotland, Wales, and Northern Ireland already have written constitutions in the form of the Acts of Parliament establishing their own governments. The Westminster Parliament remains supreme, so the power that it has given can be taken back.[8]

[8] According to Dicey, the supremacy of Parliament makes federalism impossible in the UK.

Not all definitions of federalism are quite so legalistic. For instance, S. de Smith and R. Brazier (*Constitutional and Administrative Law* (Penguin 1998)), define it in more practical, political terms, insisting that the difference between a federal and a non-federal constitution is sometimes only a matter of degree, rather than how the constitution

[9]But under a less legalistic argument, the UK is already a federal state.

might appear in legal terms. Under that definition, legislation such as the **Scotland Act 2016** and the plans for Wales recognize that self-government for those countries is permanent and that their independence from the Westminster Parliament will only increase.[9] Legally, an Act of Parliament could repeal all the Scotland Acts, but with increased demand from Scotland for outright independence, it would be politically impossible.

+ LOOKING FOR EXTRA MARKS?

■ This is a constantly developing area, so keep up to date.

■ The exact meaning of 'federal' and 'unitary' is much debated. Investigate this debate.

TAKING THINGS FURTHER

■ Allan T., 'The rule of law is the rule of reason: consent and constitutionalism' (1999) 115 LQR 221.

The rule of law theories of Raz, Fuller, and Dworkin are considered. Dicey's theory was about government, whereas the other theories are more about the 'inner morality of law', in short, justice.

■ Barber N.W., 'Laws and constitutional conventions' (2009) 125 LQR 294.

Dicey made a big distinction between law and convention, but the distinction is becoming less clear-cut, with many conventions, such as those in the Ministerial Code being reduced to a written, codified form.

■ Barendt E., 'Separation of powers and constitutional government' [1995] Public Law 599.

This comprehensive article looks at the classical theories, such as that of Montesquieu and examines how the separation of powers works in the United States, France, Germany, and the UK.

■ Beatson J., 'Reforming an unwritten constitution' (2010) 126 LQR 48.

*This is an article about the many constitutional reforms of the 1997–2010 Labour Government, such as the **Human Rights Act 1998**, the **Constitutional Reform Act 2005**, the devolution legislation, and the tentative plans to introduce a written constitution. By this process, more and more of the UK constitution became written.*

■ Bogdanor V. and Vogenauer S., 'Enacting a British constitution: some problems' [2008] Public Law 38.

This examines the problems of drawing up a written constitution for Britain. What should go into it, should it be short or long? Who would draft it? What would happen to parliamentary supremacy?

■ Dickson B., 'Devolution' in J. Jowell, D. Oliver, and C. O'Cinneide (eds) *The Changing Constitution* (8th edn, OUP 2015) 249.

This is an up-to-date account of the devolution process and includes the result of the Scottish referendum and its aftermath. Northern Ireland and Wales are also considered, but England is not forgotten. What about devolution for England?

- Jowell J., 'The Rule of Law' in J. Jowell, D. Oliver, and C. O'Cinneide (eds) *The Changing Constitution* (8th edn, OUP 2015) 13.

  *Dicey's theory is examined in detail, particularly how it fits in with parliamentary sovereignty and the **Human Rights Act 1998**, and criticized.*

- Munro C., 'Constitutional Conventions' in *Studies in Constitutional Law* (2nd edn, Butterworths 1999) 55.

  *This is a very detailed account of the role that conventions play in the UK constitution. **Re Amendment of the Constitution of Canada** is explained and the difference between law and conventions clarified.*

- Munro C., 'Legislature, Executive and Judiciary' in *Studies in Constitutional Law* (2nd edn, Butterworths 1999) 23.

  This chapter examines how Montesquieu came up with his theory and how it was received in England. There is then a detailed examination of how the theory fits into the modern UK constitution, looking at the three branches of government, the Executive, Legislature, and Judiciary.

- Munro C., 'The United Kingdom' in *Studies in Constitutional Law* (2nd edn, Butterworths 1999) 15.

  This is an account of how the UK came into being and explains that the government structure was never uniform. The first, failed, attempts at devolution are considered.

- Raz, J., Chapter 11 'The Rule of Law and its Virtue' in *The Authority of Law: Essays on Law and Morality* (OUP 1979).

  The chapter has a different interpretation of the rule of law to that of Dicey. It is not enough to know which legislative body has the power to make law. Those laws should be clearly published, they should not be retroactive, and should not change too often.

Online Resources
www.oup.com/uk/qanda/

Go online for extra essay and problem questions, a glossary of key terms, online versions of all the answer plans and audio commentary on how selected ones were put together, and a range of podcasts which include advice on exam and coursework technique and advice for other assessment methods.

3 Prime Minister and Cabinet

ARE YOU READY?

The questions in this chapter concern a central part of the constitution of the United Kingdom. What are the powers of the Prime Minister and what is the relationship between the Prime Minister and the Cabinet? How does Parliament both provide the Prime Minister and Cabinet with a majority in the House of Commons, so that they can govern the country, and also attempt to control the activities of that government? In order to attempt the questions in this chapter, you need to understand the following parts of the constitution:

- the existence and powers of the Prime Minister, which are governed by convention, not law;
- the existence and powers of the Cabinet, which are governed by convention, not law;
- the conventions of collective ministerial responsibility;
- the conventions of individual ministerial responsibility;
- the role and powers of Members of Parliament;
- questions in Parliament;
- parliamentary departmental select committees.

KEY DEBATES

Debate: Prime Minister or Cabinet

The position of Prime Minister and the existence of the Cabinet are both matters of convention. Whether the Prime Minister or the Cabinet has the greater power changes over time. The current view is that modern Prime Ministers have increased their power and that this is a bad thing.

Debate: Conventions are Flexible

The conventions of collective responsibility and individual ministerial responsibility are very flexible and are constantly changing. Is this a bad thing, meaning that there are no rules? The convention of individual ministerial responsibility is meant to ensure that government departments are efficiently run, but does it really have that effect? Does the convention make it more likely that a minister will escape responsibility for bad administration? Sometimes ministers resign, sometimes they do not.

QUESTION 1

To what extent is it true to say that the UK has moved from a system of Cabinet government to a system of Prime Ministerial government?

CAUTION!

- There is no law in this question; it is all a matter of convention.
- There is no 'right answer' to a question like this.
- It is a matter of opinion, but the opinion must be backed up by evidence.
- You will need to refer not just to the current Prime Minister, but some previous Prime Ministers as well.

DIAGRAM ANSWER PLAN

> Conventions change over time

> The existence and powers of both the Cabinet and the Prime Minister derive from convention

> The Prime Minister chooses the Cabinet

> The Prime Minister may dismiss members of the Cabinet

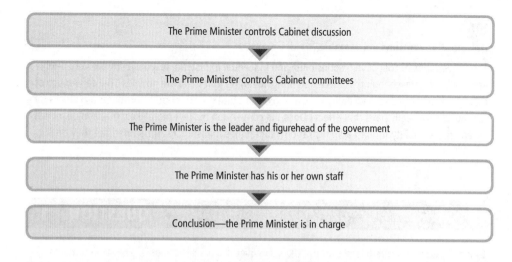

The Prime Minister controls Cabinet discussion

The Prime Minister controls Cabinet committees

The Prime Minister is the leader and figurehead of the government

The Prime Minister has his or her own staff

Conclusion—the Prime Minister is in charge

A | **SUGGESTED ANSWER**

[1] The question suggests it. It is a good idea to start by looking at the history on this.

When W. Bagehot[1] wrote his classic study of the UK constitution in 1867, he identified the Cabinet as the central controlling institution of the constitution, but when Richard Crossman (a Shadow Cabinet member at the time) provided a new introduction to Bagehot's work in 1963, he concluded that the Prime Minister was now the dominant force. Many commentators have agreed with Crossman, especially concerning the Prime Ministerships of Margaret Thatcher (1979–90) and of Tony Blair (1997–2007). In the case of Mrs Thatcher, arguably Cabinet government was ultimately reinforced, as a key factor in her being forced from office was that she no longer really had the confidence of her Cabinet.

In the UK constitution, both Cabinet and Prime Minister exist only by convention. Their functions and powers are not defined by law, but have developed gradually in order to provide a form of government answerable to Parliament rather than to the monarch. The Cabinet developed from the practice of government ministers meeting in private, in the absence of the monarch, to agree upon policies to be presented to Parliament. No legal rules defined which minister was to be regarded as most important. The position of First Lord of the Treasury, with responsibility for government finance, inevitably made its office-holder the 'first' or Prime Minister.

Initially, the Prime Minister was described as *'primus inter pares'*, first among equals. In the twentieth century, it became an established convention that the Prime Minister must be a member of the House of Commons, giving democratic accountability to the elected House and thence to the people. The potential power of a Prime Minister is enhanced by the fact that her powers derive almost exclusively from convention and the royal prerogative, not from statute, lending her flexibility. The initial creation of a new government provides the first illustration of the Prime Minister's powers. By convention, the monarch calls on the leader of the party that can command a majority in the House of Commons to form a government. One would think that the Prime Minister would only select Cabinet members who agreed with him, but he will also have to accept individuals who are powerful or popular in the party. In 2010, the largest party, the Conservatives, was only able to form a majority by going into coalition with the Liberal Democrats. So the Prime Minister[2] had to give some Cabinet posts to the Liberal Democrats. After the 2017 general election, the Conservatives again found themselves in this position, but this time entered a 'Confidence and Supply Agreement' with the Democratic Unionists, which did not require giving ministerial posts to the DUP. The longer a Prime Minister remains in office, however, the more opportunity there is for the Cabinet to be reshaped according to their real preferences. In 1979, Prime Minister Mrs Thatcher was obliged to include in her Cabinet many of the 'old guard' from the previous Tory administration, many of whom did not share her brand of Conservatism. By 1983, however, she had around her a handpicked complement of like-minded colleagues.

It is now accepted political practice for there to be Cabinet reshuffles at least annually; ministers whose performance is seen as inadequate, or who are not sufficiently in sympathy with the Prime Minister's policies, may be removed and promising talents of like mind to the Prime Minister will be brought into key posts. The dismissal of ministers can, however, weaken a Prime Minister by making enemies, providing a focus for party discontent. The very act of leading a radical change of personnel, invariably carried out with great speed, may backfire and be perceived as weakness or panic. David Cameron's reshuffle in July 2014 was criticized. He removed six members of the Cabinet,[3] including the Foreign Secretary, and replaced five other ministers, who also had the right to attend Cabinet meetings. The idea seems to have been to include more women and 'refresh' the government for the general election of 2015. It seems to have worked because the Conservatives unexpectedly won an outright majority at that election.

Once the government is formed, the Prime Minister has a decisive voice in the processes by which it operates. Because of the increasing complexity of modern government, meetings of the full Cabinet deal with only a fraction of government business. The Prime Minister controls the content and order of the agenda. He may keep controversial items off the agenda, though this will be subject to political constraints. In 1986, Michael Heseltine resigned from the Cabinet—in session—when prevented from raising the 'Westland affair' in a particular meeting.

The Prime Minister, in chairing the Cabinet, can lead and order the discussion. The Cabinet usually decides policy by consensus rather

[2] This is an example from a Coalition Government. Maybe you can find an even more up-to-date example.

[3] This is a piece of evidence to back up the argument.

than by vote. The Prime Minister normally concludes the discussion by summing up the sense of the meeting, which will be entered in the 'minutes' (general summary notes). It is a matter of personal style whether the Prime Minister allows a genuine consensus to develop or attempts to dominate the debate. Mrs Thatcher[4] tended to dominate, although vigorous arguments still took place. Perhaps in part as an 'antidote', her successor John Major was particularly collegiate.

[4] Five different Prime Ministers and their different styles of government are mentioned in the next few paragraphs. This is what the question requires.

The Cabinet forms the apex of a hierarchy of Cabinet committees, sub-committees and working groups, and most government business will be dealt with outside the full Cabinet. The Prime Minister now has considerable freedom in establishing and staffing such committees, and may, by careful selection, ensure that only those likely to favour his opinion are involved in the taking of the decision. Decisions made in a Cabinet committee are generally as final as those made in the full Cabinet, and all ministers remain bound by collective responsibility, even if they were not party to the making of the decision, however significant, illustrated by the Iraq War decision.[5] Since 1992, the identity and membership of committees have been officially revealed. A Prime Minister may even avoid the use of such formal bodies and use wholly informal working groups to take sensitive decisions. Mr Blair conducted most business by sub-committee or one-to-one ministerial discussion, merely reporting matters (*post facto*) to a Cabinet meeting, which often lasted well under an hour. For example, he met ministers individually to persuade them to support the invasion of Iraq, before any collective discussion; the Butler Report refers to his 'kitchen cabinet' and 'sofa government' style. This clearly shows how the Prime Minister can exercise a dominating influence over the decision-making process. This may, however, store up trouble. Robin Cook, for example, resigned over the invasion of Iraq and subsequently voiced frequent criticisms of Tony Blair's style of leadership. Mr Cameron vowed to restore proper Cabinet policy-making, and Theresa May has continued this approach. Against the backdrop of exponential growth in the volume and complexity of matters of governance, some delegation is unavoidable. That said, the Prime Minister has a general responsibility for government policy and is therefore entitled to intervene in almost any aspect of the work of any department, subject only to the limits imposed by energy and enthusiasm. For example, in 2016 Mr Cameron played the major role in his failed attempt to renegotiate the UK's membership of the European Union.[6]

[5] There is plenty of material to be found for your essay in discussions of the Iraq War.

[6] If you keep up to date with politics, there are plenty of examples to be found on this topic.

The Prime Minister has the assistance of a range of support services, including a Private Office, staffed by the most promising young civil servants, a Press Office, led by so-called 'spin doctors', and a Political Office, staffed by party workers. All recent Prime Ministers have engaged policy advisers from outside the Civil Service, though problems have arisen where these advisers are thought to have had too much influence and have harmed the position of civil servants by at least trying to politicize their role. Some commentators argue that under Tony Blair these support services expanded to the point where they could be described as a Prime Minister's Department. His Press Secretary, Alistair Campbell, became particularly powerful. Succeeding governments have promised that they will reduce the number and influence of these Special Policy Advisers (SPADs), but have found them too useful to do without.

There can be no doubt that recent years have seen an increasing concentration of media attention on the Prime Minister. The high-profile feature of the television broadcasting of Parliament is the weekly Prime Minister's Question Time, perhaps creating a perception that the Prime Minister *is* the government, whatever may be the reality. Elections are described as if they were a contest between party leaders, and it can be argued that elections give the Prime Minister a personal, not just a party, mandate. This strengthens the hand of a successful Prime Minister, but also increases the likelihood that a party's response to unpopularity will be to replace its leader.

The Prime Minister has enormous power, as she can promote ministers or require them to resign. She is safe, as long as she retains her Commons majority. A return to the days when the Prime Minister was only first among equals is unlikely. Even a Prime Minister who does not wish to dominate the government would find it impossible to reverse the popular perception of the dominant leader. However, in difficult times the Prime Minister still needs the support of her Cabinet, as Mrs Thatcher discovered. The picture drawn by Bagehot is still recognizable.[7]

[7] If you are able to link your opening and closing paragraphs, it creates a good impression.

LOOKING FOR EXTRA MARKS?

- Include some actual examples of the interaction between Prime Minister and Cabinet.
- For a really good answer, you need to follow politics.
- Include up-to-date examples. By the time you read this answer it will already be out of date.

QUESTION | 2

Estella Remington (ER) became Prime Minister last year when her party won a general election with a majority of 30 seats. She promised, during the election campaign, to provide a massive expansion of higher education. She has now decided that this can only be achieved if a special tax is

⊙

imposed on graduates. She has discussed this privately with the Chancellor of the Exchequer, who agrees with the scheme. No other ministers have yet been informed, and several of them are likely to be critical of the plan.

What steps may ER take to try to ensure that:

a   **the scheme is adopted as government policy;**

b   **the necessary legislation is passed through Parliament; and**

c   **the public accepts the need for the new tax?**

⚠ CAUTION!

■ This question is not just about the Prime Minister.

■ It also concerns the powers and procedures of Parliament.

■ There is convention and law in this problem.

■ Answer the problem; do not just discuss this as though it was an essay.

◯ DIAGRAM ANSWER PLAN

Identify the issues	■ Identify the legal and conventional issues ■ Discuss how policy is adopted by the Cabinet and its committees, the legal procedure to pass an Act of Parliament and public influence on the government and Parliament
Relevant law	■ Outline the relevant law and convention: statutory, general principles and case law, in particular the Ministerial Code, parliamentary procedure, past examples of ministerial behaviour
Apply the law	■ How easy would it be for the Prime Minister to get her policy approved by Cabinet? ■ Would the House of Commons and House of Lords pass her legislation? ■ How could the public be persuaded to accept the new tax?
Conclude	■ Would the Prime Minister succeed with her policy and remain in office?

A

SUGGESTED ANSWER

ER has a considerable range of powers and means of influence available to ensure the adoption of her policies. Indeed, it is arguable that the UK system of government has become one of Prime Ministerial government. There are, however, constraints on the Prime Minister's powers, and even determined Prime Ministers may find that they fail to ensure the adoption of at least some of their preferred policies, even with a clear mandate and Commons majority.

(a) The scheme should be formally proposed as policy in a meeting of the Cabinet. It will be discussed and, if agreed, usually by consensus, then it becomes policy. By the convention of Cabinet collective responsibility,[1] all Cabinet and junior ministers are bound by it and must support it in public, specifically in Parliament, irrespective of any dissent in Cabinet or private misgivings. If an individual minister cannot accept and support the policy, then by convention he must resign. It would be most unlikely in practice that any such matter would be raised in Cabinet without extensive prior consultations with the ministers directly affected, specifically the Secretary of State for Education and the Minister of State for Universities and Science. To avoid the possibility of an embarrassing defeat, the Prime Minister is sure to take soundings generally among her colleagues, so that she can take the matter to Cabinet having already satisfied herself of a majority there.

Most issues are not, however, dealt with by the full Cabinet because of pressure of business, but are instead referred to Cabinet committees. There are both permanent and temporary committees and sub-committees. As Prime Minister, ER selects the membership and remit of all of these bodies. It would therefore be possible for her to refer this scheme to a committee, the membership of which she has carefully selected to provide a majority in favour of it. The Chancellor of the Exchequer and the Education Secretary would need to be members, but ER has a fairly free hand in selecting the other members. It would be to ER's advantage to chair the committee herself, giving extra power to guide the discussion.

It is accepted practice that matters decided by a Cabinet committee are not discussed again by the full Cabinet. It is therefore quite likely that this scheme could be adopted[2] as government policy without the involvement of some members of the Cabinet, who will nonetheless remain bound by collective responsibility. This gives rise to the possibility that a minister considering himself to have been bypassed may resign, thereby revealing splits in the government that the Opposition can exploit. The resignation of Michael Heseltine in 1986 over the 'Westland affair' is an example of this. For many senior ministers this

[1] This is a problem with no law. Instead, you must identify the relevant conventional rules.

[2] A clear conclusion can be reached here, after applying the rules to the facts.

is, however, a reluctant path, as it may mean an extended period of political oblivion.

Once adopted as government policy, Education and Treasury civil servants will be instructed to prepare the necessary legislation and administrative procedures. Normally such a major proposal would be announced in the Queen's Speech at the opening of the next session of Parliament, but the government may propose legislation at any time.

(b) Assuming ER succeeds in having the scheme adopted as policy, the next hurdle is the passage of the necessary legislation through Parliament. As a measure affecting taxation, it will be introduced in the House of Commons. The government has a comfortable Commons majority, so ER need not be particularly concerned about the attitude of the opposition parties; indeed, vehement criticism of the bill by them may well encourage the loyal support of her own backbench MPs.

The task of getting the legislation through lies with the sponsoring minister and the whips. The whips must ensure a disciplined turnout of MPs to vote on the measure. After the formal introduction and First Reading,[3] the Second Reading provides the opportunity for the House of Commons to debate and vote on the principle of the bill. Defeat at Second Reading will force the withdrawal of the bill, but this is a rare occurrence. The whips will inform ER in advance of potential revolt and any measure likely to be defeated will be withdrawn for amendment before the government suffers the embarrassment of defeat. After Second Reading, the bill will be referred to a Standing Committee for detailed examination. The government will have a majority on this committee proportionate to its overall majority, thus it should have no difficulty in getting the bill safely through this stage, even if forced to accept amendments from its own side. If the opposition parties attempt to delay the bill by filibustering, the government can ask the House to pass a programme motion restricting the time allowed for discussion. Once the Committee stage has been completed, the government will have to decide whether to accept any amendments made in committee, or to have them reversed by a vote of the whole House. The vote on Third Reading will complete the bill's passage through the House of Commons.

The bill will then be sent to the House of Lords, where a similar pattern of readings will be followed. Voting in the Upper House is somewhat unpredictable because it is less shackled by party discipline and there are many cross-bench peers without a fixed party allegiance. This bill is likely to arouse the keen interest of those peers interested in higher education, and the final result of the votes cannot be foreseen.

[3] Parliamentary procedure is a matter of law. Clearly explain the law.

The House of Lords has become more willing to reject government legislation and, since the removal of the vast majority of hereditary peers in 1999, has announced that it will no longer observe the Salisbury Convention under which it would not obstruct legislation intended to fulfil government manifesto commitments. It is therefore possible that the government may have to resort to the **Parliament Acts** procedure, as was done in passing the **European Parliamentary Elections Act 1999** and the **Hunting Act 2004.**[4]

[4]Actual examples always strengthen your analysis.

If the bill were to contain no provisions except for the 'graduate tax', it would be classified as a Money Bill and the Lords could delay it for only one month. If, as is more likely, it also contains other provisions, then peers may delay it for one session. On the other hand, they may be satisfied with amending the bill, which will then have to return to the Commons. Then the government will decide either to accept the amendments or to try to persuade the Lords to concede. Unless the **Parliament Acts** are used, once the bill is passed by both Houses in identical form it may proceed to Royal Assent (which by convention presents no challenge) and become law within one session.

[5]You may be able to say more about this if your course spent a lot of time on pressure group and policy formation.

(c) In persuading the general public of the scheme,[5] ER's greatest asset is the opportunity to make effective use of the media, including trying to influence the opinion of the press. The Prime Minister has a Press Office, which holds regular lobby briefings with journalists. All of the arguments in favour of the scheme will be advanced, and opposing arguments rebutted. The press will then report, likely giving a range of slants overall. It is vital for any Prime Minister to cultivate good relations with the media as far as possible, but attempts to manipulate it have been subject to considerable criticism in recent years and may prove counter-productive. Some newspapers are traditionally—but not always—supportive of a party of their chosen political leaning, so ER might reasonably expect some favourable coverage. However, as the Deputy Prime Minister, Nick Clegg, discovered in 2010, abandoning an election manifesto promise, not to raise students' fees, could cause lasting political damage.

It is likely that this scheme will provoke many individuals to write to their MPs. It will therefore be desirable for all MPs of the government party to be supplied with material suitable for explaining and justifying the scheme to their constituents, thereby perhaps keeping both the MPs and their constituents on-board.

It may be that the scheme will provoke protest and demonstrations from students, but it is quite likely that these can be 'ignored' by government, as they are as likely to turn public opinion in favour of the scheme as against it, especially if protesters break laws and become violent. Student 'riots' in 2010, in protest against increased tuition fees at universities, probably did not help the students' cause. In the last resort, it must be remembered that there are about four years to go before the next general election. Even if the tax is initially unpopular, ER may reasonably believe that it will have ceased to be a matter of major concern by then.

[6] A clear conclusion can be reached here, based on the preceding analysis.

Once a measure has been adopted as government policy[6] its chances of becoming law are very high. Very little government-sponsored legislation is rejected by Parliament, and public opinion can rarely be mobilized so as to prevent the government pursuing its policies. The greatest problems for the Prime Minister lie in getting the initial agreement of Cabinet colleagues, but even here the influence of a determined Prime Minister may be hard to resist.

LOOKING FOR EXTRA MARKS?

■ Focus on the issues raised by the different parts of the problem.

■ The problem facts are pretty realistic. You could find some actual examples to compare it with.

QUESTION | 3

How does the convention of individual ministerial responsibility operate in relation to departmental error? How has this been affected by recent developments in Parliament and government?

CAUTION!

■ This is an answer based almost entirely on an analysis of conventional rules.

■ Be aware that conventions change over time.

■ There are only a small amount of legal rules in this area.

■ You must include examples of ministers resigning and not resigning.

■ The question is about a minister's responsibility for their department, not resignation for financial or sexual misconduct.

DIAGRAM ANSWER PLAN

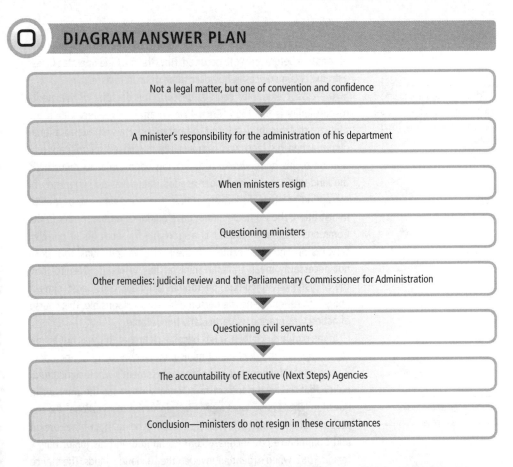

Not a legal matter, but one of convention and confidence

▼

A minister's responsibility for the administration of his department

▼

When ministers resign

▼

Questioning ministers

▼

Other remedies: judicial review and the Parliamentary Commissioner for Administration

▼

Questioning civil servants

▼

The accountability of Executive (Next Steps) Agencies

▼

Conclusion—ministers do not resign in these circumstances

SUGGESTED ANSWER

[1] The first paragraph contains a lot of information, but it does introduce all the main issues that are to be discussed in the essay.

Ministerial departments[1] can be sued, as ministers are legally responsible for the actions of their civil servants (for example, *Carltona v Works Commissioners* [1943] 2 All ER 560). Albeit not legally enforceable, the Ministerial Code and Civil Service Code set out in written detail much of what is required or expected in the dealings of departments and of their personnel. However, it is convention, unwritten and non-legal, which still governs much of what may or must be done and thus it is political enforceability and sanctions that regulate departmental and ministerial conduct. Traditional constitutional doctrine states that each minister is responsible to Parliament for the work of her department, giving indirect democratic accountability to the electorate via the Commons, as well as being a part of the overall accountability of government to Parliament. The ultimate sanction of the Commons is to force a government to resign by passing a vote of no confidence in it. Similarly, a minister who loses the confidence of the House of Commons has to resign, though in practice a Prime Minister who knew that a minister was facing defeat in such a vote would require an immediate resignation before any vote occurred. How the doctrine operates in less extreme circumstances is, however, more difficult to ascertain.

[2] Crichel Down was a long time ago, but it is still a good example. See the Finer article in Taking Things Further.

The classic example[2] used to describe the doctrine of ministerial responsibility is the 1954 'Crichel Down affair'. Civil servants in the Ministry of Agriculture refused to honour a promise made to a landowner, when his land was compulsorily purchased for military use, that he or his heirs would be given the opportunity to repurchase the land when it was no longer needed. There was no suggestion of corruption or other dishonesty; rather, it was a plain case of maladministration. The Home Secretary gave guidance on the matter in the Commons debate: a minister is responsible for what his or her civil servants do and must explain to the House of Commons. That does not necessarily mean that the minister has to resign. Despite that, the Minister of Agriculture, Sir Thomas Dugdale, considered himself obliged to resign, being the person ultimately responsible. This course of action was praised as particularly honourable.

In the period since then, it has become clear that this was not a typical example of the doctrine of ministerial responsibility in operation. Rather, it was the unpopularity of the government's whole agricultural policy that led to the loss of backbench support for the minister in question.

[3] Examine the evidence since Crichel Down, eg have other ministers resigned?

There have been very few ministerial resignations[3] for departmental error since, one notable exception being that of the Foreign and Commonwealth Secretary Lord Carrington and his junior ministers in 1982 when Argentina invaded the Falkland Islands. The stance taken, as subsequently explained by Lord Carrington, was that even though with hindsight he would not have acted differently in the conduct of matters preceding the invasion, the invasion represented a national humiliation (with very serious consequence), for which he had to take responsibility.

What then does the doctrine of ministerial responsibility amount to? Its starting point is the right of MPs to question each minister about the activities of the department, and the corresponding duty of the minister to answer. Since all Crown servants other than ministers were excluded from the House of Commons at the beginning of the eighteenth century, the minister was the only person available for questioning. When there was far less government activity, it was reasonable to expect ministers to know what was going on in their departments. As government activity increased, it remained the expectation that the minister should be able and willing, given reasonable notice, to answer questions on any aspect of the department's work. This provided one of the principal means by which an individual could seek redress for grievances, as the complainant in the Crichel

[4]Then come to a conclusion.

Down affair eventually did. Many such grievances[4] would be dealt with without publicity, and even those that did reach the floor of the House of Commons would conclude with an explanation, an apology and a promise of redress from the minister, without the issue of resignation even being raised.

From the 1960s onwards, other means of redress were developed, to supplement or even replace the traditional method. In 1967, the office of Parliamentary Commissioner for Administration (now the Parliamentary and Health Service Ombudsman) was introduced, providing an alternative course of action for an MP whose constituent is aggrieved by an act of maladministration. As the Ombudsman's reports and recommendations are almost always accepted in full by government, and appropriate redress offered, there is no need to invoke the doctrine of ministerial responsibility and no question of resignation is raised (see chapter 11).

Another development has been the immense growth in the use of judicial review, providing legal redress wholly outside the political process. If the government loses a judicial review case, they may be criticized by the Opposition, and perhaps the media, but it has never led to a ministerial resignation. Even in the case of *Re M* [1994] 1 AC 377, where it was held that the Home Secretary could be held in contempt of court, the Home Secretary did not resign.

It remains one of the bases for the doctrine of ministerial responsibility that only the minister is present in Parliament to be questioned. However, beyond the floor of the House, select committees have the right to call civil servants to give evidence, and the departmental select committees do so extensively. There can be problems; although the committee can in theory insist on the civil servant's presence, the minister may refuse permission and attend in person instead. In practice, the committee would have to be satisfied with that. Civil servants who do attend are expected to obey Cabinet Office directions restricting the answers they can give on sensitive issues. If they refuse to answer particular questions, the committee cannot force them to do so. In spite of these limitations, it has become common to see civil servants appearing before select committees, and MPs are finding this form of scrutiny in some ways more effective than questioning the minister in the traditional way. The minister is no longer the only person who can be

[5]Select committees are an important development and may be replacing the traditional doctrine of ministerial responsibility.

called to account by Parliament. The work and effectiveness of these committees[5] may gain new impetus and vigour now that its chairmen are elected by fellow MPs, not selected by their political party.

[6]'Next Steps' is also an important development.

The 'Next Steps' governmental reorganization,[6] designed to improve management and efficiency by setting up agencies to run public services in place of the Civil Service, has affected the doctrine of ministerial responsibility. Headed by a chief executive, these agencies manage implementation of government policy. No provision was made for any new form of parliamentary accountability, though new procedures have developed. Ministers answer parliamentary questions about the work of agencies by simply informing MPs that they have passed the matter to the chief executive, who answers the MP by letter. These replies are published in Hansard, like written answers from ministers, making them matters of formal record. This, however, carries the implication that the minister is not responsible or accountable for the operations conducted by the agency, as he would have been before the reorganization.

An MP has limited scope for raising a complaint on the matter on the floor of the House but an agency's chief executive may be called before a select committee, particularly useful when a large number of complaints are giving cause for concern, as happened, for instance, with the much criticized Border Control Agency. The outcome was that this agency, which had failed to keep track of illegal immigrants, was disbanded in 2013.

If there is direct accountability of the agency to Parliament by means of the detailed scrutiny of a select committee, the responsibility of the minister becomes almost irrelevant. Major difficulties remain, however, in establishing accountability where matters fall between day-to-day operational matters, with which the minister is not concerned, and matters of high policy, for which the minister alone remains account-able. Successive Home Secretaries and in particular Michael Howard in 1995 have denied that they are responsible for escapes from prison. They claim that this is a matter of the everyday running of the prison, for which the prison governor is responsible, not the Home Secretary.

[7] The conclusion links back to the arguments raised in points 5 and 6.

In conclusion,[7] it is clear that the shouts of 'Resign!' that greet a minister whose department has been at fault are little more than a ritual. Crichel Down, far from setting the precedent of expected behaviour, is in fact unique. It would perhaps be better to improve the means by which Parliament scrutinizes the Executive directly, rather than trying to revive a doctrine that took shape when minis-ters' departments did not encompass such a vast range of activities. Nowadays, civil servants are often working on matters of which the minister is unaware. The arrival of Executive Agencies may yet pro-vide the opportunity for the development of new means of scrutiny, if Parliament wishes to perform this function more effectively.

✛ LOOKING FOR EXTRA MARKS?

- Include some fresh, new examples not the same tired old textbook examples that everyone else includes.

- Show that you really understand how everyday politics operates within the conventional rules.

Q | QUESTION | **4**

Consider the following situations in relation to the convention of ministerial responsibility.

a In her Budget speech, the Chancellor of the Exchequer announced her intention to impose Value Added Tax (VAT) on books and newspapers. Twenty government backbench MPs have told the whips that they will vote against this proposal, and if necessary against the whole Budget. The government has an overall Commons majority of 15 seats.

b Sarah, the Secretary of State for Transport, proposed to the Cabinet that extra safety barriers be erected along all elevated sections of motorways, but her proposal was rejected on grounds of cost. Last week, 40 people died in a motorway crash that the safety barriers would have prevented. Sarah told James, a journalist, about the rejection of her proposal, and he has published an article blaming the rest of the Cabinet for the loss of life.

c Lesley, the Foreign and Commonwealth Secretary, informed the House of Commons two years ago that he would be adopting a new, morally sustainable foreign policy. It has now been discovered that the Foreign Office has been negotiating for a year to surrender a small UK colony to a neighbouring dictatorship. No information about this has ever been given to the House of Commons.

d Smith, a junior minister in the Department for Transport, crashed his car on the M4 motorway. PCs Ford and Austin attended the accident. Smith was breathalysed, the result negative. Smith was slightly injured, as was his passenger Jones, a financier, the financial dealings of whom are currently under investigation by the Department for Business, Energy and Industrial Strategy. PCs Ford and Austin completed reports on the accident, but were then told by their superiors that instructions had been issued from 'on high' to remove all record of it.

! | **CAUTION!**

■ This is a problem-style question, so look at the issues raised, clearly identify the 'law', apply it to the issues, and come to a reasoned conclusion.

■ Ministerial behaviour is governed by convention, not law. Treat the conventional rules like legal rules to answer this problem.

■ Parts (a) and (b) involve collective ministerial responsibility.

■ Parts (c) and (d) involve individual ministerial responsibility.

DIAGRAM ANSWER PLAN

Identify the issues	■ Identify the legal and conventional issues: collective ministerial responsibility: votes of confidence and confidentiality; individual ministerial responsibility: misleading Parliament, personal conduct

Relevant law	■ Outline the relevant law: statutory, general principles and case law, in particular the Ministerial Code and past incidents of ministerial behaviour

Apply the law	■ When a vote of confidence would be held and the consequences of losing it ■ The consequences of a breach of cabinet confidentiality ■ The differences between misleading parliament and lying to Parliament ■ Unacceptable ministerial behaviour and its consequences

Conclude	■ Are there any breaches of conventional behaviour? ■ Do the government, Sarah, Lesley, and Smith have to resign?

SUGGESTED ANSWER

(a) The convention of ministerial responsibility requires above all that the government must have the confidence of the House of Commons. If it loses that confidence it must resign, either to be replaced by another government in which the House of Commons does have confidence or, more usually, to cause an early general election.

[1] This Act is often misunderstood. Be clear on what the Act actually says.

Even though the **Fixed-Term Parliaments Act 2011** [1] provides for fixed, five-year parliaments, a lost vote of confidence could still lead to an earlier general election. The issue raised in this problem is to identify the circumstances in which a government defeat in the Commons will be taken as an indication of such a fatal loss of confidence. It was thought at one time that any defeat on a major issue would demonstrate a loss of confidence and force the government's resignation, but over the past 20 years or so this has changed. It is clear, however, that any defeat on a formal vote of confidence, moved as such by government or Opposition, will make the government resign. This last occurred in 1979, when the Labour Government lost a vote of confidence (by one vote) and immediately called a general election. Here, this government could adopt the high-risk strategy of making the vote on VAT a vote of confidence, if it judges that this would make the 20 (or at least the crucial six) rebel backbenchers rally to support it. If, however, the 20 were to persist in their rebellion, then the government would, if defeated, have no choice but to resign.

Defeat on one aspect of the Budget would not in itself force the government to resign; it would merely cause political embarrassment. In recent years, more than one government has been defeated on parts of its Budget proposals, but has not resigned. Defeat on the entire Budget, however, presents a more complex problem. Traditionally, the votes on the Queen's Speech and the Budget were seen as being tantamount to votes of confidence, but it is not clear whether this is still the case. A Finance Act must be passed each year, to authorize taxation, so were the Budget to be rejected the only way the government could survive would be to propose, and have passed, a vote of confidence, and then to introduce a new Budget acceptable to enough MPs. This would probably force the resignation of the Chancellor of the Exchequer, but the rest of the government would survive. From the facts, it appears that all of the 20 rebels have taken a principled stance upon the particular matter, challenging and presumably expecting its front bench to compromise. However, the high stakes are clear[2] to all concerned and it may be that the 20 may back down, rather than force a general election, in which they might lose their seats.

[2] The conventions are being analysed and applied to the facts, as though they are laws.

(b) As well as the relevant laws (official secrets legislation, Public Records Acts, and confidentiality) (see chapter 9), the convention of collective ministerial responsibility requires that once government policy is decided, then all ministers (Cabinet and below) must support that policy in the public domain, keep their personal opinions to themselves, and refrain from revealing discussions held in Cabinet. If a minister has a fundamental disagreement with the rest of the Cabinet, and is not prepared to accept government policy, that minister must resign. Foreign Secretary Robin Cook[3] was considered to have acted in a principled way when, in 2003, he resigned because he could not support the invasion of Iraq without the approval of the United Nations. There was criticism of Clare Short's failure to resign from the Cabinet when expressing similar opinions; Ms Short later resigned.

[3] Resignations where ministers resign disagreeing with collective responsibility are rare, so use the examples that are available.

In reality, in most governments differences of opinion between ministers will be publicly known and discussed in the media. This may be tolerated for a time, but eventually the Prime Minister's patience with dissent, and with the 'leaks', will be exhausted. Revealing the story to James is in breach of collective responsibility. Journalists jealously guard the identity of their sources. James will also wish other revelations to follow in the future, so is unlikely to reveal that Sarah is the source. So, it is likely that Sarah will not be found out as the source of the disclosure.

It can be argued that it is not justifiable to describe collective ministerial responsibility as a convention, given that ministers do not always adhere strictly to it, whether speaking off the record or expressing their views in carefully coded language. There is nonetheless recognition[4] of the political reality that an openly divided Cabinet cannot hope to survive and few ministers will take a disagreement so far as to resign, or to express dissent so openly that the Prime Minister has no option but to dismiss them.

[4] A clear, reasoned conclusion.

(c) According to the convention of individual ministerial responsibility, a minister is accountable to Parliament for the activities of his department. This gives Parliament the right to question him and imposes on him an obligation to answer. The minister is the only person available for Parliament to question, at least on the floor of the House of Commons. If the minister cannot satisfy MPs, particularly those from his own party, he may lose the confidence of the House of Commons. In extreme circumstances, the House of Commons could force the resignation of a minister by passing a vote of censure against him.

The Ministerial Code and a 1997 Resolution of the House of Commons[5] specify that a minister must give truthful and accurate information and must not knowingly mislead Parliament. If it were to be shown that Lesley had knowingly misinformed Parliament by, for example, denying that any such negotiations were taking place, that would be regarded as a grave offence and it is almost certain that he would have to resign. In 2017, Damian Green, the First Secretary of State, was obliged to resign for making a false and inaccurate statement. It was alleged that, in 2008, the police had found pornography on computers in his parliamentary office. Mr Green denied any knowledge of this, but is was proved that the police had told him about this in 2008 and 2013. It is now considered acceptable for a minister to deny personal knowledge of and responsibility for purely operational matters within his department. Successive Home Secretaries, for example, have successfully used this stance to avoid responsibility for prison escapes. Could Lesley deny all knowledge of the negotiations? They were of such importance and sensitivity that the Foreign Secretary either must have known or should have known if he were running his department effectively. His defence in these circumstances may be to assert that he has not actively misled Parliament, but has merely failed to keep MPs informed. The 1996

[5] The next two paragraphs give a detailed account of the conventional rules that affect the issue.

Scott Inquiry into 'Arms to Iraq' revealed that a number of ministers had misled Parliament, yet the government rallied behind them and they did not resign.

Lesley may claim that he has not really misled Parliament or that his failure to keep MPs informed was due to the delicacy of the negotiations, or that there is no real contradiction with the morally sustainable foreign policy. If the government[6] has a loyal majority prepared to back Lesley, he may ignore calls for his resignation from the Opposition. If, however, the government considers that public opinion is strong and requires a 'scalp', then whether or not Lesley is merely the scapegoat he may find himself sacrificed.

[6] Now we have the conclusion.

(d) Although personal misconduct by government ministers will generally lead to public and media criticism, it is unlikely that the mere fact that Smith has crashed his car would endanger his position, although there is the safety perspective, given his Transport portfolio. On the facts, he was not over the drink-drive limit, there is no other suggestion that he is particularly culpable, and no one has been seriously injured. Much more serious, however, is the question of why Jones was a passenger in his car. Any suggestion of financial impropriety, perhaps even apparently inappropriate association, is likely to be regarded by the public and media as very reprehensible, and various ministers have been forced to resign for such reasons. The Secretary of State for Culture, Maria Miller,[7] had to resign in 2014 in a dispute about her claims for housing expenses, even though she had repaid the money that the Committee on Standards said that she owed.

[7] There are always new examples of ministers resigning over matters of personal conduct. Keep up to date!

In this problem, there is the further suggestion that someone in authority is attempting to conceal what happened. Evading a prosecution for speeding, by falsely claiming that his wife was driving, caused the resignation of the Secretary of State for Energy, Chris Huhne, in 2012. Removing police records would be an even more serious matter and would be likely to provoke public outrage. If such action were proven, Smith and any other minister involved would be forced to resign, and such a scandal might embroil and threaten the whole government. A cover-up is always regarded as unforgivable, however minor the initial offence.

✚ LOOKING FOR EXTRA MARKS?

- Include some fresh, new examples, not the same tired old textbook examples that everyone else includes.
- Show that you really understand how everyday politics operates within the conventional rules.

TAKING THINGS FURTHER

- Drewry G., 'The executive: towards accountable government and effective governance' in J. Jowell and D. Oliver (eds) *The Changing Constitution* (7th edn, OUP 2011) 187.

  This looks at how Parliament scrutinizes the activities of the government and helps to provide more efficient government.

- Finer S.E., 'The individual responsibility of ministers' (1956) 33 Public Administration 377, 393.

  This is an old but famous article on the resignation of Sir Thomas Dugdale over the Crichel Down affair. What it says is still relevant today.

- Flinders M., 'Shifting the balance? Parliament, the executive and the British constitution' (2002) 50 Political Studies 23.

  This looks at the principle of accountability to Parliament, both historically and in more modern times, and considers the problems when the government has a large majority.

- Faulkener E. and Everett M., 'The Ministerial Code and the Independent Adviser on Ministers' Interests' <http://researchbriefings.parliament.uk/ResearchBriefing/Summary/SN03750>.

  This is a commentary on the Ministerial Code, which explains its history and gives examples of its use.

- Kelly R., 'Modernisation: Revitalising the Chamber' (House of Commons Library Standard Note SN/PC 04542, 12 December 2007) <http://researchbriefings.files.parliament.uk/documents/SN04542/SN04542.pdf>.

  This is the information supplied to MPs on the powers that they have to ask questions and debate issues.

- 'The Ministerial Code' <https://www.gov.uk/government/uploads/system/uploads/attachment_data/file/672633/2018-01-08_MINISTERIAL_CODE_JANUARY_2018__FINAL___3_.pdf>.

  The conventions that govern ministerial behaviour are written down. Each successive Prime Minister revises and reissues this Code.

- Oliver D., 'Reforming the UK Parliament?' in J. Jowell and D. Oliver (eds) *The Changing Constitution* (7th edn, OUP 2011) 167.

  This looks at reforms made to the workings of Parliament and considers possible future reforms.

- Woodhouse D., 'The reconstruction of constitutional accountability' [2002] Public Law 73.

  The creation of Next Steps agencies alters the principles of ministerial responsibility and accountability to Parliament.

Online Resources

www.oup.com/uk/qanda/

Go online for extra essay and problem questions, a glossary of key terms, online versions of all the answer plans and audio commentary on how selected ones were put together, and a range of podcasts which include advice on exam and coursework technique and advice for other assessment methods.

The royal prerogative

4

ARE YOU READY?

The first question in this chapter is an essay on how the courts rule on whether a prerogative power exists and how they might attempt to control its use by the use of the process known as judicial review. This is followed by a problem question about the conventions that control the Queen's use of her prerogative powers and whether the Queen ever has to make her own decision, rather than rely upon the advice of her ministers. Then there is an essay on how the government uses the Queen's prerogative powers and how this might be controlled by the courts and Parliament. Finally, there is a problem question about whether individuals have any protection when the government uses its prerogative powers against them. In order to attempt these questions, you will need to have covered the following topics in your work and your revision:

● understanding what the royal prerogative is and the main prerogative powers that exist today;

● understanding that the prerogative powers are not used by the Queen herself, but by the government acting in her name;

● understanding that the courts play a vital role in defining what the prerogative powers allow the government to do and controlling abuse of those powers by judicial review;

● appreciating that there is a debate about whether the prerogative grants the government too much uncontrolled power.

KEY DEBATES

Debate: The Government and the Royal Prerogative

The royal prerogative is the survival of the ancient common law powers of the monarch, king, or queen up to the present day. The term 'royal' prerogative is highly misleading, because, by

(●)

convention, the government of the day exercises these powers in the Queen's name. Successive governments have declined to consult Parliament about many uses of the prerogative, permitting the government too much uncontrolled power.

Debate: The Queen and the Royal Prerogative

Traditionally the Queen has 'the right to be consulted, the right to encourage and the right to warn' when the government wants to use one of her prerogative powers. If the Queen expresses too strong a view, she is accused of interfering in politics. If she says too little, she might be accused of failing to protect the constitution.

Debate: The Courts and the Royal Prerogative

According to the leading case, *Council of Civil Service Unions v Minister for the Civil Service* **[1985] AC 374**, the courts may only judicially review the government's use of the royal prerogative in certain circumstances. Since that case, the courts have become more willing to challenge the government. This leads to clashes between the Executive and the Judiciary.

QUESTION   1

As De Keyser's case shows, the courts will enquire into whether a particular prerogative power exists or not, and, if it does exist, into its extent. But once the existence and the extent of a power are established to the satisfaction of the court, the court cannot enquire into the propriety of its exercise.

(Lord Fraser in *Council of Civil Service Unions v Minister for the Civil Service* [1985] AC 374)

Discuss.

CAUTION!

- The quotation might seem a little misleading. Lord Fraser is explaining what the law was in the past and he and his fellow judges are about to change it.

- A detailed knowledge of the judgments in this case should make the answer to this question easy, but you do need that knowledge.

DIAGRAM ANSWER PLAN

> Definition of the royal prerogative: the remaining legal powers of the Queen or King

> The courts may decide on the existence and extent of a prerogative power

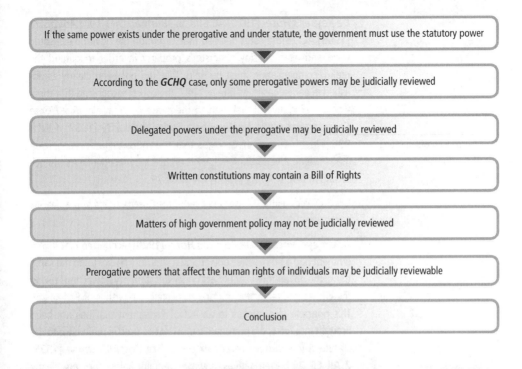

If the same power exists under the prerogative and under statute, the government must use the statutory power

▼

According to the *GCHQ* case, only some prerogative powers may be judicially reviewed

▼

Delegated powers under the prerogative may be judicially reviewed

▼

Written constitutions may contain a Bill of Rights

▼

Matters of high government policy may not be judicially reviewed

▼

Prerogative powers that affect the human rights of individuals may be judicially reviewable

▼

Conclusion

A

SUGGESTED ANSWER

The royal prerogative is the remains of royal power. C. Munro describes it as:

[1] Short, relevant quotations can sometimes explain things better than your own words.

> Those attributes peculiar to the Crown which are derived from common law, not statute and which still survive.[1]

(Studies in Constitutional Law (2nd edn, Butterworths 1999) 159)

As they are the powers of the Crown, it was thought for a long time that they enjoyed the same legal immunities as the Queen and could not be reviewed by the courts. The House of Lords had made this clear in cases like *Chandler v DPP* **[1964] AC 763** and *Gouriet v UPW* **[1978] AC 435**. This was despite trailblazing dissents, by Lord Denning, notably in *Laker Airways v Department of Trade* **[1977] QB 643**, and even Lord Devlin in *Chandler v DPP* **[1964]**, expressing some doubt. To Lord Denning, prerogative powers were government powers just like statutory powers, and if abused should be controlled.

The courts had always been able to exercise some sort of control over prerogative. Since as early as the *Case of Proclamations* **(1611) 12 Co Rep 74**, the courts have asserted entitlement to decide whether there was adequate precedent for the prerogative claimed to exist. This gives the courts more power than is commonly realized because the precedents are often unclear. For instance, in both *Attorney-General v*

De Keyser's Hotel **[1920] AC 508** and *Burmah Oil v Lord Advocate* **[1965] AC 75** the court decided that, although the government could seize and even destroy a person's property in order to defend the realm, compensation must be paid. This had not been clearly established in earlier cases. As late as 1987, the courts recognized that there was a prerogative of maintaining the peace of the realm; *R v Home Secretary ex parte Northumbria Police Authority* **[1987] 1 WLR 998.** What is certain, however, is that the courts will not recognize a 'new' prerogative for which there is no historic precedent.[2] As Diplock LJ said in *BBC v Johns* **[1965] Ch 32** at 79:

It is 350 years and a civil war too late for the Queen's courts to broaden the prerogative.

Attorney-General v De Keyser's Hotel **[1920]** recognized that if government had a prerogative power and a statutory power to do the same thing, the government should act under the statutory power, thus giving the citizen greater protection and respecting the wishes of Parliament. This principle also applies to an Act of Parliament that has not been brought into force; the prerogative must not be used in preference to the statute, *R v Home Secretary ex parte Fire Brigades Union* **[1995] 2 All ER 244**. Prerogatives, however, remain, unless they are clearly removed by an Act of Parliament, for example the power to remove a passport as shown in *R (XH) v Home Secretary* **[2017] 2 WLR 1437**.

Judicial review of the prerogative was finally allowed in *GCHQ* **[1985] AC 374**. Lord Fraser gave a number of reasons for this significant change of tack, chiefly that the Queen was not personally involved in the use of the prerogative and so the court would not be involved in questioning her legal immunity. He also noted that there had already been judicial review of decisions of judicial bodies acting under the prerogative in *R v Criminal Injuries Compensation Board ex parte Lain* **[1967] 2 QB 864** and *Attorney-General of Duchy of Lancaster v Overton Farms Ltd* **[1982] Ch 277**. With the development of judicial review in the past 30 years, there was no longer any reason to distinguish between statutory and prerogative powers.

All five House of Lords judges agreed that some prerogative powers could be judicially reviewed. It is unclear though *which* prerogative powers would be subject to judicial review.[3] All their lordships agreed that a 'minor' use of the prerogative, here concerning the conditions of service of civil servants, could be reviewed. Lords Fraser and Brightman thought that this was possible because it was only a delegated use of the prerogative. An Order in Council gave the minister for the Civil Service power to alter civil servants' conditions of service. The Order in Council itself could not be reviewed but the minister's decision under it could be. Prerogatives like control of the Armed Forces and foreign policy 'were unsuitable for discussion or review in the law courts' (Lord Fraser, 398).

The other three judges, Lords Scarman, Diplock, and Roskill, were of the opinion that whether a prerogative could be reviewed depended upon its subject matter. Only the lower level, non-political uses of the prerogative could be considered by the courts. Decisions on matters like national security, also involved in this case, had to be left to the government, because only it had the information upon which to make a decision. Lord Roskill supplied a handy list of prerogatives that were unreviewable and had to be left to government: entering into treaties; defence; grant of mercy; award of honours; dissolution of Parliament; and the appointment of government ministers. Lord Diplock thought that the prerogative should also be reviewable when its exercise affected private rights and expectations of citizens.

Judicial reviews of the prerogative resulting in success for the applicant are still rare, notwithstanding *GCHQ*. The right to British citizenship is nowadays determined by statute law, but the decision whether or not to issue a passport is a prerogative power.[4] In *R v Foreign Secretary ex parte Everett* [1989] AC 1014, the court concluded that they could review the refusal to renew Everett's passport, as this case did not concern weighty questions of foreign policy and also affected the rights of the individual. On the facts, the court refused the judicial review, but a much later case, *Rangis Begum v Secretary of State for the Home Department* [2014] EWHC 2968 (Admin) succeeded.[5]

In *R v Home Secretary ex parte Bentley* [1993] 4 All ER 442 (Bentley) the court was prepared to ignore previous case law, including the obiter dicta of Lord Roskill in *GCHQ*, and permit judicial review of the prerogative of mercy. The Home Secretary had misunderstood his legal powers when taking his decision and, although no formal order was made, he was asked to reconsider. In contrast, the Privy Council declined to follow *Bentley* in *Reckley v Minister of Public Safety (No. 2)* [1996] 1 All ER 562.[6]

The court looked at foreign affairs in *R (on the application of Abbasi and another) v Secretary of State for Foreign Affairs and Secretary of State for the Home Department* [2002] WL 3145052. Abbasi, a UK national held at Guantanamo Bay post 9/11, argued that the Foreign Office had a duty to intervene on his behalf with the US government. The court declined to interfere but conceded that judicial review would be available if the Foreign Office decision was irrational or defeated legitimate expectations.

Similarly, in *R (Sandiford) v Secretary of State for Foreign and Commonwealth Affairs* [2014] UKSC 44 the UK government declined to pay for legal help for a UK citizen sentenced to death in

[4] Prerogative powers cause a lot of confusion. It is worth distinguishing powers under statute from powers under prerogative.

[5] Analysis may reveal conflicts in the case law. A good answer will reconcile this in the conclusion.

[6] Again, analysis may reveal conflicts in the case law. A good answer will reconcile this in the conclusion.

Indonesia. The Supreme Court stated that this policy was lawful, but such decisions were not immune from judicial review on grounds such as irrationality. The court did, however, give a strong hint that the government should reconsider its decision.

Legislation for the UK's overseas territories is made under the authority of Orders in Council. In *R (Bancoult) v Secretary of State for Foreign and Commonwealth Affairs* [2001] **1 QB 1067**, the court ruled that a law ordering islanders to leave Diego Garcia was *ultra vires* the relevant Order in Council. This is similar to *GCHQ* itself, where a delegated power under the prerogative could be reviewed. The government redrafted the Order and this time it was upheld by the House of Lords, by a 3:2 majority. This was a matter of 'high policy' in which the courts would not interfere and, besides, there had never been a clear promise that the islanders would be able to return: *R (Bancoult) v Secretary of State for Foreign Affairs (No. 2)* [2009] **1 AC 453**.

[7] The last paragraph attempts to summarize the general effect of the modern case law.

It does seem, therefore, that the courts have become a little more willing to review prerogative acts[7] when they affect individual rights, embracing matters once considered out of bounds. Even when the court does not formally overturn the government's decision, it may give a strong hint that the government should reconsider. These hints are usually taken. Cases like the *Bancoult* litigation, however, touch upon important foreign policy considerations and the courts are still unwilling to become involved. Diego Garcia had been emptied of people in order to make it available as a military base for the United States.

✚ LOOKING FOR EXTRA MARKS?

- As this is a question on the attitude of the courts to the prerogative, you need a detailed knowledge of the case law.
- Knowing about the more political uses of the prerogative, for example selection of the Prime Minister, would be completely useless for this type of question.

Ⓠ QUESTION | 2

George is the leader of the Blue Party, which has a majority in the House of Commons. Therefore he is Prime Minister. A general election is held. The Blue Party wins 300 seats and the Red Party also wins 300 seats. The Yellow Party holds 30 seats and the other 20 MPs are from a number of minor parties.

▶

George does not like the result of the general election and asks the Queen to dissolve Parliament and call another election.

Advise the Queen on how she should respond to George's request.

! CAUTION!

■ This is a question about the more political uses of the prerogative, not about the legal side of this topic.

■ You will need to be comfortable with discussing how constitutional conventions work.

■ Treat past events, like what happened after the 2010 general election, as though it was case law and analyse it with the same attention to detail.

DIAGRAM ANSWER PLAN

Identify the issues
■ Identify the legal issues and issues governed by convention.
■ There are three issues here. First, can the Queen refuse a request for a general election? Secondly, how does the Queen choose a Prime Minister? Thirdly, can the Queen dismiss a Prime Minister?

Relevant law
■ Outline the relevant law and convention.
■ Under the royal prerogative the Queen has the power to choose Her Majesty's Government. Conventions, which are practices developed over many years, severely restrict the Queen's personal choices.

Apply the law
■ Analyse past incidents of dissolution of Parliament, choice of Prime Minister, and dismissal of Prime Ministers
■ See how they compare to the facts of this problem.

Conclude
■ What would it be permissible for the Queen to do?

Two of the remaining prerogative powers of the Queen are the right to dissolve Parliament and call a new one, which in modern terms would be a general election, and to choose who is Prime Minister. Old cases like the *Case of Proclamations* **(1611) 12 Co Rep 74** made a distinction between the ordinary and absolute prerogatives. The ordinary prerogatives were areas in which the Queen had no personal discretion. Nowadays she would merely act on the advice of her ministers. The two prerogative powers identified would be regarded as examples of the ordinary prerogative, but what this answer hopes to explore is the situations in which Queen might still have a choice.[1]

[1] The opening paragraph outlines the issues that we are going to consider.

It is accepted that the Queen does have the right to express a view to her ministers on how her prerogatives are used. W. Bagehot put it that the Queen has:

the right to be consulted, the right to encourage, the right to warn.

(*The Law of the Constitution* (Fontana 1867))

[2] When dealing with convention, we do not have cases; instead we have things that politicians said or did.

More recently, these principles were restated in a letter to *The Times* on 27 July 1986 by the Queen's Press Secretary, Sir William Heseltine.[2] There had been press coverage claiming that the Queen disapproved of some of the policies of the then Prime Minister, Margaret Thatcher. The letter said that the Queen 'was entitled to have opinions on government policy and to express them to her chief Minister' but was 'bound to accept and act on the advice of her Ministers'. Importantly, the letter concluded with the constitutional reminder that discussions between the Queen and her ministers are confidential. It is difficult therefore to know for certain whether the Queen, or any previous monarch, has ever gone beyond expressing a forceful opinion. That is allowed as long as the government has the final say.

By convention, the Prime Minister could always choose the date of a general election by asking the Queen to dissolve Parliament. This has been partially superseded by the **Fixed-Term Parliaments Act 2011**, which lays down that a general election can only be held every five years. The Act does allow two exceptions to this. The first is that a two-thirds majority of the Commons votes for a different date or that the government loses a vote of confidence. In 2017, Prime Minister May wanted to call an election and the Opposition parties were happy to provide her with a two-thirds majority. If George was similarly successful, then he could go to the Queen and ask for dissolution. There are no examples of the Queen refusing a dissolution in the UK, though there is an example from Canada, where the Queen is also Head of State, in 1926. Nevertheless, according to the King's Private Secretary in 1950, it is thought that the Queen could refuse a new general election if three conditions apply. First, that the existing Parliament was still 'vital, viable and capable of doing its job'; secondly, that a general election would be detrimental to the national economy and, crucially, that another Prime Minister could be found with a working majority. If two-thirds of the Commons voted for an election, it is unlikely that the Queen would refuse.[3]

[3] This is a very succinct example of applying the convention to the facts and coming to a conclusion.

If the Queen actually made a personal choice as to who should become Prime Minister, this would be highly controversial. She would be accused of political favouritism. Usually, the 'first-past-the-post' electoral system leaves no decision for the Queen to make. There is a clear result from a general election and the leader of the majority party is invited, as the person entitled, to form a government. If, however, a 'hung Parliament' results, namely no single party having an overall majority of seats in the Commons, matters are by no means so clear. Let us look at a few previous examples.[4]

[4] We cannot use legal precedents when looking at convention, but must look at past conventional practice.

In 1931, the first Labour Government, led by Prime Minister Ramsay MacDonald, faced a national economic crisis. MacDonald was convinced that it was essential in the national interest to reduce public expenditure, in particular unemployment benefit. His party could not accept this, but the leaders of the other parties agreed with MacDonald. He offered his resignation, but the King declined it. Instead, George V consulted the leaders of the other parties. They advised that MacDonald should remain as Prime Minister and form a 'National government', a coalition of parties. MacDonald took this advice and won a resounding victory at a general election later in the year. Ironically, he ended up as the Labour Prime Minister of a largely Conservative Government. Subsequently, George V has been criticized for playing too active a part in the choice of Prime Minister. Presumably the King did what he did on the advice of the other party leaders and because he thought that it was in the national interest. The electorate seems to have approved. To conclude, the Queen could seek the advice of the leaders of all three parties, Blue, Red, and Yellow.

In 1974, there were two general elections. The first, February 1974, resulted in a hung Parliament. The incumbent governing party, the Conservatives led by Prime Minister Edward Heath, lost their majority. Labour, led by Harold Wilson, won the most seats but not an overall majority of seats. Nonetheless, Heath did not offer his resignation as Prime Minister and instead spent several days in negotiations with the Liberal Party trying to form a new coalition government. During this period, it was not clear who would govern and the Queen might have had to become involved. After several days the talks broke down without agreement, Heath resigned and advised the Queen to send for the Labour leader, Harold Wilson, to form a new, minority, administration.

What we can deduce from these events is that George remains Prime Minister until he resigns.[5] The Queen might suggest that he tries to agree a coalition government with the Yellow Party.

[5]We have analysed the past incident and come to a conclusion.

The general election of May 2010 also produced a hung parliament. This had been anticipated, so in February 2010 the Cabinet Office consulted and then drafted a chapter for its Cabinet Manual setting out the constitutional position and appropriate conduct to establish a government. Civil servants were to assist the various political parties in their negotiations and the Queen's Private Secretary was to observe, but not participate. The existing Prime Minister, the leader of the Labour Party, Gordon Brown remained in office, although they had fewer seats than the Conservatives. Both Labour and the Conservatives negotiated with the Liberal Democrats to form a majority coalition. The Liberal Democrats preferred the Conservatives, so the Conservative leader, David Cameron, was able to form a government and become Prime Minister. In the 2017 general election, the Conservative Government lost their majority, but remained the largest party. They were able to remain in power by negotiating a 'Confidence and Supply Agreement' with the Democratic Unionist Party. So in our situation, the Queen would not become involved, but use her intermediaries to suggest to George that he try to negotiate a coalition or a confidence and supply agreement with the Yellow Party. If he failed to do so, the leader of the Red Party would be invited to try to form a government with the Yellow Party. If that was successful, George would be expected to resign and the Queen would ask the leader of the Red Party to become Prime Minister.[6]

[6]Another example of applying the convention and coming to a conclusion.

If George refused to cooperate and insisted upon remaining as Prime Minister, without a majority with which to govern, the Queen would need to consider dismissing him. This last occurred in this country in 1834, when William IV dismissed Lord Melbourne. In 1975, however, the Governor-General of Australia (the Queen's representative as Head of State) dismissed the Australian Prime Minister, Gough Whitlam. The Senate was refusing to agree to his Budget because of illegal ministerial misbehaviour in procuring overseas loans. A Governor-General acts in the name of the Queen and exercises her powers, and it is not thought that the Governor-General consulted the Queen. The Governor-General, however, had spoken to the leader of the Opposition and that leader was willing to take over as Prime Minister and hold an immediate general election. He won that election with a resounding majority, so it seems that the people of Australia agreed. The Gough Whitlam affair shows that the power to dismiss a Prime Minister for behaving 'unconstitutionally' still exists.[7] What George is doing is quite similar and the Queen would be entitled to request his resignation.

[7] This is a firm conclusion, but does the evidence really support it?

In reality, it is most unlikely that an experienced party leader, such as George, would dare to act in such an 'unconventional' way. If he did, though, the Queen is there to protect the national interest. The rarity of incidents of royal interference indicates that kings and queens have, rightly, been very cautious about when it is appropriate to interfere. Perhaps the *possibility* of the Queen acting is the key, as it deters inappropriate behaviour and maintains responsible government by those entrusted, by election, to wield political power.[8]

[8] The overall conclusion relates the issues in this problem to the wider constitutional role of the Queen.

➕ LOOKING FOR EXTRA MARKS?

- There are differences of opinion about what actually happened in the controversial political events described in this answer.
- A really good answer might include some different interpretations of these events.
- It is ok to criticize the conduct of the king or queen.

Ⓠ QUESTION 3

Behind the phrase 'royal prerogative' lie hidden some issues of great constitutional importance which are insufficiently recognised.

(C. Munro, *Studies in Constitutional Law* (2nd edn, Butterworths 1999) 291)

Consider whether you agree with this statement.

❗ CAUTION!

- This question is not about the Queen at all; it is about how the government uses her prerogative.
- The government has a lot of power using the prerogative.
- It is 'insufficiently recognised', because many people do not realize that the government uses royal power in this way.
- The essay is a discussion on whether this gives the government too much power and how it can be controlled.

⬚ DIAGRAM ANSWER PLAN

> Prerogative powers, the legal powers of the Queen, are used in her name by the government of the day.

▼

> These prerogative powers are some of the most important powers of government

▼

> Many of these prerogative powers are ill-defined

▼

> The courts may control the use of some of these powers by judicial review

▼

> Judicial review of matters of high government policy, for example defence and national security, is not possible

▼

> Parliament has limited control over the use of the prerogative, as ministerial responsibility does not extend to all areas

▼

> Conclusion

Ⓐ SUGGESTED ANSWER

The royal prerogative concerns 'those inherent legal attributes which are unique to the Crown' (S. De Smith, *Constitutional and Administrative Law* (Penguin 1998)). Whilst some of these remain vested in the monarch in person, by convention most (in volume and significance) are now exercisable only by ministers of the Crown. It is true that by convention the Queen must be consulted, and as W. Bagehot put it, she has 'the right to be consulted, the right to encourage, the right to warn' (*The Law of the Constitution* (Fontana 1867)) but in reality the royal prerogative now amounts to powers of Her Majesty's elected government.[1]

[1] The opening paragraph sets out the issue to be considered.

Many of the central and most important government powers lie within the royal prerogative. They include the conduct of foreign affairs, defence and national security, claims to territory, maintaining the peace, mercy and pardon, some aspects of immigration, and the grant of honours.

A problem with these ancient powers is that it is often unclear what exactly they allow the government to do. Sometimes legal challenges require the courts to attempt to clarify what powers still exist. For instance, in *Attorney-General v De Keyser's Royal Hotel* **[1920] AC 508** (*De Keyser*) historical research was needed to discover the circumstances in which the Crown could requisition property in wartime. No really clear answer was obtained, so that when a similar point came up again in *Burmah Oil v Lord Advocate* **[1965] AC 75** there was still doubt. As late as 1987 a 'new' prerogative power emerged in *R v Home Secretary ex parte Northumbria Police Authority* **[1987] 2 All ER 282** (*Northumbria*), which stated that the government has the power to maintain peace in the kingdom. This amounted to a significant, very wide, and vague tool, in addition to the extensive statutory powers already at the disposal of the police. To take a roughly similar example, the government has a duty to uphold and maintain national security, as recognized in *GCHQ* **[1985] AC 374**. What exactly is national security and what is government allowed to do to preserve it? There are no clear answers to these two questions. The attitude of the courts has usually been to leave judgements upon what constitutes a perceived or actual threat to national security to government in cases such as *Chandler v DPP* **[1964] AC 763** and *Rehman v SSHD* **[2001] 3 WLR 877**.[2]

In the *GCHQ* case, the House of Lords declared that it could control how the royal prerogative was used by means of judicial review. Control on the grounds of illegality, irrationality, and procedural impropriety is quite limited anyway and, leaving that aside, all of their lordships agreed that some government prerogative powers lay outside the control of the courts. Lords Fraser and Brightman considered that only delegated exercise of the prerogative could be reviewed; that is, the decision of the minister but not the Order in Council itself. The politically controversial prerogatives had to be left to government. Lord Roskill identified these as treaties, defence, mercy, honours, dissolution of Parliament, and the appointment of government ministers.

The courts tend to be very reluctant to interfere with government prerogative decisions. In *Chandler*, the deployment and armament of troops was outside the control of the courts. A decision by the Attorney General to take legal action or not was unchallengeable, as in *Gouriet v UPW* **[1977] 2 WLR 310**. The decision not to renew a passport was, in theory, reviewable, *R v Foreign Secretary ex parte Everett* **[1989] AC 1014**, but in reality the courts agreed with the government's policy not to renew the passports of 'wanted' criminals. Taylor LJ considered that the courts should not look at 'high-policy' executive decisions, but could review lower level decisions affecting the rights of individuals. The court continued this approach in *R (Abbasi) v Foreign Secretary*

[2] An analysis of the case law, leading to the conclusion that too much power is left to the government.

[2002] EWCA Civ 1598. Abbasi, detained by the United States at Guantanamo Bay, wished the UK government to intervene on his behalf. The court refused to tell the government what to do, but maintained that such ministerial decisions were potentially reviewable. In *Smith v Ministry of Defence* **[2013] UKSC 41**, the Supreme Court rejected the view that a court could review the decision to send British troops to Iraq or entertain any question about the legality or otherwise of the military intervention in that country. In contrast *R (Miller) v Secretary of State for Exiting the EU* **[2017] UKSC 5** decided that, although leaving the EU treaties is a prerogative power, doing so alters the rights of citizens and only an Act of Parliament can do that.[3]

[3] Another detailed analysis of the case law, leading to the conclusion that the courts may be reluctant to review the prerogative, but will uphold the supremacy of Parliament.

The courts have often justified their approach by saying, in cases like *Chandler* and *Gouriet*, that the proper body to control the use of these highly political powers is Parliament. It is true that Parliament may remove prerogatives as in the **Bill of Rights 1689** and the **Treasure Act 1996**. Where both statutory provision and prerogative apply, government must use the statutory power rather than the prerogative; *De Keyser*. The courts have also held that the government must not ignore the will of Parliament when statutory powers have replaced a prerogative but have not yet been brought into force; *R v Home Secretary ex parte Fire Brigade Union* **[1995] 2 All ER 244**. However, a government with a Commons majority usually controls what Parliament does and it is inconceivable that the Legislature would be allowed to remove or restrict an important prerogative power against the government's wishes.[4]

[4] Evidence to support the argument that the government has too much power. Parliament will not intervene.

By convention, ministers are accountable for their actions to Parliament. Whilst in principle this includes actions under the prerogative, by long-standing practice many prerogative areas are hidden from the view of Parliament. Since 1955, successive governments have refused to answer MPs' questions concerning the Prime Minister's advice to the Queen, the grant of honours, mercy in death sentences, commercial contracts, investigations by the Director of Public Prosecutions, and senior appointments such as judges, bishops, and Privy Councillors. Similarly, governments may refuse to answer questions on many defence issues, such as sales of arms, issues of national security, and confidential relations with foreign states. The Parliamentary Commissioner for Administration is also prevented from investigating many of the same areas.[5]

[5] Plenty of evidence to support the argument is developed in this paragraph.

At law, the Queen decides on military action, using her prerogative. By convention, the Prime Minister actually takes the decision, perhaps first consulting Cabinet or selected senior ministers. After the controversial decision to go to war with Iraq in 2003, all political parties agreed that the Prime Ministerial prerogative to commit the country to war should end (save in urgent circumstances), instead making it a decision for debate and vote by the House of Commons. For example, in August 2013, the Commons rejected the Prime Minister's request to authorize military action against Syria.[6]

[6] An up-to-date example is good.

It can be seen that the royal prerogative gives the government of the day great power. This power is subject only to limited accountability, not amounting to control. Some change is afoot, though there will always be a temptation for those in power jealously to guard that power.[7]

[7] The conclusion, though brief, is based on the evidence considered in the essay.

 LOOKING FOR EXTRA MARKS?

- This question overlaps into other areas of the syllabus, such as ministerial responsibility and judicial review.
- You should be prepared for topics that overlap in Constitutional Law.
- Look in the media for new examples of how the government uses the prerogative and how Parliament attempts to control the government.

Q **QUESTION** | **4**

The UK and the Republic of Fantasia (Fantasia) are in dispute about possession of an island called Lackland, which has been sovereign UK territory for the past 200 years. Fantasian troops invade and take control of Lackland. UK Armed Forces are deployed to remove them. The Crown takes a number of actions. It withdraws the passports of some UK citizens resident in Fantasia thought to be helping the Fantasian invasion forces; Fantasian citizens resident in the UK are arrested and expelled and a number of UK-owned and registered ships are requisitioned, without compensation, for military use. The UK troops retake Fantasia, and occupy and destroy properties belonging to both Fantasian and UK citizens, taking many Fantasians prisoner.

The UK action is successful and a peace treaty is concluded between the UK and Fantasia. Among other provisions, it stipulates that neither country accepts liability for loss or damage inflicted during the hostilities. No UK legislation is enacted to give effect to the treaty within the UK, as it is not thought necessary.

A number of UK and Fantasian citizens are aggrieved by the actions taken against them by the UK during the hostilities and each seeks a legal remedy.

Advise them.

CAUTION!

■ This question requires a very detailed and accurate knowledge of the case law on the royal prerogative.

■ Do not treat this problem question as an essay. Try to apply the law to the facts.

DIAGRAM ANSWER PLAN

Identify the issues	■ Identify the legal issues: the use of the royal prerogative in time of war; specifically the decision to go to war, withdrawal of passports, expulsion of enemy aliens, destruction of property, and detention without trial
Relevant law	■ Outline the relevant law: case law and statute, in particular: *CCSU v Minister for the Civil Service, Attorney-General v De Keyser's Hotel, Nissan v Attorney-General, Rahmatullah v Ministry of Defence, R (Miller) v Secretary of State for Exiting the European Union* and the **Human Rights Act 1998** ■ Apply the law
Apply the law	■ Can the government withdraw a passport? ■ Can the government expel enemy aliens? ■ Can the government destroy property without compensation? ■ Can the government detain without trial? ■ Is Act of State a defence to these actions?
Conclude	■ What do these prerogative powers allow the government to do? ■ How are these powers modified by the **Human Rights Act**?

SUGGESTED ANSWER

The declaration and conduct of war is one of the established royal prerogatives. Whilst there is no formal declaration of war here, other armed conflicts and troop deployment are also governed by the royal prerogative. It is most unlikely that a court would entertain any challenge as to whether war was justified or troops should be sent: *Chandler v DPP* **[1964] AC 763**. This was confirmed by *CCSU* *v Minister for the Civil Service* [1985] AC 374 (the *GCHQ* case) where, in particular, Lord Roskill included war as one of the prerogatives that was beyond the control of judicial review. An indirect challenge to the legality to the 2003 Iraq War was also not allowed in *R v Jones* [2006] 2 WLR 772. That the decision to go to war or not and how the war is conducted is a prerogative power that the courts will not challenge was confirmed in *Smith v Ministry of Defence* [2013] UKSC 41.[1] This does not, however, mean that the Crown can do as it pleases (see later).

It is clear that there still is a prerogative power to withdraw passports: *R (XH) v Home Secretary* [2017] 2 WLR 1437. In *R v Foreign Secretary ex parte Everett* [1989] AC 1014, however, the Court of Appeal held that the Foreign Secretary's refusal to renew a passport was subject to judicial review, for Everett had a right to natural justice. Here, however, the facts may be distinguished.[2] Taylor LJ stated that matters of high policy were not justiciable. War is a matter of high policy, so it is possible that the courts might refuse to intervene here. In *GCHQ* itself, a similar matter of high policy, namely national security, overrode the requirement of natural justice. Also, as in *Everett*, whilst the court might find the applicants' cases reviewable, it might, in its discretion, award no remedy.

The expulsion of enemy aliens has been held to be an unchallengeable prerogative matter; *Netz v Chuter Ede* [1946] Ch 224. In the famous case of *R v Bottrill ex parte Kuechenmeister* [1947] KB 41, it was held that the Home Secretary could intern an enemy alien during a war. What is more, only the Home Secretary could decide when the war was over, that too being a matter of royal prerogative. Even in peacetime the courts of Australia upheld a prerogative power to expel aliens in *Ruddock v Vadarlis* (2001) 66 ALD 25. At the time of the first (1991) Gulf War some Iraqi nationals were threatened with deportation. The courts were at least willing to look at their cases, although they decided that they could not investigate an issue of national security; *R v Home Secretary ex parte Cheblak [1991] 2 All ER 319*. Subsequently, the European Court of Human Rights ruled in *Chahal v UK* (1997) 23 EHRR 413 that the courts should be able to review such government decisions based on national security. However, in *Rehman v SSHD* [2001] 3 WLR 877 the House of Lords kept to the view that they were unwilling to question the Secretary of State's decision to deport a foreign national on grounds of national security.[3]

The requisitioning of a UK subject's property is certainly allowed in wartime. Compensation, however, must be paid: *Attorney-General v De Keyser's Royal Hotel* [1920] AC 508. According to *Burmah Oil v Lord Advocate* [1965] AC 75, when UK-owned property abroad is destroyed for wartime purposes, compensation is due. This seems to

[1] Case law over a considerable period is examined, because the law in this area is developing and changing.

[2] A precedent might not quite fit the facts of a problem, so it needs to be distinguished.

[3] The European Court of Human Rights (ECtHR) may come to a different decision to a UK court, but it only becomes law in the UK if the House of Lords/Supreme Court accepts the ECtHR's views.

be confirmed by ***Nissan v Attorney-General* [1970] AC 179**, when UK forces requisitioned and damaged a hotel in Cyprus. The House of Lords confirmed that this action did not qualify as an Act of State and therefore Nissan might have a remedy. Act of State was here defined as an action of government policy that should not be considered by the courts ('non-justiciable'). The case law seems to make a distinction based on the nationality of the victim. Act of State cannot be committed against a UK citizen. Nissan was a UK subject and so had his remedy in a UK court. Actions in Fantasia that harm Fantasian citizens used to qualify as Acts of State, as held in ***Buron v Denman* [1848] 2 Ex 167**, where the Royal Navy destroyed Spanish property in Africa, acting on clear government policy to stamp out the slave trade. This can be contrasted with ***Johnstone v Pedlar* [1921] 2 AC 262**, where the property of a US citizen was confiscated within the UK. This was not an Act of State. The true *ratio* of this case is hard to define.[4] Can an Act of State be committed in the UK? It seems that it cannot be committed against the citizen of a friendly country, here the United States. However ***Johnstone*** is interpreted, it certainly does not apply to the citizens of a country with which the UK is at war and against which the UK commits acts in that foreign country.

Act of State is a rather old-fashioned doctrine, which is not often pleaded as a defence by Her Majesty's Government nowadays. It was considered by the Court of Appeal in ***Rahmatullah v Ministry of Defence; sub nom Re Iraqi Civilian Litigation* [2015] EWCA Civ 843**, where Iraqis were suing for alleged unlawful detention during the British occupation. The court thought that ***Buron v Denman* [1848] 2 Ex 167** was maybe outdated and that Act of State would only apply to important government foreign policy actions, such as annexing foreign territory. The detention of individuals was not a pressing matter of foreign policy and with increasing concern for human rights, could not be held to be non-justiciable.[5] The court must at least consider the merits of their case. The same court confirmed that Act of State could not be used as a defence against human rights infringements in ***Belhaj v Straw MP (UN intervening)* [2016] 1 All ER 121**.

The Human Rights Act 1998 would apply to Lackland, because it was held by the European Court of Human Rights in ***Al-Skeini v UK* (2011) 53 EHRR 18**, that as the UK had assumed authority and responsibility for South-East Iraq it was under the jurisdiction of the UK. ***Smith v Ministry of Defence* [2013] UKSC 41** confirmed that the UK courts accepted the ***Al-Skeini*** view.[6] The rights of the local inhabitants of Lackland are protected just as much as the inhabitants of the UK. This would include things such as unlawful killing as in ***Al-Skeini***, unlawful detention as in ***Al-Jedda v UK* (2011) 53 EHRR 23**, and inhuman and degrading treatment in

[4] Not all cases have a clear *ratio* and a good answer will analyse the different interpretations.

[5] Many old principles of public law have to be adapted to conform to Human Rights.

[6] This is the same point as in 3; the Supreme Court has to accept the ECtHR view of the law in order for the law in English courts to change.

Al Saadoon & Mufdhi v UK **[2010] ECHR 282**. The British soldiers conducting the invasion would also be protected by the **Human Rights Act 1998**, because the soldiers are always under the authority and control of the government, particularly when they are on active service: *Smith v Ministry of Defence* **[2013] UKSC 41**.

It is clear that the conclusion of a treaty is an unchallengeable act in the UK courts; *Blackburn v Attorney-General* **[1971] 2 All ER 1780** confirmed in *R v Foreign Secretary ex parte Rees-Mogg* **[1994] 1 All ER 457**. However, it is also clear that the treaty cannot affect legal rights within the UK unless it is given statutory force: *R (Miller) v Secretary of State for Exiting the EU* **[2017] UKSC 5**. It does not matter whether the rights are statutory or common law, such as trespass and negligence; *The Parlement Belge* **[1879] 4 PD 129**, confirmed in *Littrell v USA (No. 2)* **[1994] 3 All ER 203**. So the attempt to prevent legal action in the UK courts would not work.[7]

In conclusion, the UK and Lackland citizens affected by these 'wartime actions' have a fairly good chance of some kind of legal remedy.[8] The decision to go to war and things like military tactics are unchallengeable matters of high policy, with which the courts would not interfere, but the modern trend is not to allow the more minor prerogative actions to be unchallengeable, particularly when they affect individuals. This is reinforced by the view that human rights are universal. They do not just apply in the UK and can even apply when military action is being taken. Oddly, however, the removal of passports may be more difficult to challenge. There is not a right under the **Human Rights Act 1998** granting the freedom to travel, so the courts might not feel able to depart from older decisions.

[7] Complex case law is examined, but a conclusion can be reached.

[8] The final paragraph summarizes the legal position of all the claimants.

✚ LOOKING FOR EXTRA MARKS?

- Human Rights law is now pervasive. It affects all of the law and in particular it affects all areas of Public Law.

- You need to consider how Human Rights law is changing what was previously understood to be the law, as illustrated by this answer.

➚ TAKING THINGS FURTHER

- Blackburn R., 'Monarchy and the personal prerogatives' [2004] Public Law 546, 255.
  This article examines whether the Queen could ever take a personal decision on how the prerogative is to be exercised or whether she would always be bound by convention and the views of her government.

- Brazier R., 'Monarchy and the personal prerogatives: a personal response to Professor Blackburn' [2005] Public Law 45.

  As the title suggests, this author disagrees with Professor Blackburn's interpretation of the role of the Queen in the exercise of the royal prerogative. Read it to gain a different view.

- Markesinis B.S., 'The royal prerogative revisited' (1973) 32 Cambridge Law Journal 287.

  The exact extent of the royal prerogative and what it allows the government to do is not as clear-cut as it might seem. It can require much historical and legal research.

- Moules R., 'Judicial review of prerogative Orders in Council; recognizing the constitutional reality of executive legislation' (2008) 67 Cambridge Law Journal 12.

  The government legislates under the prerogative by using Orders in Council. This can be for overseas territories, as in the **Bancoult** *cases or for the UK, as in* **GCHQ***. This article explains how this works and how it is not subject to the same kind of approval process as an Act of Parliament.*

- Munro C., 'Crown and Prerogative' in *Studies in Constitutional Law* (2nd edn, Butterworths 1999) 255.

  This is a really good overview of the whole subject of the royal prerogative, looking at its history, the conventions that govern its use, and the attempts by the courts and Parliament to control government abuse of its prerogative powers.

Online Resources

www.oup.com/uk/qanda/

Go online for extra essay and problem questions, a glossary of key terms, online versions of all the answer plans and audio commentary on how selected ones were put together, and a range of podcasts which include advice on exam and coursework technique and advice for other assessment methods.

Parliament

5

ARE YOU READY?

The questions in this chapter concern various aspects of the work of Parliament. There is an essay about the work and procedures of the House of Commons. Then there is a problem that explores the same area of the work of the Commons from the point of view of an MP. There is an essay on the work of select committees, a problem on parliamentary privilege, and an essay on reform of the House of Lords. In order to attempt these questions, you need to have covered all of the following topics in your work and your revision:

- understanding the functions and processes of the House of Commons;
- understanding the role of an MP in the House of Commons;
- understanding what select committees do and being able to evaluate their effectiveness;
- understanding how parliamentary privilege controls the behaviour of MPs and non-MPs;
- understanding the role of the House of Lords and why reform has proved so difficult.

 KEY DEBATES

Debate: The Effectiveness of Parliament

Is Parliament still a democratic, effective institution with a strong effect on the life of the nation or is it now firmly under the control of the government of the day, while real power lies elsewhere?

Debate: Parliamentary Privilege

Parliamentary privilege in effect means that Parliament makes its own laws to control the activities of its own members. Is that acceptable nowadays?

Debate: Reform of the House of Lords

It would be difficult for the House of Commons to cope with the workload if the House of Lords did not exist and it contains some expertise that the Commons lacks. Yet it is odd in a modern state to have an unelected legislative chamber.

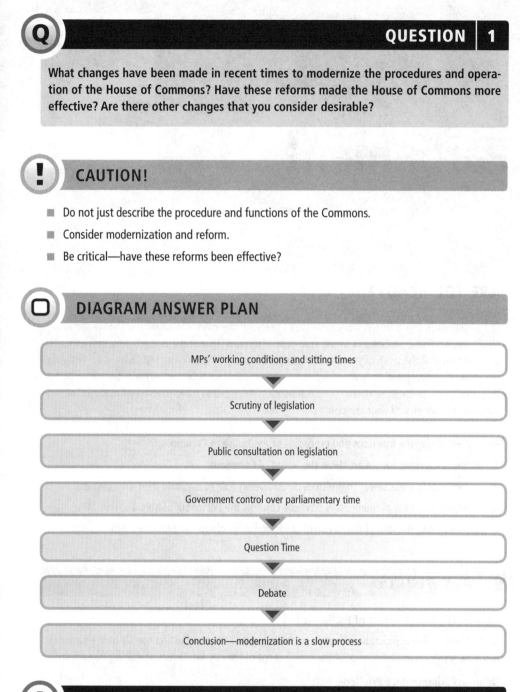

QUESTION 1

What changes have been made in recent times to modernize the procedures and operation of the House of Commons? Have these reforms made the House of Commons more effective? Are there other changes that you consider desirable?

CAUTION!

■ Do not just describe the procedure and functions of the Commons.

■ Consider modernization and reform.

■ Be critical—have these reforms been effective?

DIAGRAM ANSWER PLAN

> MPs' working conditions and sitting times
>
> Scrutiny of legislation
>
> Public consultation on legislation
>
> Government control over parliamentary time
>
> Question Time
>
> Debate
>
> Conclusion—modernization is a slow process

SUGGESTED ANSWER

The UK is known for its traditions, pageantry, and ceremony. To many, the way in which the House of Commons does its business is a prime example, steeped in history from its building to its procedures and language. The structure seems even to be class-ridden, with the distinction made between the Lords and the Commons. This is, of course, a product of continuity and development over a long period of time, although some might find it old-fashioned.[1]

[1] The Commons may seem old-fashioned.

In recent years, however, there have been some significant changes to the way the House of Commons operates. These have been intended to improve working conditions for MPs as well as enabling it to perform its principal functions, legislating and scrutinizing the Executive, more effectively and efficiently.[2] Much of the impetus for changes to the legislative process comes from government, ever trying to get substantial amounts of (its) legislation through Parliament as smoothly as possible. Governments are, however, likely to be less enthusiastic about measures to improve scrutiny of the Executive itself. Some long-standing criticisms of parliamentary procedures, such as the ineffective scrutiny of delegated legislation, remain to be addressed.

[2] But modernization is occurring.

The first aspect that will be examined relates to the working conditions of MPs. Until relatively recently, the work of MPs was seriously hampered by a shortage of office accommodation. Many had to share offices and some had no office space at all. With the opening in 2000 of Portcullis House, all MPs have an office, usually with a room for a secretary and research assistant nearby. This is of particular value in dealing with the substantial volume of correspondence from constituents that MPs now receive. MPs are paid a substantial allowance towards their office costs. This payment and how some have utilized it has caused great controversy recently, with calls for a flat salary only. However, the fact remains that appropriate assistance is necessary for MPs if they are to perform their functions effectively. The expenses scandal forced the House of Commons, which jealously guards its self-regulation and independence, to hand over control of MPs' expenses to an independent body, the Independent Parliamentary Standards Authority.[3]

[3] Rapid change is possible, a point picked up in the conclusion.

The change that has probably had the greatest impact on MPs' working conditions concerns the sitting hours of the House of Commons. Traditionally, Commons proceedings began at 2.30 p.m., except on Fridays when sittings began at 9.30 a.m. and ended by 3.00 p.m. to allow MPs to travel back to their constituencies for the weekend. Debates on legislation would not normally begin until 5.00 p.m., normally continuing until 10.00 p.m. and sometimes well into the night. These hours were designed for the convenience of those MPs who had another occupation. Until well into the twentieth century it was common for an MP to carry on a business or practice a profession, such as law, being in effect only a part-time MP. This became less common as politics developed into a full-time occupation, including much increased constituency work, which could thus no longer be combined with another job. Also, meetings of select and standing committees were normally scheduled for mornings, and more MPs were involved in these.[4]

[4] Parliament has more work now.

As well as being outdated, these sitting hours disrupted the private lives of MPs; it was impossible to enjoy a normal family life if one frequently had to be at the House of Commons until 10.00 p.m. or later. Great difficulty was caused to women with young children, and it was widely believed that these hours contributed to the reluctance of women to stand for Parliament. From 1999 onwards, there have been reforms to the sitting hours of the Commons, so that they nowadays resemble normal 'office hours'. The standard day is approximately 9 till 5, with an afternoon start on Mondays and an early afternoon finish on Fridays, which enables MPs who do not represent London area constituencies to return home for the weekend. There have also been adjustments to the arrangement of the yearly sessions, again partly to help MPs with family commitments. For example, there are now half-term breaks in February and May, to coincide with school holidays, and the summer recess has been shortened. Maybe as a result of these more family-friendly hours, there are a record number of women MPs—208 were returned at the 2017 general election.[5]

[5] An up-to-date example is always useful.

Turning to the legislative process, there has long been criticism of the way in which the House of Commons examines legislation, or fails to do so. Even important laws may be rushed through without adequate scrutiny. The **Data Retention and Investigatory Powers Act 2014** was published in bill form on 10 July and went through all its parliamentary stages in the Commons and the Lords between 14 and 17 July. It was emergency legislation to allow communication service providers to retain communications data for up to two years, after the European Court of Justice had declared this illegal under EU law. To defy EU law was a significant step that may have required more time for scrutiny and debate.[6]

[6] A good example always strengthens the argument.

There have, however, been some welcome developments in the legislative process. It is now the practice of government to publish proposed legislation in draft form well in advance of its formal introduction to Parliament, allowing earlier consideration and comment by expert and other interested parties and the public at large. It is then subjected to the new procedural stage of pre-legislative parliamentary scrutiny by committee, for example a Joint Committee specifically formed to examine a specific bill. For the Children and Families Bill 2014, a Public Reading Stage was added, inviting members of the public to submit their comments to the MPs considering the bill in committee. This seems a welcome addition to the scrutiny process.[7]

[7] Reforms are being made.

The timetable for passing legislation is always contentious. Successive governments have refused to address the effective stranglehold that government has upon what legislation is considered and in turn passed. The vast bulk of bills are government bills and government, of course, wishes to get its way, specifically in getting its mandated legislative programme through. Opposition parties argue that it would improve the effectiveness of the Commons in checking government if it had more of a say over its own business, specifically as to what gets debated and examined, when, and for how long. The Commons established a Backbench Business Committee enabling backbenchers to bring forward debates of their own choice.[8] The committee considers the case made for the proposed subject. Time for such debates is, however, limited and still ultimately controlled by government.

Governments also object to delays that they attribute to Opposition obstruction. The Opposition and backbenchers generally do not wish their examination of bills curtailed. Programme Motions limit time for debate and so ensure managed progression of a bill with planned allocation of time for consideration of each clause. This device has largely replaced the old Allocation of Time Order, the 'guillotine', resulting in a more rational and less contentious timetabling of legislative scrutiny.

One of the main reasons for the pressure on the Commons' timetable is the rule that public bills must complete their passage through both Houses within one session, or else fall and start again from scratch next session. There has been innovation to allow some bills to be carried over from one session to the next, despite the concern that this makes life too easy for the government of the day.

There have been other changes to parliamentary procedures. Soon after the 1997 election, Prime Minister's Question Time was moved from the traditional 3.00 p.m. 15-minute Tuesday and Thursday afternoon slots, to 30 minutes every Wednesday (noon–12.30 p.m.). The intention was to allow for more extended and sober questioning, rather than the short and noisy performance of the past, but there is little noticeable difference. A further adaptation has been the introduction of a parallel chamber for simultaneous debates, at nearby Westminster Hall. This enables backbenchers to raise more issues and provides the opportunity to debate select committee reports. The government has held a few debates on matters raised by the new 'e-petition', a measure introduced to try to enhance public engagement and involvement. Any petition attracting at least 100,000 signatures has to be considered for debate in the Commons.[9]

Although many of the changes discussed, and the removal of other arcane, if harmless, rules (like having to wear a hat to raise a point of

[8] Another reform.

[9] More opportunities for debate.

order during a division!) have been largely welcomed, there remain many areas where further reform could be achieved. For instance, many outside Parliament consider that the slow process of voting by walking through the division lobbies should be replaced by instant electronic voting. However MPs, who value the voting process as an opportunity to buttonhole a government minister, have rejected this. Whatever the merit, perhaps this illustrates the inherent conservatism of an institution that has existed for centuries. It may be noted though, that if there is a big enough scandal and the public react to it, such as the MPs' expenses scandal of 2009, change can be very fast. The **Parliamentary Standards Act 2009**, creating a new body to control MPs' expenses and salaries, the Independent Parliamentary Standards Authority, followed within months.[10]

[10] Modernization is slow, but public interest can speed it up.

LOOKING FOR EXTRA MARKS?

- Parliament's website is full of information about this topic.
- It contains lots of up-to-date examples.
- You are asked to suggest reforms—be creative.

QUESTION 2

At the recent UK general election, ten seats in the House of Commons were unexpectedly won by the Save the National Health Service Party (SNHS). These 'first-time' MPs seek your advice as to the means available to them to try to influence government policy, especially on health issues.

Advise them.

CAUTION!

- Look at this from the point of view of 1 in 650 MPs. What can they achieve?
- How do small political parties operate in Parliament?
- Do not just describe the procedure; advise the party how they can use it.

DIAGRAM ANSWER PLAN

Identify the issues	■ Identify the issues: the ability of a small political party to influence government policy
Relevant law	■ Outline the relevant parliamentary procedure and practice
Apply the law	■ Involvement in the legislative process ■ Participation in debates ■ Parliamentary questions ■ Membership of select committees ■ Lobbying
Conclude	■ The influence of a small political party is limited

A SUGGESTED ANSWER

The most important factor in determining the extent to which the new MPs may influence the government will be the size of the government's majority. Assuming a single party to be in power, a government with a substantial majority need not worry about the attitude of Opposition parties, as long as its own backbenchers remain loyal. At the other extreme, a minority government will be dependent on the votes of other parties, which may therefore be able to exact a high price in policy terms, as was seen in 2017 with the Conservative Government dependent upon the support of the ten-member Democratic Unionist Party, who required more expenditure on Northern Ireland in return. However, even where a government has a comfortable working majority, parliamentary procedures offer Opposition and backbench MPs a variety of opportunities for the exercise of influence, and a skilful use of such procedures will maximize their effect. Although government business generally has priority, the new SNHS MPs will find opportunities to make their presence felt in Parliament.[1]

[1] The introduction sums up the political realities for a small party.

The largest single item in the House of Commons' timetable is the consideration of government legislation. The government will be bound to introduce bills on health matters. The SNHS MPs may seek to speak in the Second Reading debate, but the party's greatest opportunity for influence will be achieved by getting one or two of its MPs on to the Standing Committees that subject bills to detailed scrutiny. They may then propose amendments, though these will only succeed if they attract the support of some government MPs on the committee in question; the government, provided that it has an overall majority in the House of Commons, will have a majority on each Standing Committee. Any amendments agreed to in committee can be reversed by the House of Commons chamber at the report stage, but it may be that the government will accept reasoned amendments in order to avoid delay in passing the legislation.[2]

[2] The SNHS's influence on legislation will be small.

Other forms of legislation may provide opportunities for intervention. If a health authority were to promote a private bill, say, to give more legal powers to a health authority, then that would give opportunities for backbench MPs to call for debates on the floor of the House, as well as for participating in the quasi-judicial committee stages.

There are various methods by which an MP may propose legislation, but most of these provide no real likelihood of success. The best way to try to have a Private Member's Bill debated and even enacted is for the MPs to enter the annual ballot to promote a bill on one of the Fridays reserved for that purpose. Competition is great; most backbenchers enter the ballot, whether or not they have a bill ready to propose. If one of the SNHS MPs were to be successful in gaining a high place in the ballot, that would give an excellent opportunity to change the law. One important limitation must, however, be noted. Any bill requiring public expenditure, or the imposition of a tax, cannot be passed unless a money resolution is agreed, usually after the Second Reading. Only a government minister can move such a resolution, in which case there would be no real likelihood of the SNHS procuring an increase in spending against the wishes of the government. In any case, all successful Private Member's Bills need at least the benevolent neutrality of government, and preferably its tacit support. A modest measure, not involving public expenditure, would seem the most promising option for the SNHS MPs.[3]

[3] It is unlikely that the SNHS could change the law.

Some matters of health policy will also be dealt with by secondary legislation, but the opportunities for MPs to scrutinize this are not great. Although the most important statutory instruments may require the approval of the House of Commons, most do not and will become law unless a negative resolution is proposed and passed. The Joint Committee on Statutory Instruments examines all instruments laid before Parliament and has the power to draw matters of concern to the attention of the House, though not in respect of the substantive content of the instrument.[4]

[4] The SNHS's influence on statutory instruments will be small.

Apart from legislation, much of the House of Commons' time is spent on various forms of debate. Although most debate is at the government's initiative, there are a certain number of Opposition days, when it can choose the subject for debate. Most of these are used by the largest Opposition party, but, by agreement, the SNHS may be allocated a half-day to debate a subject of their choice. There have always been daily adjournment debates, with MPs' right to choose the topic being allocated by ballot. The Backbench Business Committee might also allow SNHS members time for debate. The opportunity for debate has been greatly increased with the introduction of the parallel chamber in Westminster Hall. [5]

[5] The SNHS can use debates.

One of the most obvious ways for the SNHS MPs to raise health matters is by asking parliamentary questions. To obtain maximum publicity, questions should be set for oral answer, often in an oblique form in the hope of surprising the minister with an embarrassing supplementary question. MPs are, however, subject to restrictions on the number of questions they may table; because of the likelihood of the system becoming clogged, and question time being strictly limited, only 10 to 20 questions may be dealt with on any given day. Any questions not reached are instead answered in writing, as are all questions where a written answer is requested. This procedure, while not attracting such immediate publicity as Question Time, is extremely useful as a means of obtaining information about the government's actions and policies. Application under the **Freedom of Information Act 2000** also holds potential. [6]

[6] The SNHS can ask awkward questions.

In recent years, the department-related select committees have provided MPs with enhanced opportunities for scrutiny of the Executive; the SNHS MPs will hope, having made known their interest and any expertise in the field, to obtain a place on the Health Committee, which is currently chaired by a doctor. Competition for places is intense and, while places are formally allocated by the Committee of Selection, in practice the whips of each party have a considerable influence over allocation between the parties. The government will have a majority on each committee, and the official Opposition party will take the bulk of the remaining places. Determined lobbying by the SNHS MPs might, however, secure them perhaps a single place. Select committees do generally try to operate in a non-partisan way as far as possible, and are more likely to influence government if they operate in this way. The opportunities for questioning witnesses in public and obtaining information from government and other sources tend to make select committees an effective forum. Of particular importance in the health field would be the power of the Health Select Committee to summon and question witnesses, including ministers from the Health Department, but also departmental civil servants who are more actively involved in implementation of policy and, often most useful, the day-to-day healthcare providers, such as key figures in health authorities and hospital trusts. The first elections of chairmen of select committees took place in 2010. Replacing the former practice of appointment by party whips, this may further enhance the effectiveness of scrutiny by these committees, as well as freeing up backbenchers from pressure to be loyal in votes and debates with the promise of such future patronage.[7]

[7] Committee membership might allow the SNHS to influence policy.

Given their specific interest, the SNHS MPs are likely themselves to be lobbied on health issues by constituents as well as the various interested parties from the NHS and private sector alike, for example pharmaceutical companies. Such lobbying is regulated by the Committee for Standards in Public Life, established after the 1995 Nolan Committee Report into Standards in Public Life (1996). Restrictions include prohibition of paid advocacy of any cause. Unpaid advocacy and the general making and facilitating of contacts—indeed the whole 'networking' process—are going to be one of the most important tools of the SNHS MPs in the ultimate goal of influencing those with power, government ministers.[8]

[8] Being MPs enhances their ability to network.

In conclusion, there is a range of possible means available to the new SNHS MPs. It may be events, perhaps a newsworthy healthcare 'public cause', or a political happening such as a hung Parliament of which the Democratic Unionist Party were the fortunate beneficiaries in 2017. Otherwise, it is up to them to make effective use of the tools described, with political skill and acumen. Their efforts may be frustrated by the dominance of the major parties unless they win allies within those parties. They should at least be successful in obtaining information, which they would not have had but for their electoral success.[9]

[9] The evidence leads to the conclusion.

✚ LOOKING FOR EXTRA MARKS?

- If you follow what happens in Parliament, you can include that in your answer.
- There are some actual examples of what small parties have achieved that you could use.
- Show that you really understand the detail of how Parliament works.

Ⓠ QUESTION 3

What role do departmental select committees play in the scrutiny of the Executive? How effective are they?

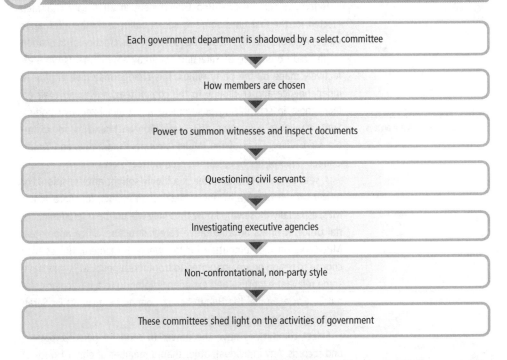

- Do not confuse departmental select committees with other parliamentary committees.
- Parliament is not just there to pass legislation, but to scrutinize and control the government.
- Be accurate about what these committees do.

DIAGRAM ANSWER PLAN

> Each government department is shadowed by a select committee
>
> ▼
>
> How members are chosen
>
> ▼
>
> Power to summon witnesses and inspect documents
>
> ▼
>
> Questioning civil servants
>
> ▼
>
> Investigating executive agencies
>
> ▼
>
> Non-confrontational, non-party style
>
> ▼
>
> These committees shed light on the activities of government

SUGGESTED ANSWER

The present system of departmental select committees was established in 1979, when it was agreed that there should be one House of Commons select committee to examine the work of each government department (ministry) and its associated agencies, boards, and 'quangos'. As suggested by the question, the purpose of select committees is to scrutinize the Executive, examining expenditure, administration, and policy. They do this by probing investigation, including examining documentary evidence and close questioning of witnesses, work of a nature that cannot be performed adequately in the Commons chamber. Witnesses include civil servants and key personnel of executive agencies and other bodies ranging from energy utilities to police forces, all of whom are in any event barred from the chamber of the House. The end product of a committee's work on a given matter is its report, including any recommendations for change.[1]

Membership of select committees is in practice confined to backbench MPs. Each committee has between 11 and 16 members. Membership is proportionate to party strength; for example, both the Health and Home Affairs Select Committees have 11 members comprising five Conservative, five Labour, and one SNP backbenchers.

Reform under the Coalition Government in 2010 saw chairmen elected for the first time, some by secret ballot using the alternative vote electoral system. This replaced the former practice of allocation by the old Committee of Selection, whereby appointments were effectively made by the party whips. This change may give enhanced independence and credibility to the committees, bolstering their effectiveness in scrutinizing government and other executive bodies. Some chairmen come from the Opposition backbenches, for example Meg Hillier, Chair of the Public Accounts Committee, and Yvette Cooper, Chair of the Home Affairs Committee.[2]

A seat on a select committee is a highly sought-after position. For newer MPs, it offers a means of making an impact; for more senior MPs, especially those who know that they will not be offered ministerial office, it offers an alternative career structure. Once appointed, MPs serve on the committee for the whole Parliament, unless they choose to resign or are appointed to frontbench posts. MPs may have some relevant expertise and experience to bring to a particular committee. For example, the Health Select Committee includes Dr Sarah Wollaston, who is the chair.[3]

Select committees have the power to send for persons, papers, and records. Any individual, other than a member of either House of Parliament, may be formally summoned to appear, though in practice committees need do no more than issue an invitation, which will invariably be accepted. Many witnesses will indeed welcome the opportunity to give evidence, whereas some have been less cooperative. In 2011, the Chief Executive of Kraft Foods refused to appear before the select committee investigating their takeover of Cadburys. Similarly, an investigation into News International's involvement in phone hacking found some witnesses uncooperative and in contempt. All they can do is refer the matter to the House of Commons, which has the power to punish those found to be in contempt, but is unlikely to be willing to do so except in an extreme case. In 1985, Arthur Scargill (then leader of the National Union of Mineworkers) was called to the Bar of the House of Commons and obliged to apologize, following his refusal to give evidence to the Energy Select Committee, but this is very unusual.[4]

Members of either House, including in particular government ministers, can only be invited, not summoned, to appear. The government promised in 1979 that ministers would appear when invited, and very largely this has happened ever since. The House of Commons has the power to compel one of its members to attend a committee, but this power is unlikely in practice to be used against a government minister whilst the government retains its overall majority. In any event, it is the degree of cooperation they proffer in answering questions candidly that is key.

An interesting issue arises in relation to the appearance of civil servants before select committees. Civil servants are responsible to the government of the day (their departmental minister), which in turn is accountable to Parliament. The select committee system, however, can bypass the departmental minister by calling the civil servants themselves to give evidence, creating an awkward, three-sided relationship between minister, official, and committee. Successive governments have issued guidance for officials appearing before committees. Though exhorting officials to be as helpful as possible, it reiterates that civil servants remain subject to the instructions of ministers in giving evidence. The guidance suggests that where issues of the conduct or misconduct of officials are concerned, the official should suggest to the committee that the minister should give evidence instead. Some serious disputes have arisen where ministers have refused to permit particular officials to attend, instead appearing themselves or sending the departmental Permanent Secretary to give evidence.[5] The Defence Select Committee had difficulty investigating the 1986 'Westland affair' because the relevant officials were not allowed to attend: some very senior ministers' jobs were 'on the line'.

[5] Detailed knowledge of the rules is useful here.

The guidance to officials also identifies various classes of material on which no information should be given to the committee without the minister's approval; these include advice given to ministers, confidential personal information, sensitive economic information, and matters under international negotiation.[6] The government's decision is the last word. Some matters are too sensitive to be discussed publicly in committee, but there remains the suspicion that the government sometimes uses this as an excuse, to prevent the exposure of politically embarrassing facts.

[6] Detailed knowledge of the rules is useful here.

Even more complex issues arise in relation to executive agencies that, while remaining part of government departments, are supposed to operate with a degree of autonomy. Although the creation of these agencies was not intended to alter the arrangements for accountability, their existence has limited the scope for scrutiny through parliamentary questions and has increased the need for other methods of scrutiny to be developed. The government has accepted that for matters concerning the day-to-day operation of an agency, the head of the agency is the appropriate witness to give evidence to a select committee, though reserving the minister's right to control the answers given.[7]

[7] A conclusion to the argument in this paragraph.

The most striking feature of these committees is the ability of MPs from different parties to work together, symbolized by the fact that when hearing witnesses they sit together round a table, unlike the confrontational arrangement of the chamber of the House of Commons. Whilst the examination of witnesses becomes adversarial on occasion, the committee itself operates 'as one', as far as possible, and tries, in reaching its findings, to achieve a consensus and to issue a unanimous report. Sometimes, party divisions prevent this (and so a minority report will also be issued). The impact of the Culture, Media and Sport Select Committee Report, 'News International and Phone-hacking', HC 903-I (May 2012), was significantly undermined by reason of it not being unanimous.[8] This, however, does not happen so often as to diminish the effectiveness of the select committee system as a whole.

[8] An example of a divided committee.

Each committee can choose what topics to examine within its own remit; it will usually conduct one or two major investigations each session, as well as responding quickly to matters of immediate concern. The government has no direct control over the choice of topics and, while it may try to exert an influence behind the scenes, this has not prevented committees from choosing subjects that have embarrassed the government of the day, such as the Foreign Affairs Committee expressing scepticism about the case for military action in Syria in 2015.[9]

[9] An up-to-date example.

Select committees have enhanced the powers of the backbench MP to scrutinize government actions. Just how much impact these committees have had in practice is, however, more difficult to assess. Whilst some of their reports have been followed by statutory reform, other influences have contributed to the pressure on government to act. Government invariably makes a formal response to select committee reports, whereby it is at least forced to consider and justify its attitude to the issue in question. Some committee members have claimed that governments deliberately put out major news stories on the day that difficult reports are released, so as to deflect attention. It is very difficult for a government to dismiss a unanimous select committee report out of hand; there is always the risk that the subject will arise again to embarrass the government.

It was never likely that the introduction of these committees would transform the House of Commons into as powerful a legislative chamber as, for instance, the US Senate, before the committees of which even the most powerful may tremble. The Commons select committees have, however, succeeded in providing backbenchers with a source of detailed information and in encouraging the development [10]Conclusion on the effectiveness of of expertise within Parliament. Committee reports have provided insights into the inner workings of government, and the televising of committee hearings shows the people that the House of Commons does not amount simply to the bear garden of the full chamber in set piece events like Prime Minister's Question Time, but does far more.[10]

[10]Conclusion on the effectiveness of select committees.

LOOKING FOR EXTRA MARKS?

- Find some recent examples of what these committees have been doing.
- Go into detail about the powers of these committees.
- Try to evaluate how successful these committees have actually been.

QUESTION | 4

Consider the following situations in the light of the rules on parliamentary privilege.

a   Giles, a backbench MP, said during a debate in the House of Commons that the directors of the three largest UK fertilizer companies met together regularly to fix prices, in breach of both UK and EU law. The Minister for Agriculture and Food asked Giles to send him further details of the accusation and also suggested that Giles inform the EU Commission. Giles wrote to both the minister and the Commission from his parliamentary office. The managing director of one of the companies is threatening to sue Giles for defamation.

b   A Private Member's Bill to ban the use of chimpanzees in medical research is to be debated next week in the House of Commons. Dr Foster MP is the parliamentary consultant to the British Medical Research Society (BMRS); she is paid £10,000 a year for her services, but she has not declared this in the Register of Members' Interests. She has been told by BMRS that they will end her consultancy immediately unless she votes against the bill. Animal rights activists have warned Dr Foster that they will picket her home and her office unless she votes for the bill.

c   During a debate in the House of Commons on the decline in moral standards, Pecksniff MP accused Deadlock MP of fathering an illegitimate child. This accusation was false, and Deadlock was so annoyed that he punched Pecksniff in the voting lobby. The following day, the Daily Bluetop published a report of the debate, including a mention of Pecksniff's accusation. The Daily Redtop published a front-page article, under the headline 'Deadlock in Love Child Scandal', not mentioning the rest of the debate.

! CAUTION!

- Be careful to distinguish the law of Parliament from case law and statute.
- A court might reach a different conclusion about parliamentary privilege to Parliament.
- Each of the three parts raises different aspects of parliamentary privilege.

◯ DIAGRAM ANSWER PLAN

Identify the issues	■ Identify the legal issues: freedom of speech inside and outside Parliament; MPs' consultancies and outside pressure; publication of parliamentary proceedings
Relevant law	■ Outline the relevant law: statutory, case law, and the law of Parliament: **Bill of Rights 1689**; The Committee of Privileges; *Church of Scientology v Johnson-Smith; Beach v Freeson; Makudi v Baron Triesman; Wason v Walter;* and *Cook v Alexander*
Apply the law	■ Does the MP's communication have absolute and qualified privilege? ■ Declaration of financial interest and attempts to influence an MP ■ Right of Parliament to regulate its own proceedings ■ Publication of parliamentary papers and media reports of Parliament
Conclude	■ The communication is protected ■ The consultancy is a contempt of Parliament ■ What is acceptable reporting and what is not?

A SUGGESTED ANSWER

(a) This problem is concerned with the fundamental privilege of Parliament, freedom of speech. This is protected by **Article 9 of the Bill of Rights 1689**, which states that:

[1] **Article 9** is worth quoting.

The freedom of speech and debates in Parliament ought not to be impeached or questioned in any place out of Parliament.[1]

As a consequence, the courts have accepted that words spoken in the course of parliamentary proceedings are absolutely privileged. No action for defamation can be brought in respect of such words, nor can they even be cited in court to support an action for defamation arising from words spoken outside Parliament, as in *Church of Scientology v Johnson-Smith* **[1972] 1 QB 522**. Giles can therefore face no legal action over what he said in the debate.

As for the letter written by Giles to the minister, the position is less clear. If Giles had given the details orally in the course of the debate, this would be protected as a proceeding in Parliament. Does the writing of a letter count as a proceeding in Parliament? In 1957, G.R. Strauss MP had written a letter to the minister outlining complaints from a constituent about a public utility. The utility (an electricity board) considered the letter defamatory and threatened legal action, which the MP suggested might be a breach of privilege. The Committee of Privileges adjudged the MP's letter a proceeding in Parliament that should have the protection of absolute privilege. The House of Commons disagreed and voted to dismiss the complaint of breach of privilege.[2]

Correspondence (including emails) is increasingly used by MPs as the best way of raising issues with a minister, parliamentary questions being reserved as the second line of attack. It may, accordingly, be argued that the absolute privilege should be extended. Indeed, MPs are now encouraged to deal with the executive agencies directly by letter rather than by asking a question of the minister in the House of Commons. An MP's correspondence on official matters will, however, have the protection of qualified privilege, and it can be argued that this is sufficient: *Beach v Freeson* **[1972] 1 QB 14**. Why should an MP be immune if maliciously passing false information to a government minister or official?[3] The call for absolute privilege, on the other hand, is that even the unfounded threat of legal action might operate to deter MPs from performing their proper function without fear or favour; arguably, anything that reduces the effectiveness of MPs is undesirable.

As far as the letter to the EU Commission is concerned, it would be difficult to argue that this was a proceeding in Parliament: EU institutions are separate from UK institutions. However, in *Makudi v Baron Triesman of Tottenham* **[2014] EWCA Civ 179**, Lord Triesman accused FIFA of corruption, while giving evidence to a House of Commons departmental select committee. Later, he repeated exactly the same allegations to a Football Association investigation. The Court of Appeal accepted that there was a legitimate public interest in repeating these allegations and Triesman was still protected by absolute privilege. Giles would probably be able to use the same defence.[4]

[2] It is possible for the Committee of Privileges and the Commons to reach different conclusions.

[3] Qualified privilege and absolute privilege are different.

[4] The courts also have a view on matters of privilege.

(b) There are three separate breaches of privilege in this question. First, Dr Foster would be obliged to declare her financial interest if she spoke about the bill. She would also have to enter her consultancy contract and the amount that she is paid on the Register of Members' Interests. She would be dealt with by the Parliamentary Commissioner for Standards and found in contempt of Parliament. Her punishment could be a warning, suspension, or expulsion.

The second breach of privilege would be by the BMRS. It is a clear breach of privilege for any outsider to attempt, by bribery or threats, to influence an MP, and any such attempt would be subject to punishment as contempt of Parliament, as well as possibly amounting to a criminal offence. It is, however, not clear how this rule relates to the practice of parliamentary consultancy. This issue was raised in 1947. W.J. Brown MP was appointed by a trade union to further its interests in Parliament, but when political disagreements arose between them the union threatened to withdraw from the contract, causing Brown financial loss.[5] The Committee of Privileges was concerned mainly with the propriety of the original contract, and having decided that it was proper, found no breach of privilege in the contract being terminated. They also confirmed that any agreement that purported to bind an MP to behave, vote, or speak in a particular way would be improper. In some later instances, the threat by a trade union to withdraw sponsorship from an MP has been classed as a breach of privilege. On each occasion the union withdrew the threat as soon as the issue of privilege was raised, and no punitive action was taken.

It therefore seems probable that any express threat from the BMRS, or any subsequent decision to withdraw sponsorship with immediate effect, would be regarded as a breach of privilege, though there would be nothing wrong with a decision to terminate the contract in due course in accordance with its terms.

Any physical action taken by the protesters may be a breach of the criminal law; an offence under the **Public Order Act 1986**, assault, or criminal damage. Dr Foster's best course of action if subjected to harassment may well be to involve the police. It will also be contempt of Parliament to molest or threaten an MP. In the case of the *Daily Graphic*, HC 27 (1956–7)[6] a newspaper was held to be in contempt when it published an MP's telephone number and incited its readers to ring him up to complain about his actions in Parliament. The House of Commons has the power to order an outsider to appear at the Bar of the House to be reprimanded, but this power is rarely used. It is probable that, as happens if people demonstrate in the public gallery, any protesters will be handed to the police to be dealt with.

(c) Because Pecksniff's statement was made during a debate, he is protected by the absolute privilege conferred by the **Bill of Rights**.

[5] This is not a court case, but a decision of Parliament.

[6] Another parliamentary law report.

Deadlock cannot bring any legal action against Pecksniff for defamation, even if Pecksniff knew that the accusation was false; only if Pecksniff were to repeat the statement outside Parliament could Deadlock sue him. The European Court of Human Rights upheld the legality of this aspect of parliamentary privilege in *A v UK* [2002] **All ER (D) 264.**[7] In contrast to (a), *Makudi v Baron Triesman of Tottenham* is unlikely to apply, as there seems no public interest in repeating this allegation outside Parliament and it is not repeated to any sort of official investigating body. Deadlock might argue that Pecksniff is abusing his parliamentary immunity, and may thus refer the matter to the Speaker as a possible breach of privilege; MPs have been reprimanded in such circumstances.

As far as the assault by Deadlock on Pecksniff is concerned, there are various possible consequences. Deadlock has apparently committed a criminal offence. Although MPs were once entitled to freedom from arrest, this no longer applies to criminal proceedings. Deadlock may therefore be arrested, charged, and prosecuted just as any other person. It is, however, possible for the House of Commons to exercise its right to regulate its own proceedings. It has from time to time had to deal with disorderly conduct by MPs. It may suspend the MP from the House for a time; the MP is not paid during that time and cannot take part in any business of the House. The ultimate parliamentary sanction available against an MP is expulsion from the House. This has only ever been used in extreme circumstances, such as on conviction for a grave criminal offence, or following gross contempt of the House. It is unlikely that Deadlock's behaviour would be regarded as justifying such an extreme sanction, though he would certainly be expected to apologize, as was Ron Brown MP in 1988. During an 'overheated' debate, Brown exhibited disrespect for the House by damaging the Mace, the symbol of the authority of the House.

So far as newspapers are concerned, the **Parliamentary Papers Act 1840** provides that absolute privilege only extends to material (such as Hansard) published by or under the authority of either House. A newspaper has qualified privilege for any fair and accurate report of parliamentary proceedings made without malice, as in *Wason v Walter* (1868) **LR 4 QB 73**. The report does not have to be verbatim to be protected. In *Cook v Alexander* [1974] **QB 279**, it was held that a parliamentary sketch, provided it was honest and fair comment, could attract qualified privilege. It therefore appears that the *Daily Bluetop* may be able to claim qualified privilege for its report. The *Daily Redtop*, however, appears not to be reporting parliamentary proceedings at all, let alone in a fair and accurate way. It will therefore be susceptible to an action in defamation and cannot plead any privilege as a defence.[8]

[7] The **European Convention on Human Rights** applies as well.

[8] Case law must be analysed and distinctions made.

LOOKING FOR EXTRA MARKS?

- Freedom of speech for MPs is a complicated subject. There are more cases that you could cite.
- MPs' pay and outside interests is a controversial subject. Look out for new examples.
- Show that you understand the difference between absolute and qualified privilege.

QUESTION | 5

If it is to fulfil the functions of a second legislative chamber, the House of Lords needs substantial further reform.

Discuss.

CAUTION!

- You need to describe the composition and work of the House of Lords.
- But you also need to criticize it.
- And consider reform proposals.

DIAGRAM ANSWER PLAN

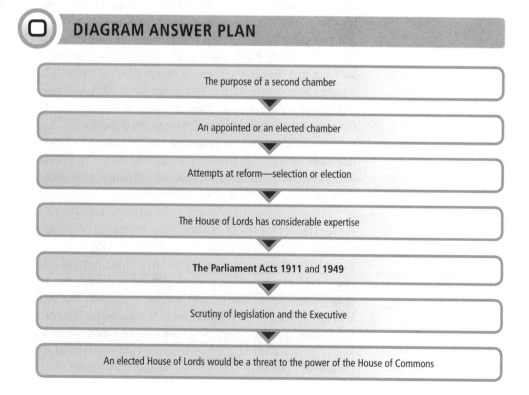

The purpose of a second chamber

An appointed or an elected chamber

Attempts at reform—selection or election

The House of Lords has considerable expertise

The Parliament Acts 1911 and 1949

Scrutiny of legislation and the Executive

An elected House of Lords would be a threat to the power of the House of Commons

In most liberal democracies the Legislature comprises two chambers. The respective powers of the two chambers will vary according to the constitutional structure of the state in question. In the UK, the House of Lords and House of Commons have developed over the centuries, and as with much of the UK constitution their relationship is set by statute and convention.[1]

[1] A short introduction raises the main issues.

It is an essential element in any democratic state that the Legislature should consist of representatives of the people. Often in a bi-cameral legislature each chamber represents the people in a different form. Commonly this is by geographical distinction; for instance, in a federal state such as Germany or the United States the first chamber is representative of the nation as a whole, whereas the second chamber specifically represents the constituent parts of the federation, in Germany the 16 *Länder* and in the United States the 50 states (and one district). Even in non-federal states, such as France, it is common for the second chamber to consist of representatives of geographic regions.[2]

[2] A brief comparison with other countries.

The principal weakness of the House of Lords is that it lacks legitimacy. This lies at the heart of its lack of 'teeth' and why it has become merely a revising and delaying chamber, albeit arguably very good at what it does. It is not a democratically representative assembly. All members are there by dint of birth or by appointment, none by direct election by the people.[3] Therefore, it is essential to change the basis of membership of the Lords to give it the legitimacy and acceptability it needs to be able to perform effectively its functions as a second chamber.

[3] The main reason for reform.

The **House of Lords Act 1999** removed all but 92 of the hereditary peers, and all major parties agree that the remainder will be removed when the reform of the Upper House is 'completed'. The life peers now form the bulk of membership of the House of Lords. Whilst most of these sit and vote on party political lines, with only a minority of independent 'cross-benchers', the Lords is less party-political, and therefore less adversarial in character than the Commons. Other interests are represented in the Lords; for example, the 26 Bishops of the Church of England will represent the stance of the established Church. The key 'rule' that prevailed throughout the Wakeham Commission Report 2000 and the White Papers of 2001, 2007, and 2011 (and accompanying Draft Bill) has been that however the Lords is reformed, the primacy of the Commons must be maintained.[4] The Commons has unsurprisingly and repeatedly endorsed this, and in any event will be the decider of the Lords' fate.

[4] The last major attempt at reform.

Wakeham recommended a wholly or largely appointed second chamber, primarily to avoid rivalry through similarity with the Commons. Following Wakeham and the 2001 White Paper, the Commons voted overwhelmingly for a wholly or largely (80 per cent) elected second chamber, whereas the Lords themselves voted convincingly the other way, for a wholly or largely appointed House. Therefore, no agreement could be obtained on how to proceed. The Conservative/Liberal Democrat coalition government set up a cross-party committee and published its House of Lords Reform Bill in 2012, proposing an 80 per cent (or wholly) elected House significantly reduced in size from 828 to 450 Lords, and various measures to differentiate the Lords from the Commons so as not to challenge the primacy of the Commons. Members of the reformed House would be elected from specific regions of the UK by a different, proportional voting system (the single transferable vote) for a non-renewable term of 15 years. There would only be 12 Church of England bishops, instead of the current 26, among the 90 appointed members. One-third of the House would face re-election every five years, so that at no time would the complete Lords' membership be more recent than that of the Commons.[5] Frontbench and backbench members on all sides roundly criticized the bill and it was withdrawn.

[5]It is worth remembering some detail of reform proposals.

In 2017, a House of Lords committee, chaired by Lord Burns, proposed reforms. They advocated that the number of Lords should be gradually reduced by appointing one new Lord for every two that retired. These new Lords would be appointed for a fixed-term of 15 years and would mirror the respective party strengths in the Commons. Despite the fact that this would be an unelected House and not a rival to the Commons, it is unlikely that these reforms will be enacted. The Prime Minister and other party leaders are unwilling to give up their powers of patronage.[6]

[6]Plans for reform are always being produced and then rejected.

An advantage of a nominated House is that it could retain some of the wealth and diversity of experience and expertise of the life peers, in particular in fields such as medicine and science, perceived as a significant asset of the Lords, rather than mirroring the Commons in attracting 'career politicians' only.[7]

[7]The expertise of the Lords is a major point in its favour.

Minor reform of the membership of the House of Lords was achieved by the **House of Lords Reform Act (No. 2) 2014**, which allowed peers to resign and the House to expel members if they were convicted of a serious criminal offence or failed to attend.

A principal role of a second chamber is to act as a check on the first, a safeguard against the concentration of too much power in the hands of one body. Under the **Parliament Acts 1911** and **1949** the Lords may delay for one year legislation introduced in and passed by the House of Commons. It is significant that the Upper House retains the power to reject any bill to extend the life of the House of Commons, thus making the Lords a safeguard against any attempt to subvert democracy by postponing elections (confirmed in *R (Jackson) v Attorney-General* [2005] **UKHL 56**).

For other legislation, the House of Lords retains some power to act as a check on the House of Commons, because it is still generally necessary for public bills to be passed in identical form by each House if they are to become law in a single session. The Lords has become increasingly bold in rejecting government legislation. In 2015, they rejected delegated legislation on reducing the entitlement to tax credits. A further task performed by a second chamber is to share the onerous work of scrutinizing legislation, thus reducing the work burden of the Commons. Modern governments require the enactment of large amounts of increasingly complex legislation. In the UK, some 50–70 Acts are passed each year. It is an essential element in the democratic process that all legislation should be scrutinized by the Legislature and that governments should have to justify their proposals in both substance and detail. It is common practice for some legislation, particularly non-controversial measures, to start its passage in the House of Lords, where detailed scrutiny can be given, thus saving time in the over-pressed House of Commons.

The House of Lords has been considered to play a very useful role in the scrutiny of legislation. Whereas in the Commons the intensity of the party struggle detracts from the technical scrutiny of legislation, members of the House of Lords, who do not have to face re-election, may be able to take a more detached view, thereby ensuring that legislation, whatever its substantive merits, is well drafted.

A fourth purpose that can be served by a second chamber is to assist in the scrutiny of the Executive. Government is ultimately accountable to the Commons alone through the convention of ministerial responsibility, but some ministers sit in the Lords. So, most government departments will be represented there and members of the House of Lords can ask oral and written questions of them. The Lords also uses its power to set up select committees to scrutinize aspects of government behaviour, though there are no departmental select committees like those in the Commons. The House of Lords, however, does exercise the only effective parliamentary scrutiny of the European Union, through its EU Select Committee and its sub-committees.[8] Were the upper chamber to be wholly or largely elected, its members would likely shed their caution and expect a greater role in the scrutiny of the Executive.

In the absence of a legally enforceable written constitution and strong separation of powers, and with a government commanding a majority in the House of Commons being thus able to control the

[8] A good example of the Lords' little known but worthwhile work.

legislative programme with arguably little effective restraint, the case for an effective second chamber in the workings of the UK constitution is strong. The problem is that a reformed House of Lords would be an elected House of Lords. This would challenge the primacy of the Commons, and the Commons could never accept that.[9]

[9]Which is why reform proposals always fail.

LOOKING FOR EXTRA MARKS?

- It is possible to answer this question in another way, by comparing the Lords to second chambers in other countries.
- Keep up to date on the latest reform proposals.
- Find examples of the work of the House of Lords.

TAKING THINGS FURTHER

- <https://www.parliament.uk>.

  The website of the UK Parliament has a large amount of information about what Parliament is doing, providing plenty of up-to-date examples for your answers. It also has many explanatory sections about how Parliament works, providing the sort of information found in a textbook.

- Lord Bingham of Cornhill, 'The House of Lords: its future?' [2010] Public Law 261.

  Everyone seems to agree that the House of Lords does good work, but lacks democratic legitimacy. An elected House would clash with the Commons and an appointed House would give the Executive even more power. Lord Bingham comes up with a suggestion of a completely new body to replace the House of Lords, the Council of the Realm.

- Judge D., 'Whatever happened to parliamentary democracy in the UK?' (2004) 57(3) Parliamentary Affairs 682.

  Unlike the reading above, which goes into the details of what Parliament does, this article asks the deeper question of whether Parliament is actually democratic in the sense that it responds to what people actually want. Does Parliament still take the important decisions, or does real power reside elsewhere?

- Norton P., 'Parliament: A New Assertiveness' in J. Jowell, Oliver, and C. O'Cinneide (eds) *The Changing Constitution* (8th edn, OUP 2015).

  The writer gives a brief history of Parliament and then gives a fairly comprehensive account of what it does, noting its increased powers over the government's use of the royal prerogative and the use of votes of confidence. The House of Lords is also considered.

- Parpworth N., 'The Parliamentary Standards Act 2009: a constitutional dangerous dog's measure?' (2010) 73 MLR 262.

  *There was a scandal over MPs claiming unjustified expenses in 2009. Parliament reacted quickly by passing the **Parliamentary Standards Act 2009**, which established the Independent Parliamentary Standards Authority. The author considers that the Act is ill–*

thought-out and that more time should have been taken. The simplest solution would have been to abolish the system of allowances and pay MPs a decent salary, but that would have been too controversial.

- Russell M. and Comes R., 'The Royal Commission on the House of Lords. A House for the future?' (2001) 64 MLR 82.

  Lord Wakeham chaired the Commission, whose recommendations were never implemented. Perhaps the reason lies in part of the Commission's remit, 'the need to maintain the position of the House of Lords as the pre-eminent chamber of Parliament'. The article describes the suggested reforms in detail.

Online Resources

www.oup.com/uk/qanda/

Go online for extra essay and problem questions, a glossary of key terms, online versions of all the answer plans and audio commentary on how selected ones were put together, and a range of podcasts which include advice on exam and coursework technique and advice for other assessment methods.

6 Parliamentary sovereignty

ARE YOU READY?

The questions in this chapter concern an essay on the traditional doctrine of parliamentary supremacy, an essay on the effect that EU membership has had on the traditional doctrine of parliamentary supremacy, a problem question on the effect of an EU directive on English law, and an essay on the functioning of the EU. In order to attempt these questions, you need to have covered all of the following topics in your work and your revision:

- understanding how the doctrine of parliamentary supremacy arose and how it is interpreted today;
- understanding how the doctrine of parliamentary supremacy has been modified since the passing of the **European Communities Act 1972**;
- understanding the effect that the different types of EU legislation have in English law;
- understanding the structure and working of the EU;
- understanding how withdrawal from the EU will affect parliamentary supremacy.

 KEY DEBATES

Debate: The Nature of Parliamentary Sovereignty

The traditional doctrine of parliamentary sovereignty is that the Parliament of the UK is the supreme legislative authority and can make any law that it wants. What is the constitutional basis of this idea? Are there any limitations on the laws that Parliament can pass? Is there anything that Parliament cannot do?

Debate: Parliamentary Sovereignty and the European Union

The EU claims legislative supremacy for itself, yet this is not found in any of the international treaties that formed that organization. It is a doctrine developed by the European Court of Justice. The

UK adapted its traditional doctrine of parliamentary supremacy when it joined the then European Economic Community (EEC), to accept the supremacy of EEC law. Is this a permanent change to the UK constitution or can it be reversed? It seems clear that, as predicted by various judges, the **European Communities Act 1972** can be expressly repealed by another Act of Parliament, currently the European Union (Withdrawal) Bill 2017–19. Yet most of the law of the EU will remain in force in the UK for some time to come. This is a matter of great political controversy.

Q | QUESTION | 1

What is meant by the term 'parliamentary supremacy'? What are its implications in matters other than those raised by the UK's membership of the European Union?

! | CAUTION!

- There is no clear source for the doctrine of parliamentary supremacy such as a written constitution.
- The UK has parliamentary supremacy as the highest source of law, *instead* of a written constitution.
- Distinguish clearly between the legal theory that Parliament can do what it likes and the practical reality: some laws are unacceptable to the public or other countries.
- Do not consider the effect of the EU on parliamentary supremacy at this stage.

◯ | DIAGRAM ANSWER PLAN

Parliamentary supremacy emerged from the history and politics of England

▼

The courts accepted parliamentary supremacy and it became a matter of common law

▼

Parliament may make or unmake any law on any subject

▼

An inconsistent later Act will impliedly repeal an earlier Act

▼

Parliament cannot bind its successors

▼

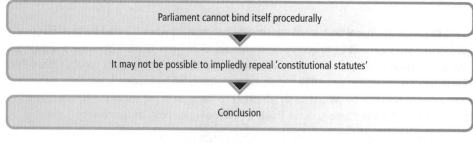

Parliament cannot bind itself procedurally

It may not be possible to impliedly repeal 'constitutional statutes'

Conclusion

A   SUGGESTED ANSWER

[1] The introductory paragraph outlines the two main problems. Most countries have a written constitution, which states who can make law.

[2] The UK does not, so the answer comes from an examination of history.

In most states, the validity of any law can be traced back to a written constitution,[1] which forms the basis of the organization of the state. In the UK, however, there is no written constitution and we just accept, as a basic principle of the constitution, that Parliament is the supreme law-making body. Why Parliament has that power is an interesting historical and political question,[2] but the lawyer is generally happy to accept the existence of Parliament's power as very much established and thus unquestioned and unquestionable.

The historical origins of parliamentary supremacy lie in the political conflicts and Civil War of the seventeenth century. The King tried to assert that he could make laws, without the agreement of Parliament, but Parliament eventually won the conflict. In the Glorious Revolution of 1688, they expelled one king, James II and made his daughter, Mary, queen. Parliament now declared that they were the supreme law-making authority in the country in the **Bill of Rights 1689, Article 1**:

[3] Quotations can be good, but for exam purposes most students would only be able to remember short ones.

the pretended power of suspending of laws, or the execution of laws by regal authority without consent of Parliament is illegal.[3]

After the Glorious Revolution, judges were content to accept the validity of any Act passed by traditional parliamentary procedure. Parliament was thus established and treated as the supreme lawmaker and parliamentary sovereignty as a common law rule. The concept of parliamentary supremacy was popularized by A.V. Dicey:

[4] In an exam, it is perfectly acceptable to summarize a longer quotation in your own words. No one expects you to be word perfect.

Parliament thus defined has, under the English constitution, the right to make or unmake any law whatever; and, further, that no person or body is recognized by the law of England as having a right to override or set aside the legislation of Parliament.[4]

His views received judicial confirmation in ***Madzimbamuto v Lardner-Burke* [1969] 1 AC 645**, where Lord Reid remarked that if Parliament did things that were regarded as improper for moral or political reasons, they would not be unconstitutional, because Parliament has the power to make any law that it likes and the courts cannot hold such laws invalid.

It is clear that Parliament can do, and has done, many things that in other countries might be regarded as unconstitutional. It may, for instance, break international law, *Mortensen v Peters* (1906) 8F (J) 93; legislate retrospectively, **War Damage Act 1965**; and provide for detention without trial, **Terrorism Act 2006**.[5]

[5] Short, snappy examples can be good.

It is virtually impossible to imagine any circumstances (other than a breach of EU law) where the UK courts would refuse to accept the validity of an Act of Parliament. Further, the courts will not involve themselves in questions relating to the way in which the legislation was passed. In *British Railways Board v Pickin* [1974] AC 765, Pickin alleged that a private Act of Parliament had been passed only after Parliament had been misled by the appellant. The court upheld the validity of the Act, stating that it would be for Parliament itself to investigate any defects in the procedure.

[6] This is a difficult case, so do some further reading on it. An article by Ekins is suggested at the end of this chapter.

In *R (Jackson) v Attorney-General* [2006] 1 AC 262,[6] it was argued that the **Parliament Act 1949** was invalid because it used the procedure laid down in the **Parliament Act 1911** to amend the 1911 Act itself. This procedure allowed an Act to be passed by the House of Commons, without the consent of the House of Lords. In contrast to *Pickin* above, the Supreme Court was at least willing to investigate the procedure by which the Act was passed. The **Parliament Act 1911, s. 2(1)** allowed the use of the procedure for 'Any public bill', so the courts would not question the validity of the **Parliament Act 1949**.

There remains one disputed area. Can Parliament bind its successors? The orthodox view is that it cannot. The Parliament that is supreme is the current Parliament, so it has the power to amend or repeal the legislation of any previous Parliament. Normally, such repeal is expressed in the later Act. However, if two Acts of Parliament contradict each other, the later Act is taken to impliedly repeal the earlier Act: *Ellen St Estates Ltd v Minister of Health* [1934] 1 KB 590.

What is the origin of this rule that Parliament cannot bind its successors? If it is regarded as a rule of common law, then logic would suggest that like all other rules of common law it would be subject to alteration by Act of Parliament. However, H.W.R. Wade argued in his article,[7] 'The basis of legal sovereignty' ((1955) 13 CLJ 172), that if the rule is regarded as the rule of recognition, on which the whole basis of constitutional legality rests, then it is not like other common law rules and could not be changed by an Act of Parliament. It could only be changed if there was a legal revolution and a new constitutional settlement was accepted. Yet, in various contexts the issue of

[7] There are other theories, different from Wade's. Investigate them, as in 6.

Parliament's ability to bind its successors has arisen and given rise to legal and academic debate.

The first concerns the granting of independence to former colonies, which are given legal effect by an Act of Parliament stating that Parliament will no longer legislate for the country in question. Could such an Act be repealed by the Westminster Parliament? Legal theory suggests that it could, but, as was pointed out in *British Coal Corporation v R* **[1935] AC 500**, that has no relation to reality (except perhaps if the former colony wished and requested it), as the country in question would not accept it. It appears that the UK courts would consider themselves bound to obey[8] the express terms of the UK statute, but such legislation is most unlikely even to be tabled.

There have been some differences of opinion between Scottish and English lawyers over the status of the **Acts of Union 1707**, various provisions of which are deemed to be unalterable. It is argued that as the Acts were the work of the then separate English and Scottish Parliaments, they could not be repealed by the UK Parliament that replaced them and that owes its very existence to those Acts. In Scotland, these Acts are regarded as a fundamental part of the constitution, rather like a written constitution, but it is unlikely that an English court would take this view. They would regard the **Act of Union** as repealable, just like any other Act.

The question that has given rise to most debate is whether Parliament could prescribe special procedures for the passing of future legislation, that might then bind it and future Parliaments, so that that Parliament would have to use the special procedure, even if only to pass an Act to get rid of it. There is nothing to prevent Parliament creating special procedures. The **Fixed-Term Parliaments Act 2011** removes Prime Ministerial discretion and fixes the date of the next general election. **Section 2(1)** stipulates a special majority of at least two-thirds for the Commons to decide on an early general election. The **Northern Ireland Act 1998, s. 1** requires an approving referendum before any legislation changing the constitutional status of Northern Ireland can be passed.

There is a school of thought[9] that Parliament may be bound by such special provision regulating the 'manner and form' of future legislation, providing partial entrenchment by the likes of a referendum or special majorities in each House for amendment or repeal. However, the only authority for this contention is Commonwealth case law, such as *Attorney-General for New South Wales v Trethowan* **[1932] AC 526**, *Harris v Minister of the Interior* **1952 (2) SA 428**, and *Bribery Commissioner v Ranasinghe* **[1965] AC 172**. Significantly, in all of these cases the requirements as to the manner and form of future legislation were contained in the original statutes emanating from the Westminster Parliament by which independence

[8] The courts of this country would always uphold the supremacy of Parliament, but that does not mean that the courts of another country would agree.

[9] There are different theories in constitutional law. Do not be afraid of this.

was granted. Accordingly, these 'entrenching' provisions could not be changed by the Commonwealth legislatures in question. The problem in applying these precedents to the UK Parliament is that it is a supreme legislature. Its powers were not granted by another legislature. For example, the **Fixed-Term Parliaments Act 2011** could be repealed by an ordinary Act of Parliament, but there seems little need to do so, as Prime Minister May easily obtained the required two-thirds majority to call an election in 2017.

In *Thoburn v Sunderland City Council* **[2002] EWHC 195 Admin, [2002] 4 All ER 156**, Laws LJ suggested that the courts had begun to recognize[10] a special category of constitutional statutes, those concerning fundamental constitutional rights. These statutes, he said, could not be impliedly repealed. If Parliament wished to repeal them, it would have to use express, unambiguous words. Laws LJ suggested some examples: the **Bill of Rights 1689**, the **Acts of Union 1707**, the **European Communities Act 1972 (ECA 1972)**, and the **Human Rights Act 1998**. In *R (Miller) v Secretary of State for Exiting the EU* **[2017] UKSC 5** the Supreme Court agreed that the **ECA 1972** could only be expressly repealed.

Parliamentary supremacy is a matter of common law and common law can evolve and change. We have seen in this essay that ideas about parliamentary supremacy have changed. Joining the EU in 1973 necessitated changes in the theory and it is conceivable that it might become unacceptable to change some laws of constitutional importance.

[10] The UK constitution is always changing. Do not be afraid of this.

➕ LOOKING FOR EXTRA MARKS?

This is an established debate, with nothing much new to say BUT:

- you can make sure that you can understand and explain the complex theory underlying this;
- for example, Wade's rule of recognition;
- for example, the manner and form argument.

Q QUESTION 2

What impact has UK membership of the European Union had on the doctrine of parliamentary sovereignty?

! CAUTION!

- Concentrate on what the case law actually says, not the often ill-informed pronouncements of politicians or media.
- Some questions have been definitely answered, but the exact boundaries to the domestic courts' obedience to EU rather than UK laws remain uncertain, and therefore debatable.
- You will need to start by explaining the general doctrine of parliamentary supremacy, but concentrate on the EU dimension of this question.

O DIAGRAM ANSWER PLAN

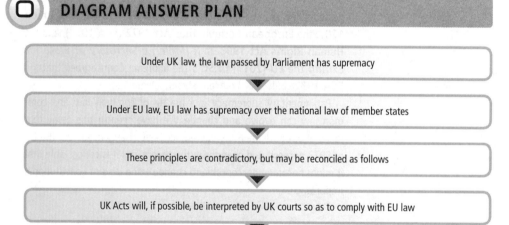

Under UK law, the law passed by Parliament has supremacy

▼

Under EU law, EU law has supremacy over the national law of member states

▼

These principles are contradictory, but may be reconciled as follows

▼

UK Acts will, if possible, be interpreted by UK courts so as to comply with EU law

▼

The *Factortame* cases held that a UK Act, that was inconsistent with EU law would not be enforced by a UK court

▼

The **European Communities Act 1972 (ECA 1972)** can be expressly repealed or amended, but not impliedly repealed or amended

▼

The European Union (Withdrawal) Bill is expressly repealing the **ECA 1972**

▼

Conclusion

A.V. Dicey popularized the doctrine of parliamentary supremacy in his book, *The Law of the Constitution* (Macmillan 1885). According to him, it meant that the Queen in Parliament can: make or unmake any law; no other person or body can override or set aside an Act of Parliament; Parliament does not share its right to make law; and no Parliament can bind a future Parliament. He did, though, concede that representative parliamentary government usually reflects the will of the people, so Parliament would usually take this into account when deciding whether or not to make a law.[1]

[1] Parliamentary supremacy is only a *legal* theory. Politically, Parliament cannot do whatever it wants.

Dicey based his theory on his interpretation of English history. In the Glorious Revolution of 1688, Parliament overthrew the King, replaced him with a Queen and took away the monarch's power to legislate. From that date onwards, it was accepted as a political and legal fact that Parliament was now the supreme legislative authority. This was discussed by Lord Denning in *Blackburn v Attorney-General* **[1971] 1 WLR 1037**, where Mr Blackburn was trying to claim that entering the European Economic Community (EEC) would be unconstitutional as a permanent surrender of the UK's parliamentary sovereignty. Lord Denning commented that 'Legal theory must give way to practical politics'[2]. He meant that what we had believed for 300 years about parliamentary supremacy could change and that Parliament could renounce or modify its sovereignty.

[2] In a country without a written constitution, legal theories change to accommodate political change.

Under the traditional theory, Parliament could do anything it wanted with its legislation. The one thing Parliament could not do was to prevent a later Parliament repealing its legislation, because otherwise that later Parliament would not be supreme: *Ellen St. Estates Ltd v Minister of Health* [1934] 1 KB 590.

The doctrine of parliamentary supremacy was so universally accepted that legal challenges to it were very rare. Joining the EEC in 1973 led to a debate about parliamentary supremacy and so it was no coincidence that Mr Pickin disputed the validity of an Act of Parliament, unrelated to the EEC, in *Pickin v British Rail Board* **[1974] AC 765**. The House of Lords refused to countenance his claim. The courts could not question an Act of Parliament, or investigate the procedure by which it was passed.[3]

[3] The courts support the theory of parliamentary supremacy

Six member states had formed the EEC by the Treaty of Rome in 1957. The UK had been invited to join, but declined at the time. A few years later, the UK government had changed its mind, but was not granted permission to join, together with Ireland and Denmark, until the **Treaty of Accession 1972**. By joining, all three countries had to accept existing EEC law in its entirety. Under UK law, the government (Crown) uses the royal prerogative to agree to treaties and Parliament's

[4] Treaties are agreed under the prerogative, but only Parliament can change the law.

[5] Case law shows that the EEC asserts legislative supremacy.

[6] A succession of cases illustrate how the UK courts slowly adapted their understanding of supremacy.

[7] *Factortame* is a key case.

permission is not legally required. However, an Act of Parliament is required to change the law within the UK, domestic law, as it is called.[4] This Act was the **European Communities Act 1972 (ECA 1972)** and **ss. 2(1)** and **3** enacted that all EC law, present and future, now took effect in the UK and could be enforced in any UK court. There was also the somewhat mysteriously worded **subs. 2(4)** which said that 'any enactment passed or to be passed . . . shall be construed and have effect subject to the foregoing provisions of this section.'

A few years before the UK joined the EEC, the European Court of Justice had decided, in *Costa v ENEL* **[1964] CMLR 425**, that if a national law conflicted with an EEC law, then the law of the EEC would have supremacy.[5] All member states had transferred part of their sovereignty to the Community. **Subsection 2(4)** was passed to give effect to this principle, but what, exactly, did it mean? Was the **ECA 1972** an Act unlike any other that could not be repealed by a later Act of Parliament? Lord Denning had feared, in *Blackburn v Attorney-General* **[1971] 1 WLR 1037**, that the effect of joining the EEC would be an irreversible transfer of parliamentary supremacy to the EEC.

This did not turn out to be the case. Lord Denning came up with a more nuanced interpretation of the supremacy issue in a later case,[6] *Macarthys v Smith* **[1979] 3 All ER 325**, where the UK **Equal Pay Act 1970** did not coincide with EEC equal pay provisions. The easiest way to deal with such a conflict was for the UK court to interpret the UK Act in a way that took account of the EEC law. **Subsection 2(4)** could easily be interpreted to support this approach and clever judicial interpretation could eliminate any conflict between the two systems of law. Lord Denning went further and stated that if interpretation was not possible, EEC law was an 'overriding force' and had supremacy over a UK Act. He also added that Parliament could not impliedly repeal the **ECA 1972**, but it could be expressly repealed.

All three propositions were controversial at that time, but came to be accepted by the judiciary. The normal approach of the courts is to avoid conflict, by trying to reach an interpretation of the UK Act that conforms to EC law: *Pickstone v Freemans plc* **[1989] AC 66**. The **ECA 1972** has been recognized as one of a number of statutes of constitutional importance that cannot be impliedly repealed, Parliament must show that it is deliberately repealing the Act in question: *Thoburn v Sunderland City Council* **[2002] 4 All ER 156**. The House of Lords accepted in *R v Secretary of State for Transport ex parte Factortame* **[1991] 1 AC 603** [7] that EC law was supreme over UK Acts and Acts that conflict with EC law could not be enforced. That was the clear instruction from Parliament in the **ECA 1972**.

Public opinion about what was now known as the European Union changed and so Parliament used the **European Union Referendum Act 2015** to authorize the holding of a national referendum on whether the

UK should remain a member. The vote in 2016 was to leave. Under the UK constitution, referenda have no legal effect, as only Parliament can change the law. This was pointed out by the Supreme Court in *R (Miller) v Secretary of State for Exiting the EU* [2017] UKSC 5, but the Law Lords also observed that this referendum had 'great political significance'. Dicey had claimed, back in 1885, that although legally Parliament had unlimited supremacy, in reality Parliament would fear to go against the will of the people.[8] In accordance with this theory, although a majority of MPs actually supported remaining in the EU, Parliament enacted the **European Union (Notification of Withdrawal) Act 2017**, which allowed Prime Minister May to notify the EU that the UK was withdrawing under the procedure laid down in **Article 50 of the Treaty on the European Union**. *Miller* required Parliament to authorize this step, because in that case the government had conceded that once they had notified under **Article 50**, leaving the EU was inevitable. The Supreme Court considered that this would change the existing rights of UK residents and only Parliament could authorize that.

To complete the process of leaving the EU, the **ECA 1972** has to be expressly repealed by Parliament. This is being done by the European Union Withdrawal Bill 2017–19,[9] but it is not a simple process, as the legislation has to take into account that some of the UK's law is direct legislation from the EU and even more of UK law is based on EU requirements. To remove all of that law on the day of leaving the EU, 29 March 2019, would produce huge gaps in the legal system. The plan seems to be to keep the existing EU law and gradually remove it, if Parliament considers it necessary. The bill makes clear that, after exit day, the EU cannot make any new law for the UK and the UK courts would certainly not accept the supremacy of any of those new laws. UK courts or tribunals would no longer be bound by decisions of the Court of Justice of the European Union and UK cases could no longer be referred to that Court.

However, 'EU-derived domestic legislation' as it is called, that is enacted before exit day, would remain in force after leaving the EU. This would include direct EU legislation, such as Regulations and 'EU-derived rights', which would be UK legislation required by EU directives. To help UK courts understand what EU-derived legislation means, they could still consider the decisions of the Court of Justice of the European Union, but would no longer be bound by them, which is the existing position under the **ECA 1972**. More controversially, the bill also proposes that for this 'retained law', as it is also called, the principle of EU supremacy would still apply.

In this essay, we have put forward the theory that Parliament can legislate on whatever it wants. It can give a foreign organization the power to legislate for the UK, but can also, if it wishes, remove that permission. Or even, as we will probably see as withdrawal is painstakingly negotiated over the next few years, accept some EU laws, but not others.[10]

[8] This picks up and continues the argument introduced in the first paragraph.

[9] This bill illustrates the point that only express repeal of the **ECA 1972** is possible.

[10] This concludes the argument begun in the first paragraph: Parliament is supreme.

LOOKING FOR EXTRA MARKS?

- The answer above is designed to be straightforward, but there is plenty of academic opinion on these issues, which could be added to an answer.

- Negotiations on the UK leaving the EU are ongoing so look out for amendments to the European Union (Withdrawal) Bill.

- It is possible that the UK might remain in the EU after 2019, for a transition period. This will add complications to the supremacy issue.

QUESTION | 3

In January 2011, the EU Commission issued (fictitious) Directive 1/2011, which provided:

In the event of property of a European Union citizen being compulsorily acquired into public ownership that citizen shall be entitled to prompt, adequate, and effective compensation from the nationalizing government. This Directive must be implemented by Member States within two years.

In 2014, due to the financial crisis in the Eurozone, the government of the UK wished to obtain powers to take banks, affected by the crisis, into public ownership. The Nationalization of Banks Bill 2014 is proposed. The bill contains a controversial section that stipulates:

No compensation shall be payable to any shareholders in any bank, taken into public ownership.

In the Commons debate on the bill, the Minister for Europe explained that this clause was to prevent anyone making excess profits from the collapse of a bank.

Joan is a major shareholder in Farrows Bank, which is named in the Nationalization of Banks Bill 2014 as one of the banks that is to be nationalized. She wishes to challenge the legality of this proposed measure.

Advise Joan.

CAUTION!

- Do not oversimplify your answer. The *Factortame* case seems to give supremacy to EU law, but it is a lot more complicated than that.

- The problem of the EU claiming supremacy over UK law only makes any sense if you can explain the traditional doctrine of parliamentary supremacy.

- Different types of EU law have different types of effect in UK law.

- A directive is involved here and it can only have direct effect in certain circumstances. Directives can be enforced in other ways too.

- Remember to come to a conclusion, as this is a problem question. What does Joan get?

- At the time of writing, the UK is still subject to EU law and will be until at least 29 March 2019.

DIAGRAM ANSWER PLAN

Identify the issues	■ Identify the legal issues ■ There are two issues here; first, does an Act of Parliament or EU legislation have supremacy? Secondly, can an EU Directive be enforced in a UK court?
Relevant law	■ Outline the relevant law: statutory, general principles and case law, in particular: the views of A.V. Dicey; **European Communities Act 1972;** *Ellen St Estates v Minister of Health; Costa v ENEL; R v Secretary of State for Transport ex parte Factortame; Marshall v Southampton; Macarthys v Smith*
Apply the law	■ How does parliamentary supremacy work? ■ Can a directive be enforced in a UK court? ■ Is an Act of Parliament or EU law supreme?
Conclude	■ Can Joan depend on the directive, or will the Act of Parliament defeat her? ■ What sort of remedy would Joan be awarded?

SUGGESTED ANSWER

A good starting point for the traditional theories of parliamentary sovereignty is the views of A.V. Dicey, expressed in his *Introduction to the Study of the Law of the Constitution* (Macmillan 1885). Parliament can make, or unmake, any law that it wants and nobody can override or set aside that law.

As Parliament can unmake any law,[1] no Act of Parliament can be protected from being amended or repealed by a later Act of Parliament. Parliament may repeal an Act either by explicitly referring to the previous Act (express repeal) or, where two Acts conflict, by the latter being taken to be the law (implied repeal). Even if an Act was worded so as to prevent repeal, that wording would be ineffective: *Ellen Street Estates Ltd v Minister of Health* **[1934] 1 KB 590**. So, according to Dicey's view, there is nothing to prevent the Nationalization of Banks Bill 2014 repealing any previous legislation. Similarly, an Act of Parliament always overrides any other form of law, and this would include foreign

[1] There are two issues in this problem: supremacy and direct effect. The author has chosen to start with supremacy, because it is fairly easy to explain the traditional theory.

legislation: *Mortensen v Peters* **(1906) 8F (J) 93**. No person or body can set aside legislation made by Parliament, so the courts reject any attempt to challenge an Act of Parliament: *Pickin v BRB* **[1974] AC 765**. Once a bill has been passed by both the House of Commons and the House of Lords and has received Royal Assent, it cannot be questioned.

According to traditional views then, Joan has no case at all. Membership of the EU has, however, changed this, though at first this was not clear. **Section 2(1) of the European Communities Act 1972 (ECA 1972)** states that all EU law is part of the law of the UK and **s. 3(1)** adds that the UK courts have to abide by the decisions of the European Court of Justice (ECJ). The Act does not clearly state what would happen if EU law conflicted with a UK statute. Under the traditional theory of implied repeal, EU law would take priority over any Act of Parliament enacted before the **ECA 1972**: *Ellen Street Estates*. **Section 2(4) ECA 1972** has attracted attention, although its exact meaning is obscure. It states that:

[2] A short quotation. It might be possible to remember it for an exam.

> any enactment passed or to be passed . . . shall be construed and have effect subject to the foregoing provisions of this section.[2]

This could mean that EU law has supremacy over Acts of Parliament passed after 1972, or it could just mean that such Acts should be interpreted ('construed') so as to try to avoid any conflict with EU law. Both interpretations seem to have found favour with the UK courts.

It is clear that some time before the UK joined the EU, the ECJ had decided that the law of the EU had primacy over incompatible national laws. *Costa v ENEL* **[1964] ECR 585** [3] declared, at 593 that, by joining the EEC, member states had transferred part of their sovereignty to the Community:

[3] Note that this is the ECJ, not a UK court.

[4] The same point as in 2.

> Consequently a subsequent unilateral law which is incompatible with the aim of the Community cannot prevail.[4]

The Nationalization of Banks Bill 2014 seems to be a 'subsequent unilateral law which is incompatible' with the 2011 directive, in that it denies any compensation.

[5] We now move to the second issue, direct effect.

First, however, it must be decided whether the directive is actually applicable; that is, can it be enforced in UK law?[5] The UK is obliged under **Article 288 of the Treaty on the Functioning of the European Union (TFEU)** to give legal effect in its own national legal system to a directive, but appears not to have passed any legislation to do this. The ECJ has ruled that in certain circumstances a directive may have direct effect and be enforceable in the courts of a member state, despite the lack of national legislation.

The ECJ decided this in two UK cases, *Van Duyn v Home Office* **[1975] Ch 358** and *Marshall v Southampton and SW Hants AHA* **[1986] QB 402**, and this has been accepted by the UK courts.

[6] You must remember all three conditions and apply all three, methodically, to the facts.

The directive must meet three conditions to have direct effect.[6] First, the date for the implementation of the directive must have passed, which is the case here. Secondly, the wording of the directive must be clear, precise, and unconditional so that there is something that a court may enforce. Directive 1/2011 grants a clear right to compensation to Joan. The third condition is the 'vertical direct effect' condition: the directive can only be enforced against a public body, 'an emanation of the state'. Joan is going to be denied compensation by an Act of Parliament (if passed). She cannot sue the sovereign body, Parliament, so she would have to sue the government minister responsible for the legislation as an emanation of the state: *R v Secretary of State for Transport ex parte Factortame* [1991] 1 AC 603.

The problem is that Directive 1/2009 seems to be in direct contradiction to the 'no compensation' clause proposed in the bill. The ECJ held in *Costa* that EU law has supremacy, but in *Pickin* the House of Lords insisted on the supremacy of Acts of Parliament. The ECJ suggested a solution to this difficulty in *Marleasing SA v La Commercial Internacional de Alimentacion SA* [1990] ECR I-4135, in that the national court is obliged to interpret its own national law 'as far as possible, in the light of the wording and the purpose of the directive'.

The House of Lords accepted this obligation in *Webb v EMO Air Cargo (UK) Ltd* [1995] 1 WLR 1454, but it seems impossible to reconcile a directive that requires compensation to be paid and an Act of Parliament stipulating that it should not.

There appears a clear conflict between the UK Act and the directly effective EU directive. Lord Denning was one of the earliest judges to say, in *Macarthys Ltd v Smith* [1981] QB 180, that the UK courts should accord supremacy to EU law in such a case of conflict. It was not until *Factortame* that the House of Lords was willing to accept that EU law now had supremacy. Lord Bridge merely said, at 659:

> Under the terms of the Act of 1972, it has always been clear that it was the duty of a United Kingdom court, when delivering final judgment, to override any rule of national law found to be in conflict with any directly enforceable rule of Community law.[7]

[7] You might need to paraphrase a longer quotation than this.

This is what **s. 2(4) ECA 1972** required.

[8] Do not be satisfied with just saying 'EU law wins'; try to work out the remedy that this will give Joan.

Joan could therefore follow the precedent of *Factortame*, but the exact remedy that the court could grant her is more problematic.[8] In the light of the traditional theories of parliamentary supremacy, it is unthinkable that the UK courts would order Parliament not to legislate or order that an Act of Parliament is of no legal force. In *Factortame* itself, the House of Lords merely issued an interim injunction against the government minister responsible for that piece of legislation, telling him not to enforce the offending Act of Parliament. Joan could follow this precedent and do the same. The court might even prefer to issue a lesser remedy, a Declaration, as in *R v Employment Secretary ex parte Equal Opportunities Commission* [1995] 1 AC 1.

The ECJ has also provided another remedy for claimants in Joan's position. If a government or public body breaches EU law and causes loss to the claimant, particularly if acting intentionally and persistently, it must compensate the claimant. The directive here confers upon Joan a right to compensation and it would seem to be a serious breach of EU law here: *R v Secretary of State for Transport ex parte Factortame Ltd (No. 4)* [1996] 2 WLR 506. Joan could sue the relevant government minister for compensation.

There is one final possibility that is not favourable to Joan's case. In *Macarthys*, Lord Denning observed that EU law only has supremacy in the UK because an Act of Parliament says so. Parliament could always change its mind about the **ECA 1972** and repeal or amend it. Lord Denning went on to say that the words of the repealing Act would have to be clear, 'express'. This is confirmed by *Thoburn v Sunderland City Council* [2002] 1 CMLR 50, which held that the **ECA 1972** was a 'constitutional statute', which could not be impliedly repealed. Only express repeal could remove EU law and replace it with a UK statute.[9] The wording of the Nationalization of Banks Bill 2014 seems clearly to contradict EU law, but the court might consider that it would need to consult the record of parliamentary proceedings (as happened in *Pickstone v Freemans plc* [1989] AC 66) in order to ascertain whether Parliament intended to contradict or implement EU law.

[9] This answer is attempting to apply the law to the facts. What would express repeal look like?

If an Act of Parliament clearly did intend to remove this EU directive, then the UK courts would be bound to follow the intention of Parliament. The ECJ would assert the supremacy of EU law, so there would be a clash between the two courts. As seen in the *Factortame* litigation, it would probably be the UK that had to back down and remove the offending part of the Act of Parliament.

➕ LOOKING FOR EXTRA MARKS?

■ Not all British judges have the same view about parliamentary supremacy. Study the contrasting views carefully.

■ The judges of the UK courts and the judges of the ECJ perceive the issue of sovereignty differently. Make clear which courts you are talking about.

Q | QUESTION | 4

Should the European Union become more democratic?

! CAUTION!

- The EU system of government is based on different concepts to the UK system.
- In particular, the European Parliament is not the supreme body.
- Do not assume that member states want a more democratic EU.

◯ DIAGRAM ANSWER PLAN

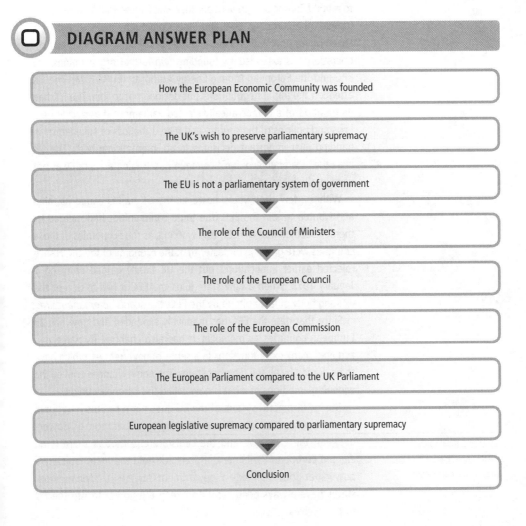

How the European Economic Community was founded

The UK's wish to preserve parliamentary supremacy

The EU is not a parliamentary system of government

The role of the Council of Ministers

The role of the European Council

The role of the European Commission

The European Parliament compared to the UK Parliament

European legislative supremacy compared to parliamentary supremacy

Conclusion

A SUGGESTED ANSWER

When the European Economic Community (EEC), the predecessor of the EU, was founded in 1957, the preamble of the founding **Treaty of Rome** stated that an objective of the Community was to 'lay the foundations of an ever closer union among the peoples of Europe'. This is a very ambiguous statement.[1] Does it mean the political union of the countries of Europe, to form a 'United States of Europe' or that the different peoples of Europe should cooperate more, become closer, and have some control over the destiny of Europe?

The origins of the EEC lie a little earlier[2] in the aftermath of the Second World War, in a continent devastated by that conflict. There was a general move, between countries, to cooperate more in order to rebuild Europe and prevent another war. France and West Germany founded the European Coal and Steel Community in 1951. Belgium, Luxembourg, the Netherlands, and Italy also joined. In 1957, this co-operation was extended, by founding two further organizations, the EEC and the European Atomic Energy Authority (EURATOM). The UK attended the initial negotiations but decided not to join. The UK had its tradition of a democratically elected Parliament that decided the laws and policies of the country and feared the loss of sovereignty in handing over important decisions to an international body. The UK liked the idea of an economic community, a trading area, but was not keen on the ideas about political union.[3]

Within a few short years, however, the UK had changed its mind and wanted to join the EEC (the three communities had merged by then). It seemed that the EEC was working, as the economies of those countries were growing far faster than the economy of the UK. France rejected earlier applications, but the UK finally gained entry on 1 January 1973. When a new state joins the EEC it has to accept the existing body of law built up by the EEC, the *acquis communautaire*.

Since that date the EEC has massively expanded and now has 28 European countries as members. It has also changed its name and acquired many extra functions in a series of new treaties, which have to be agreed by all the member states. The name changes convey the widening ambitions of what is now called the European Union.

The 'government' system of the EU does not resemble a national government system at all and there is no separation of powers between the Executive and the Legislature. Although there is an elected European Parliament, it does not hold the main legislative power, nor does it provide a 'government' for the EU.[4] The member states have always been careful to keep the power to run the EU to themselves.

---

[1] The introductory paragraph raises the central problem of the EU: different countries want different things from it.

[2] A bit of history is necessary to show that the EU developed in the way it has, before the UK joined.

[3] This has been the UK's main objection to the EU from the start.

[4] This key comparison is made several times: the EU is not a parliamentary democracy.

The Council of Ministers meets in Brussels and 'shall consist of a representative of each Member State at ministerial level': **Article 16(2) Treaty of European Union (Maastricht Treaty)**. So if the countries are discussing transport, the transport ministers meet and if they are discussing education, education ministers meet, and so on. The Council has legislative and budgetary functions, jointly with the European Parliament and also carries out policy-making and co-ordinating functions. This is arguably the most powerful institution of the EU.[5] For some decisions it has to be unanimous, for example the decision to admit a new member state, for others a simple majority is required, but the main method is qualified majority voting. Currently, each state has a number of votes, roughly proportional to its size, for example the UK, Germany, and France have 29 and Malta 3, and 255 of 345 votes must be cast in favour. Usually states negotiate and compromise and to aid this each country maintains staff at the Committee of Permanent Representatives (COREPER), which supports the Council's work.

[5] Here the evidence is evaluated and a conclusion is reached.

Confusingly, there is also a body called the European Council, in which the Heads of State or Heads of Government meet twice every six months to take the major decisions and decide the strategic direction of the EU. Governments formed this body because they wanted to make sure that they kept control of the EU.

The European Commission is probably the best known of the EU institutions and is also based in Brussels. It recommends actions for the EU, carries out the wishes of the Council of Ministers, and makes laws together with the Council of Ministers and the European Parliament. The Commission also has the important task of enforcing the Treaties and EU law in general and, if necessary can take defaulting member states to the European Court of Justice. Each of the 28 Member States appoints a Commissioner, each of whom is given a specialist brief, such as the internal market, environment, trade, etc. The Commissioners are independent and are not permitted to take instructions from governments, nor are member states allowed to influence them. There is a President of the Commission, who provides political guidance and allocates responsibilities to each Commissioner.

The European Parliament was originally just an advisory body, which consisted of delegates from national Parliaments, but successive treaties have increased its power. Since 1979, Members of the European Parliament (MEPs) have been directly elected by the electorates of the 28 Member States. Although in the UK candidates stand under their traditional party labels, once elected they become members of Europe-wide party groupings. The maximum number of elected MEPs is 750, with Germany having the largest number of 96 and the UK having 73. The European Parliament has some similarities with the UK Parliament, having an elaborate committee structure and the ability to question and scrutinize the European Commission. By a two-thirds majority it can cause the Commission to resign, but this is a rarely used power. By the same majority, the Parliament can reject the Commission's proposed budget, which does give it some power over expenditure in the EU.

[6] An explicit comparison of the EU and UK Parliaments is made.

The European Parliament differs from the UK Parliament[6] in its lack of legislative power. Although it can suggest legislative proposals to the European Commission, it is the European Commission that initiates EU legislation. Unlike the UK, the EU has different legislative procedures for its different areas of competence. Under the cooperation procedure, the European Parliament can amend the legislation. To increase the power of the Parliament, the co-decision procedure is now more used, where the Parliament can reject the legislation proposed by the Commission.

The EU has increased the powers of the Parliament over the years in an effort to make the Union more democratic and responsive to the wishes of the 500 million people that live there. It would be a mistake to think that this is what national leaders want.[7] Instead, they wish to take the key decisions in the Council of Ministers or the European Council. For instance, no legislation can be passed without the agreement of the Council of Ministers. Under **Article 17(7) of the Treaty on European Union (TEU)** the President of the European Commission is elected by the European Parliament, but the European Council selects the candidate.

[7] Another conclusion is reached, supported by evidence.

The last main institution of the EU is the European Court of Justice, staffed by 28 judges, one from each of the member states. Under **Article 267 TFEU**, individuals cannot bring a case involving EU law directly to this court, but must first commence their action in their national courts. That court may refer the matter to the ECJ, and once a case has reached the highest court the national court must do this. The existence of this procedure has enabled the ECJ to create its own unique legal order. In ***Van Gend en Loos v Nederlandse Tariefcommissie* [1963] ECR 1**, the ECJ recognized the supremacy of EU law over national law, which enables citizens of the EU to enforce their EU rights, maybe against their own state.

[8] The final paragraph reaches a conclusion, supported by evidence.

The ECJ saw this as a positive thing, but countries like the UK, with its proud tradition of parliamentary supremacy, resent handing over legislative and judicial power to a 'foreign' organization,[8] so much so that under the **EU Referendum Act 2015** a referendum on whether to leave or remain in the EU was held in 2016. The vote was to leave and Parliament is in the process of enacting the European Union (Withdrawal) Bill 2017–19. So it might be said that the UK prefers to return to its own parliamentary democracy, rather than create a new European democracy.

✚ LOOKING FOR EXTRA MARKS?

- Although this is a question about the 'constitution of the European Union', you need to be clear about the constitution of the UK first, in order to make the comparison.

- Include the latest disputes between the UK and the EU to provide fresh evidence for your answer.

TAKING THINGS FURTHER

- Allan T., 'Parliamentary sovereignty: Lord Denning's dexterous revolution' (1983) 3 Oxford Journal of Legal Studies 22.

  Although attention nowadays focuses on the **Factortame** *case, Lord Denning prepared the way for it in preceding cases such as* **Macarthys v Smith***. He accepted the supremacy of EU law, while maintaining that the UK Parliament still retained ultimate supremacy.*

- Craig P., 'Britain in the European Union' in J. Jowell, D. Oliver, and C. O'Cinneide (eds) *The Changing Constitution* (8th edn, OUP 2015) 104.

  The chapter opens with a brief explanation of the institutions of the EU, followed by a more detailed account of the case law on the supremacy issue and direct effect.

- Curtin D., 'Challenging executive dominance in European Union democracy' (2014) 72 MLR 1.

  This article discusses the secretive and informal nature of some EU decision-making. This makes it difficult for both the European Parliament and national Parliaments to scrutinize the EU.

- Ekins R., 'Acts of Parliament and the Parliament Acts' (2007) 123 LQR 9.

  This article considers the **Parliament Acts 1911** *and* **1949** *and* **R (Jackson) v Attorney-General** *and fits that decision within the general theory of parliamentary sovereignty.*

- Elliott M., 'The Principle of Parliamentary Sovereignty in Legal, Constitutional, and Political Perspective' in J. Jowell, D. Oliver, and C. O'Cinneide (eds) *The Changing Constitution* (8th edn, OUP 2015) 38.

  Not only does the author look at the traditional approach to parliamentary sovereignty, but also whether this doctrine has been changed by devolution, EU membership, or the European Convention on Human Rights.

- Elliott, M. 'The Supreme Court's judgment in *Miller*: in search of a constitutional principle.' (2017) 76 Cambridge Law Journal 257.

  This article is a detailed analysis of what **R (Miller) v Secretary of State for Exiting the EU** *has to say about various aspects of the UK constitution, such as the royal prerogative, EU law,* *parliamentary supremacy, constitutional conventions, and the role that the Supreme Court has to play in regulating the constitution.*

■ Gordon M., 'The conceptual foundation of parliamentary sovereignty: reconsidering Jennings and Wade' [2009] Public Law 519.

Jennings thought that Parliament had supremacy, not sovereignty and that Parliament could bind itself. This article compares his theory with that of Wade.

■ Gordan M. and Dougan M., 'The UK's European Union Act 2011: who won this bloody war anyway?' (2012) 37 European Law Review 3.

This is a detailed criticism of the Act. It is argued that not only will this Act spoil relationships with other EU states, but that the Act will also be ineffective. In particular, the requirement to hold a referendum will not bind future Parliaments.

■ Wade H.R.W., 'The basis of legal sovereignty' (1955) 13 Cambridge Law Journal 172.

This is the classic explanation of the theory of parliamentary sovereignty. The rule of recognition is explained. Why do the courts accept parliamentary sovereignty and could this ever change?

Online Resources

www.oup.com/uk/qanda/

Go online for extra essay and problem questions, a glossary of key terms, online versions of all the answer plans and audio commentary on how selected ones were put together, and a range of podcasts which include advice on exam and coursework technique and advice for other assessment methods.

The Human Rights Act 1998

7

ARE YOU READY?

The questions in this chapter concern an international treaty, the **European Convention on Human Rights**, and the **Human Rights Act 1998**. In order to attempt these questions, you need to have covered all of these topics in your work over the year and your revision:

- understanding the difference between the Council of Europe and the European Union;
- understanding that the **European Convention on Human Rights** does not have direct effect in English law;
- understanding that the European Court of Human Rights is a different court from the Court of Justice of the European Union (formerly known as the European Court of Justice)
- a victim of a breach of human rights may complain to an English court;
- a victim of a breach of human rights may also complain to the European Court of Human Rights;
- the **Human Rights Act 1998** does not change the supremacy of Parliament;
- the High Court and other superior courts may make a 'Declaration of Incompatibility'.

KEY DEBATES

Debate: The European Court of Human Rights versus the Supreme Court

The **European Convention on Human Rights** allows direct complaint to the European Court of Human Rights. The **Human Rights Act 1998** allows a complainant to bring their case in the courts of the UK. The UK courts and the European Court of Human Rights might decide the same issue in different ways. Which court should have the final say?

(▶)

Debate: Human Rights and Counter-Terrorism Legislation

Counter-terrorism legislation often restricts human rights. Is this legislation necessary to protect national security and who should decide: the government or the courts?

Debate: A British Bill of Rights

Successive UK governments have considered repealing or amending the **Human Rights Act 1998** and replacing it with a British bill of rights. What would this bill look like and how much could it differ from the current law?

QUESTION 1

Dai, Llewellyn, and Aneurin are leaders of the 'Free Wales Organization', which seeks independence for Wales and the end of English rule. They believe that independence can be achieved by political means and do not support violence against people. However, they do support the destruction of English-owned property in Wales.

All three men are seized by the police. Dai, though he is unarmed, is shot dead.

Llewellyn is held at a police station, without charge, for two weeks, and is not allowed to contact his family or solicitor. When he is released the police order him to live in England and not contact his family, friends, or members of the Free Wales Organization.

Aneurin is beaten up by the police when they question him. He admits being a member of a terrorist organization. Then he is released.

Llewellyn and Aneurin are prosecuted for being members of a terrorist organization. At their trial, they are not allowed to see the evidence against them. The government wants the evidence to remain secret on grounds of 'national security'.

Dai's widow, Llewellyn, and Aneurin consider that their human rights have been infringed.

Advise them.

CAUTION!

■ This is a problem concerning human rights, not criminal law or criminal procedure.

■ There are a number of different human rights issues in the problem. Carefully identify each one.

■ Plan carefully and stick to a clear structure. Look at each issue in turn.

DIAGRAM ANSWER PLAN

Identify the issues	■ Identify the legal issues: the definition of terrorism; the killing of a terrorist suspect; imprisonment without trial; freedom of movement, torture, and inhuman and degrading treatment; the right to a fair trial
Relevant law	■ Outline the relevant law: statutory, general principles and case law, in particular: the **Terrorism Act 2000**; the **European Convention on Human Rights, Articles 2, 5, 8,** and **6**
Apply the law	■ Analyse the meaning of the statutory and Convention provisions above ■ Compare relevant case law to the facts
Conclude	■ Are there breaches of human rights? ■ What is the remedy?

SUGGESTED ANSWER

The facts of this problem raise a number of legal issues. The three men are accused of terrorism: how is terrorism legally defined? Dai has been killed by the police. Can this ever be legally permissible? Llewellyn has been held without trial, which has been forbidden since **clause 39 of Magna Carta 1215.**[1] Is his exile to England any more legal? Can the police use violence against a suspect, as they do against Aneurin? Finally, the same clause of **Magna Carta** guarantees everyone a fair trial. Have Dai, Llewellyn, and Aneurin received this? For ease of explanation, I shall examine each of these legal issues in turn, explain the law that applies to each of these issues, and try to assess whether the three men's human rights have been infringed.

'Terrorism' is defined by **s. 1 of the Terrorism Act 2000**. Terrorism consists of threats or action involving serious violence against a person or serious damage against property. These threats must be designed to influence the government or to intimidate the public. Crucially, the threat or action must be made for the purpose of advancing a political, religious, ideological, or racial cause. This

[1] There are fundamental constitutional issues at stake here. Make that clear at the start.

would seem to cover the activities of the Free Wales Organization. Although they do not advocate violence against the person, they do endorse violence against property, which is covered by the Act. They want to influence the government to grant independence to Wales and this would indicate a political motive. Dai, Llewellyn, and Aneurin probably believe that their cause is just and that they are opposing English dictatorship, but that is no defence, according

²Do not be content to just quote a statutory definition; look for the case law that explains it.

to *R v F (Terrorism)* [2007] 3 WLR 164.² Nor could they claim self-defence against, foreign, English invaders: *R v Gul* [2013] **UKSC 64**.

It is possible that the Home Secretary has 'proscribed' the Free Wales Organization, under **s. 3 of the Terrorism Act 2000**, which would make it an offence to be a member or profess to be a member. In interpreting these sections, the court has incorporated human rights considerations, in particular **Article 11 of the European Convention on Human Rights (ECHR)**, which guarantees 'Freedom of Association' with others. It must be proved that a 'member' actually engaged in the activities of the organization to commit the offence: *Attorney-General's Reference (No. 4 of 2002)* [2005] 1 AC 264. To fit the definition of terrorism, it must also be shown that the organization actually is a violent, terrorist organization and not just a political one: *Alton v Secretary of State for the Home Department* [2008] 1 WLR 2341. We know that the Free Wales Organization is violent against property and

³If you can come to a clear conclusion, after applying the law to the facts, do so.

that the three accused men are its leaders, so the offence would seem to be proved.³

Article 2 ECHR states that: 'Everyone's right to life shall be protected by law.' According to **Article 2(2)**, deprivation of life is permissible 'when it results from the use of force which is no more than absolutely necessary' **(a)** 'in defence of any person from unlawful violence' or **(b)** 'in order to effect a lawful arrest or to prevent [an] escape'. In *McCann, Farrell and Savage v UK* (1995) **21 EHRR 97**, members of the armed forces shot dead three alleged terrorists. This was not 'absolutely necessary', because the three were not actually threatening unlawful violence, were unarmed

⁴In Human Rights law, use both cases from the European Court of Human Rights and from the English courts.

and could have been arrested, rather than killed. This would seem to apply to Dai, too, and so his killing would also be a breach of **Article 2**, the right to life.⁴

Imprisonment without trial is contrary to **Article 5 ECHR**. Extended detention, for the purpose of police questioning, is permissible for up to 14 days in terrorist cases under the **Protection of Freedoms Act 2012**, but it must be authorized by a judge. Human rights law insists on the same judicial authorization in *Brogan v UK* **(1988) 11 EHRR 117**, so the detention of Llewellyn is illegal. The courts frown on detention without trial, as was strongly stated by the House of Lords in *A v Home Secretary (No. 1)* **[2005] 2 AC 68**. Under **Schedule 8 to the Terrorism Act 2000**, delaying access to a lawyer, for a terrorist suspect, would be acceptable for up to 48 hours, if there was a good reason to do so, such as the need to protect the public or prevent the arrested person alerting other suspects. These delays have been accepted by the European Court of Human Rights as not breaching **Article 6(3)**, in cases such as *Ibrahim v UK* **[2015] 61 EHRR 9**, but two weeks is too long a delay. Llewellyn's rights have been infringed.

'Exiling' a person to another part of the country used to be possible with a 'Control Order', under the **Prevention of Terrorism Act 2005**. The idea was to break their contacts with their terrorist network. A Control Order that sent a man 150 miles from his home was condemned as a breach of **Article 8**, the right to family life, in *Secretary of State for the Home Department v AP* [2011] 1 AC 1. It is important to note that Control Orders were used against terrorist suspects who had not been convicted of any offence, because there was no evidence that could be used in court. Control Orders were replaced by 'Terrorism, Prevention and Investigation Measures' by the **Terrorism Prevention and Investigation Measures Act 2011**. This regime does not currently allow a suspect to be removed from his home. So sending Llewellyn to England is unlawful and contrary to his human rights.

English law does not allow the ill treatment or torture of suspects. The House of Lords noted, in *A v Home Secretary (No. 2)* **[2006] 1 All ER 575**, that this country has had a long opposition to torture. Torture, inhuman and degrading treatment, or punishment is forbidden by **Article 3 ECHR**. This would include the beating of suspects as held in *Ireland v UK* **(1978) 2 EHRR 25**, so the treatment of Aneurin would be unlawful. Any confession that he made would be inadmissible evidence, under **s. 78 of the Police and Criminal Evidence Act 1984**: *R v Ibrahim* **[2008] 4 All ER 208**.

A fair trial is required by **Article 6 ECHR**. In particular, a person is entitled under **Article 6.3(a)** 'to be informed promptly, in a language which he understands and in detail, of the nature and cause of the accusation against him'. This has proved problematic in terrorist trials, particularly in cases involving control orders. The government side often considers that the evidence is so secret and might involve revealing methods of intercepting communications or the identity of informers, that it would be a threat to national security to disclose it to suspected terrorists or their lawyers. This is known as 'closed procedure material'. A system of special advocates has been established. These are barristers who have security clearance. They are allowed to see the 'closed procedure material' and make out a case for the defendant as best they can. The problem is that the special advocates are not permitted to tell the defendants or their lawyers what is in the closed procedure material. The English and European Courts have decided that this is not sufficient to guarantee a fair trial and that the defence must be told 'the essence of the case against him': *Secretary of State for the Home Department v MB* [2008] 1 All ER 657. This was repeated for Temporary Provision Investigation Measures in *Mohamed v Secretary of State for the Home Department* [2014] 3 All ER 760, the defence must be told the gist of the case against them. So this would be yet another human rights breach for Llewellyn and Aneurin. The judge would make every effort to ensure that the pair received a fair trial,[5] in particular that they were told the basics of the case against them.

[5] The right to a fair trial is a key constitutional issue, which is why it has been given lengthy treatment.

The three men can raise their human rights concern in any English court under the **Human Rights Act 1998**. They probably are terrorists under the **Terrorism Act 2000**, but, as we have seen earlier, they are likely to be successful on all their other human rights points. Compensation might well be paid, but it is likely to be limited in amount, as the main point of human rights litigation is to establish whether rights have been infringed: *R (Greenfield) v Home Secretary* [2005] 1 All ER 927.[6]

[6] A clear, concise conclusion is always desirable.

LOOKING FOR EXTRA MARKS?

■ The cases on this subject come to different interpretations of the law. Try to make sense of this and come to a clear conclusion.

■ There are controversial issues here, such as the right to a fair trial in a terrorist case. Look for up-to-date information on this subject.

QUESTION | 2

What effect has the Human Rights Act 1998 had on English law?

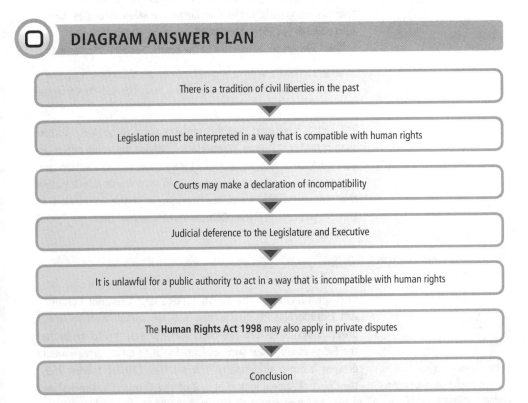

- You need to explain what the **Human Rights Act** does, but by itself that does not answer the question.

- You also need to explain the important cases which have established the meaning of this Act.

- This Act has had an effect on the whole of English law, so you need to be selective about what you put into your answer.

- Choose the most well-known examples, which is what this answer does, or concentrate on one area of law.

◯ DIAGRAM ANSWER PLAN

There is a tradition of civil liberties in the past

▼

Legislation must be interpreted in a way that is compatible with human rights

▼

Courts may make a declaration of incompatibility

▼

Judicial deference to the Legislature and Executive

▼

It is unlawful for a public authority to act in a way that is incompatible with human rights

▼

The **Human Rights Act 1998** may also apply in private disputes

▼

Conclusion

Ⓐ SUGGESTED ANSWER

[1] The essay has quite a long introduction, which is necessary to explain why the **HRA 1998** was such a major change.

The **Human Rights Act 1998 (HRA 1998)** came into force on 2 October 2000 and made it far easier to enforce the **European Convention on Human Rights (ECHR)** in British courts. Before this Act,[1] Britain had a tradition of civil liberties, popularized by the late-nineteenth-century writer A.V. Dicey. Citizens did not have rights guaranteed by the constitution, but rather they had liberties: they could do anything that the law did not forbid. Judges would prevent governments taking actions for which they did not have legal power, as in the classic case of *Entick v Carrington* **(1765) 19 St Tr 1030**. If any problems remained, Parliament would enact legislation to deal with the matter.

The United Kingdom has been a party to the **ECHR** since 1951. Even before the **HRA 1998**, the courts of this country could refer to the provisions of the Convention to help interpret ambiguous legislation: *R v Home Secretary ex parte Brind* **[1991] 1 AC 696**. The courts had also said that breaches of the European Convention would encourage them to judicially review a minister's decision and hold it to be unreasonable and therefore illegal: *R v Ministry of Defence ex parte Smith* **[1995] 4 All ER 427**.

The 1998 Act required more of the courts. **Section 3** states that:

So far as it is possible to do so, primary legislation and subordinate legislation must be read and given effect in a way which is compatible with the Convention rights.

The courts have held that this requires them to go much further than ordinary statutory interpretation, where the court might depart from the ordinary language of the statute to avoid absurd consequences. If necessary, the judge could read words into a statute that were not there to ensure compliance with the Convention. As Lord Steyn put it in *R v A (Complainant's sexual history)* **[2002] 1 AC 45, 68**:

[2] Quotations can be effective in an essay. Keep them short and to the point.

The techniques to be used[2] would not only involve the reading down of express language in a statute but also the implication of provisions.

Section 43(1)(c) of the Youth Justice and Criminal Evidence Act 1999 forbids the questioning of a rape complainant about her previous sexual history. The court reinterpreted this to mean that the judge could allow such questioning if to do otherwise would prevent a fair trial. Similarly, in *R v Offen* **[2000] 1 WLR 253**,[3]

[3] This is evidence of the interpretation technique explained earlier in the essay.

the Court of Appeal looked at **s. 2 of the Crime (Sentences) Act 1997**, which says that a defendant should be given a life sentence if they commit two serious offences, unless there were 'exceptional circumstances'. The court took account of the **ECHR** and interpreted it to mean that a life sentence should only be imposed if the defendant was a serious risk to the public. So far a lot of the cases on the **HRA 1998** have involved a consideration of the fairness or otherwise of criminal and, sometimes, civil trials, which is covered by **Articles 5** and **6** of the Convention. If the court concludes that there is no breach of the Convention, as they often do, then the judges do not have to do any 'interpreting' under **s. 3** and the existing law remains: *Poplar Housing v Donoghue* [2001] 3 WLR 183.

If there is a clear breach of a Convention Article and the courts cannot interpret the difficulty away under **s. 3**, the court has no power to declare the Act void. Such a power would conflict with the supremacy of Parliament. Instead, **s. 4** allows the courts to make a 'declaration of incompatibility'.[4] The court merely states that the Act of Parliament in question is 'incompatible' with human rights. Only the High Court and above can do this. Then it is up to Parliament to amend or repeal the offending Act, if Parliament chooses to do so. There is a special 'fast-track' procedure to do this under **s. 10 HRA 1998**, using delegated legislation. This was done after the declaration of incompatibility in *R (on the application of H) v London North and East Mental Health Review Tribunal* [2001] QB 1, where the court held that it was a breach of **Article 5** to place the burden of proof on a restricted patient to show that he was no longer suffering from a mental disorder warranting detention. In fact, declarations of incompatibility have not been that common, but a controversial example of this would be[5] *R (Anderson) v Home Secretary* [2002] 4 All ER 108, where the House of Lords said that the Home Secretary could not decide the minimum period that a murderer must stay in prison. This was not a fair trial under **Article 6**, because a trial should be conducted by a judge, not a politician. Similarly, release of a murderer has to be decided by a judicial body, independent of the government, the Parole Board and the prisoner has a right to an oral hearing: *Osborn v Parole Board* [2013] UKSC 61.

In fact, the courts have been rather cautious in their application of the Convention. Indeed, Richard Edwards has eloquently argued in his article 'Judicial deference under the Human Rights Act' that a culture of 'judicial deference' has developed, in that judges can be reluctant to interfere with laws enacted by a democratically elected Parliament: (2002) 65 MLR 859. In *R v DPP ex parte Kebilene* [2000] 2 AC 326, 381, a case involving the **Prevention of Terrorism Act 2000**, the Court of Appeal issued a declaration of incompatibility. The House of Lords disagreed that there was a breach of the Convention and Lord Hope observed that:

In some circumstances[6] it will be appropriate for the courts to . . . defer, on democratic grounds, to the considered opinion of the elected body or person.

[4] How the **HRA 1998** deals with the constitutional doctrine of the supremacy of Parliament is a key debate.

[5] As this is such a key debate, plenty of evidence is used to support the argument.

[6] Whether the courts should defer to Parliament and the Executive is another key debate.

Section 6 HRA 1998 makes it 'unlawful for a public authority to act in a way which is incompatible with a Convention right'. This, combined with the succeeding **ss. 7** and **8**, creates a new right of action and allows the 'victim' of a human rights abuse to sue and recover damages among other remedies. The courts have had some difficulty in deciding the meaning of 'public authority', as it is not defined in the Act. In *Yarl's Wood Immigration Ltd v Bedfordshire Police* [2008] EWHC 2207 (Comm), the court held that a private company operating an immigration detention centre under a contract with the Home Office was a public authority. In contrast, in *YL v Birmingham City Council* [2008] 1 AC 95 the House of Lords held that private care homes that accommodated persons paid for by the local authority were not public authorities.

The European Court of Human Rights can award damages, but sees its function more as to make rulings on the law, rather than to compensate victims. The objective is to try to end the human rights abuse, rather than compensate the victim. In *R (Greenfield) v Secretary of State for the Home Department* [2005] 2 All ER 240, the House of Lords decided that the purpose of the **HRA 1998** was not to give victims better remedies at home than they could recover at Strasbourg. It was more important to ensure 'just satisfaction' and issue an order remedying the breach of rights. The Supreme Court[7] endorsed this approach in *Michael v The Chief Constable of South Wales Police* [2015] UKSC 2.

A much-discussed question is whether the **HRA 1998** applies to legal disputes between private individuals or just when a public authority infringes a person's human rights. The courts have so far not been willing to recognize completely new rights based on the Convention in disputes between private individuals. Instead, the UK courts have tentatively moved towards using the Convention in private disputes to reinforce claims that already exist in English law. In *Campbell v Mirror Group Newspapers* [2004] 2 AC 457, Convention rights were used to reinvent breach of confidence as a new right of privacy.

The public maybe has a misleading impression of the **HRA 1998**. Some cases generate enormous publicity, such as *R (Nicklinson) v Ministry of Justice* [2014] UKSC 38, on whether the **Article 8** right to a private life allowed assisted suicide, and *Preddy v Bull* [2013] UKSC 73, on whether Christian hotel owners could refuse to give a homosexual couple a bed for the night. What is lost in all the publicity is that the human rights claim was defeated in both cases and UK Acts of Parliament applied.

[7] New cases decided by a high-level court are always good evidence.

Most judges, particularly in the higher courts, have taken a cautious approach. In *R (Nicklinson) v Ministry of Justice* [2014] **UKSC 38,**[8] the Supreme Court stated that the European Court of Human Rights had not yet given a clear judgment on the issue of assisted suicide. Their lordships stated that there might be a breach of human rights, but they would make no ruling and no declaration of incompatibility. Parliament should be given the opportunity of considering whether to legislate on this issue. Parliament was the representative body in the UK constitution and they, rather than a court, should decide. The Legislature, however, has done nothing, so now the Supreme Court is willing to consider this matter again: *R (Conway) v Secretary of State for Justice* [2017] EWCA Civ 275.[9]

[8] A clear conclusion backed by new evidence is always a good idea.

[9] The very last part of the essay shows that you keep up to date.

➕ LOOKING FOR EXTRA MARKS?

■ Make sure that you are clear on what the **Human Rights Act** has done and what it has not.

■ Be up to date on the latest cases and academic opinion.

ⓠ QUESTION 3

Should the Human Rights Act 1998 be replaced with a UK bill of rights?

❗ CAUTION!

■ What does the phrase 'bill of rights' actually mean? It can mean different things in different countries.

■ How would a bill of rights differ from the existing **Human Rights Act 1998**?

■ Be accurate about reform proposals. Do not just give your own opinion.

DIAGRAM ANSWER PLAN

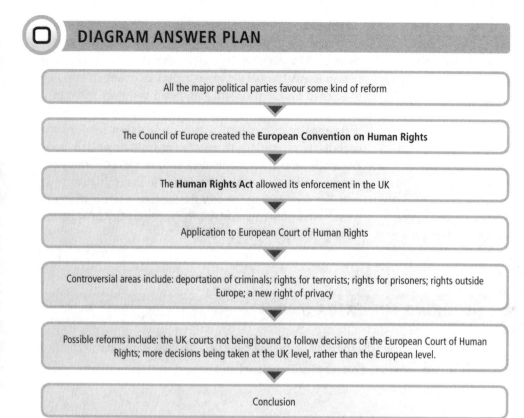

All the major political parties favour some kind of reform

⬇

The Council of Europe created the **European Convention on Human Rights**

⬇

The **Human Rights Act** allowed its enforcement in the UK

⬇

Application to European Court of Human Rights

⬇

Controversial areas include: deportation of criminals; rights for terrorists; rights for prisoners; rights outside Europe; a new right of privacy

⬇

Possible reforms include: the UK courts not being bound to follow decisions of the European Court of Human Rights; more decisions being taken at the UK level, rather than the European level.

⬇

Conclusion

A SUGGESTED ANSWER

The **Human Rights Act 1998 (HRA 1998)** was introduced by the government of Tony Blair, but the governments that succeeded him, led by Prime Ministers Brown, Cameron, and May have considered replacing it with a UK 'bill of rights'. The politicians are reacting to what they perceive as public concern over the working of the 1998 Act. Some court decisions have aroused unfavourable publicity in the press and others have been unpopular with government ministers, angered to see their policies frustrated by judges.

[1] A brief explanation of the **HRA 1988** allows us to consider whether the UK already has a bill of rights.

A brief explanation of the **HRA 1998** is called for.[1] The **HRA 1998** allows the rights in the **European Convention on Human Rights (ECHR)** to be enforced in UK courts. The rights are listed and the main body of the Act explains how they are to be enforced, so it is roughly equivalent to the charter or bill of rights found in many constitutions. The **ECHR** is not a product of the EU or a consequence of the UK joining the EU, so the UK will remain a party to the **ECHR**, even when it leaves the EU. A different European organization, the Council of

Europe, created the **ECHR**, which was signed in Rome in 1950 and came into force in 1953. The UK was a founder member of the Council of Europe and British lawyers, such as the future Lord Chancellor, Lord Kilmuir, played a prominent role in drafting the Convention. It was intended to reflect the basic civil liberties or rights respected for many years in countries such as the UK.

Although the UK was always a prominent supporter of the **ECHR**, successive governments did not think it necessary to enact the Convention into British law, until the Labour Government of 1997. One motive was to save UK citizens and residents the trouble and expense of taking their case to the European Court of Human Rights in Strasbourg. The UK had also lost a few prominent cases in that court, which was bad publicity in Europe and the wider world. Membership of the EU[2] also required the UK to respect human rights: **Article 6 of the Treaty on European Union.**

[2] The relationship between the **ECHR** and the EU is a key debate.

Since 1998, the **HRA 1998** has attracted some unfavourable publicity. A number of examples[3] can be given. The European Court of Human Rights held that people who were not British citizens could not be deported if they might face inhuman or degrading treatment or torture (**Article 3**) in their home state. The UK courts have followed the precedents set for 'ordinary criminals' in *Soering v UK* **(1996) 23 EHRR 413** and alleged terrorists in *Chahal v UK* **(1996) 23 EHRR 413** and often refused to sanction the government's wish to deport.

[3] Why has the **HRA 1988** been criticized? We need to look at the evidence.

Parliament's anti-terrorist laws have been questioned on the basis of human rights. Control orders allowed the government to restrict the movement of suspected, but unconvicted 'terrorists'. The European Court of Human Rights held, in *A v UK* **(2009) 49 EHRR 29**, that there was a potential breach of **Article 6**, the right to a fair trial, in that, because of national security considerations, the suspected terrorist might not be told the evidence against them. The UK House of Lords implemented this in *Secretary of State for the Home Department v AF (No. 3)* **[2009] 3 All ER 643**. On their own initiative, the UK courts have condemned control orders that confine the suspect to their home for 16 hours a day in *Secretary of State for the Home Department v JJ* **[2008] 1 All ER 613** as a breach of **Article 5**, the right to liberty, and **Article 8**, the right to a private life.

British law states that convicted criminals in prison do not have the right to vote, but the European Court of Human Rights has repeatedly held that such a blanket ban is disproportionate and breaches human rights in cases such as *Hirst v UK* **(2006) 42 EHRR 41** and *Greens v UK* **(2011) 53 EHRR 21**. This leaves the government with a dilemma; they are obliged under the Convention to change the law, but

4Parliamentary supremacy is
preserved. This is a key debate.

Parliament will not vote for it. The Supreme Court[4] neatly summed up the dilemma in *Chester v Secretary of State for Justice* **[2013] 3 WLR 1076**: UK law clearly did not allow prisoners to vote and this remains law in the UK and, even though this is a clear breach of human rights, it is the law until Parliament changes it.

Human rights have also affected the UK's foreign policy in that the **ECHR** applies wherever the UK has 'jurisdiction' (**Article 1**). That included the parts of Iraq that were under British occupation after the second Gulf War: *Al Skeini v UK* **(2011) 53 EHRR 18**. British soldiers are protected by the **ECHR**, wherever they are serving in the world: *R (Smith) v Ministry of Defence* **[2013] UKSC 41**.

The courts have used a combination of the old equitable action for breach of confidence and the right to a private life in **Article 8** to begin to develop a right of privacy in English law: *Campbell v Mirror Group Newspapers* **[2004] 2 AC 457**. Even the sex life of a public figure might be protected, as in *Mosley v News Group Newspapers* **[2008] EMLR 20**, much to the consternation of media that make their money by exposing such activities. Yet no legislation[5] has been passed to make this 'change' in the law.

5This is a strong argument. Should the courts be allowed to use the **HRA 1998** to develop new laws?

Under **s. 2 HRA 1998**, the UK courts have been obliged to 'take into account' decisions of the European Court of Human Rights, but are not bound, in the precedent sense, to follow them.[6] The House of Lords has held that the UK courts should normally abide by decisions of the European Court of Human Rights: *R (Alconbury Developments Ltd) v Secretary of State for the Environment* **[2003] 2 AC 295, 313**. The new Supreme Court refused to follow *Al-Khawaja and Tahery v UK* **(2009) 49 EHRR 1** in *R v Horncastle and others* **[2010] 2 WLR 47**. The Supreme Court considered that the European Court judges, who come from a civil law tradition, did not fully understand the common law way of doing things and that the protections in English law guaranteed the defendant a fair trial. In further proceedings, the Grand Chamber of the European Court of Human Rights conceded that the UK courts were partially right: *Al-Khawaja and Tahery v UK* **(2012) 54 EHRR 23**.

6This is another key debate. The UK courts maintain their independence and are not bound to follow the decisions of the European Court of Human Rights.

It is not unknown for the UK courts[7] to reinterpret European Court of Human Rights decisions. To refer back to the examples such as *Chahal v UK* given earlier, the courts do approve deportations if the judge(s) are satisfied, on the evidence, that the deportee will not be ill-treated back home: *RB (Algeria) v Secretary of State for the Home Department* **[2009] 4 All ER 1045**. It was hoped at the time of the **HRA 1998** that British judges would interpret human rights in a way appropriate to the UK, and this seems to be happening.

In 2010, the Conservative–Liberal Democrat Government set up an independent Commission to investigate the creation of a British bill

7A number of different types of evidence are brought together in this paragraph: English cases, European cases, government papers, and EU treaties.

[8] No one can predict the future, but this conclusion tries to summarize the evidence at the time of writing the essay.

of rights and possible reform of the **HRA 1998**. There were many differences of opinion within the Commission, but the majority recommended[8] that a UK bill of rights should be enacted that would build on the existing rights in the European Convention and maintain the supremacy of Parliament preserved by the **HRA 1998**. It was thought that there were so many misunderstandings about what the current **HRA 1998** did, that a fresh start was needed, with a bill of rights that the British public would understand and support. After the Conservative Party won the 2015 general election, they began planning a British bill of rights. This might involve wholesale change or just amendments to the parts of the **HRA 1998** that have caused problems, as outlined earlier in this essay. An enhanced role for the Supreme Court, as a constitutional court able to protect human rights and UK constitutional principles, has been suggested. Total withdrawal from the **ECHR** is unlikely, because it would cause the UK so many international problems, not only with the Council of Europe, but also the EU and the United Nations, which also endorse and promote human rights. However, the 2017 Conservative Government has said that it will not repeal or replace the **HRA 1998** until the Brexit process is complete and will remain a party to the European Convention for the duration of this Parliament.[9]

[9] The conclusion draws on the evidence presented in the essay: this is a controversial issue, but it will not be settled at the moment.

✚ LOOKING FOR EXTRA MARKS?

■ In order to put forward proposals for reform, it is necessary to know what the criticisms of the existing law are.

■ This requires a detailed knowledge of controversial court decisions based on the existing law.

■ The **HRA 1998** can still be criticized, even though there are no immediate plans to reform it

Ⓠ QUESTION | 4

Parliament decides to strengthen the law prohibiting the hunting of wild mammals with dogs and enacts the (fictitious) Hunting Act 2009. The Act makes any organization engaged in hunting an illegal organization, and membership of such an organization a criminal offence. Members of such an organization can be arrested and held without trial for a period of up to three months. Under the Act, the Home Secretary decides whether a person detained can be released.

Anonymous informers say that Dougie, Karen, and Paul are all members of the Borchester Hunt, so the three are arrested and detained at a disused army camp. The camp, which is run for the government by a private security company, lacks any heating and the food and conditions are

⊙

very poor. Dougie is placed in a cell with another inmate, Boris, who is known to be violent. Boris kills Dougie.

Karen and Paul are denied access to lawyers, but friends of theirs petition the Home Secretary to release them. He refuses.

Karen, Paul, and Dougie's widow, Sharon, are wondering whether any legal action would be worthwhile.

Advise Karen, Paul, and Sharon.

! CAUTION!

- ▦ This is a problem question, not an essay, so concentrate on the legal issues raised by the facts. A general explanation of human rights law is not required.

- ▦ You need to be acquainted with the different Articles in the **European Convention of Human Rights** and what those Articles actually say, but only mention those Articles that relate to the facts of the problem.

- ▦ You also need to know about the leading cases on each of the relevant Articles.

- ▦ Try to spot each human rights issue as it is raised, identify the relevant Article of the **European Convention of Human Rights** and apply the relevant case law.

- ▦ The **Human Rights Act 1998** is only relevant when discussing how Dougie, Karen, and Paul might enforce those rights.

DIAGRAM ANSWER PLAN

Identify the issues	▪ Identify the legal issues: a hunting ban; imprisonment without trial; arbitrary arrest; lack of a fair trial; inhuman and degrading treatment; and unlawful killing
Relevant law	▪ Outline the relevant law: statutory, general principles and case law, in particular: **Articles 3, 5, 6, 8**, and **11 of the European Convention on Human Rights**
Apply the law	▪ Use appropriate cases to decide the meaning of the Articles above and compare them to the facts of the problem
Conclude	▪ Are there any breaches of human rights? ▪ What are the remedies available to Dougie, Karen, and Paul under the **Human Rights Act 1998?**

SUGGESTED ANSWER

What has happened to Dougie, Karen, and Paul would seem to raise some serious human rights issues. Since the **Human Rights Act 1998 (HRA 1998)** came into force these issues can be raised in an English court, and, if the three fail to gain satisfaction, they could still raise a complaint with the European Court of Human Rights in Strasbourg. First, we need to advise them on whether there are any human rights breaches, and then on who would be liable for those breaches and what remedies the courts might grant.

First, we must ask whether it is a breach of human rights to make hunting illegal. The real **Hunting Act 2004** made hunting mammals with dogs a criminal offence and was challenged in the courts on a number of grounds, including that it infringed human rights, in *R (Countryside Alliance and others) v Attorney-General and another* **[2008] 3 All ER 1**. Participants in hunting claimed that it was part of their private life and to stop them doing it was a breach of **Article 8**, the right to a private life.[1] The House of Lords disagreed, stating that fox hunting, for instance, was a very public activity carried out in daylight with considerable colour and noise, and so could hardly be termed 'private'. **Article 11** guarantees freedom of

[1] The Articles of the **European Convention on Human Rights (ECHR)** create a simple and logical structure for this answer.

association, and it was argued that this included the right to form and join 'hunts'. The court held that freedom of association was intended to protect political activity. Both **Articles 8(2)** and **11(2)** allow the restriction of human rights to protect morals. The court deferred to Parliament's decision that hunting was immoral. So it would seem acceptable to have laws banning hunting, but any law that restricts rights must be proportionate to the aim; it must not restrict rights any more than necessary to stop hunting. In *R (Countryside Alliance and others) v Attorney-General and another* [2008] 3 All ER 1,[2] it was acceptable to make hunting illegal, but to make hunting organizations illegal and to imprison their members without trial would not seem to be a proportionate response to the problem and might be a breach of **Article 11**.

Imprisonment without trial has always been regarded as a serious breach of civil liberties (*Liversidge v Anderson* [1942] AC 206) and is now clearly prohibited by **Article 5**, the right to liberty and security. *Brogan v UK* (1988) 11 EHRR 117 held that detention without trial for only four days was excessive. The detainee must be brought before a judge who can determine the legality of the detention, but we know from our facts that Karen and Paul's only remedy is to the Home Secretary, an elected politician, and that is unacceptable: *R (Anderson) v Home Secretary* [2003] 1 AC 837. *Brogan* is a decision of the European Court of Human Rights,[3] which, under **s. 2 HRA 1998**, must be 'taken into account' by any UK court when deciding on the meaning of a 'Convention right'. Despite this wording, which would suggest that a UK court is not bound to follow a European Court decision, the House of Lords would nearly always follow such a decision.

The trio have been arrested and **Article 5(1)(c)** requires there to be 'reasonable suspicion' that they have committed the offence. The European Court of Human Rights accepted that information from unnamed informants could amount to reasonable suspicion in *Fox, Campbell and Hartley v UK* (1991) 13 EHRR 157, but that was a case involving terrorists and the Court did say that that could justify a lower standard of evidence on which to reasonably base suspicion. So maybe there is not enough evidence to justify Dougie, Karen, and Paul's arrests.

Dougie, Karen, and Paul have clearly not received a fair trial. Legal advice is an essential preparation in making a proper defence and to deny access to a lawyer is a breach of **Article 6(3)(d)**:[4] *Golder v UK* (1975) 1 EHRR 524 and *Silver v UK (1981)* 3 EHRR 475. There is no doubt that the English courts accept that defendants, prisoners, and arrested persons must be allowed to communicate with their lawyers without any interference from the authorities, as shown by

[2] Having a detailed and accurate knowledge of the leading cases and being able to apply that knowledge to the facts of the problem leads to good marks.

[3] The effect of European Court of Human Rights judgments in English law is important. Get it right!

[4] **Article 6** is a very important Article. Show that you understand what it means by discussing the case law on it.

the prison case *R (Daly) v Home Secretary* [2001] 2 AC 532. The House of Lords accepted that it was a basic right existing in English law, irrespective of anything in the European Convention. The House of Lords held in *R v Davis (Iain)* [2008] 3 WLR 125 that it is not permissible to convict anyone solely on the evidence of anonymous witnesses. This is a breach of common law principles and **Article 6**, the right to a fair trial, specifically **Article 6(3)(d)** which states that everyone charged with a criminal offence has the right to examine witnesses. The three, in fact, have not received any trial at all, as we are not told that the Home Secretary has held 'a fair and public hearing' as required by **Article 6**. The hearing must also be held by an 'independent and impartial tribunal' and a number of cases have held that a politician, who may be influenced by electoral considerations, should not act as a judge: *R (Anderson) v Home Secretary* [2003] 1 AC 837. The applicants here have not had a trial from any sort of court at all.

The treatment of Dougie, Karen, and Paul while detained leaves something to be desired. 'Inhuman or degrading treatment' is prohibited under **Article 3** and, although what has happened to the three is not as severe as the beatings and psychological interrogation techniques in *Ireland v UK* (1978) 2 EHRR 25, sending a prisoner to the harsh conditions of 'death row' in the United States was a breach in *Soering v UK* (1989) 11 EHRR 439. So, poor prison conditions could be an infringement of human rights.

Allowing a prisoner to be murdered is also a breach of human rights, because, under **Article 2**, the state has a duty to protect the right to life. *R (Amin) v Home Secretary* [2004] 1 AC 653 has quite similar facts to the killing of Dougie by Boris, for it concerned a young prisoner who was killed by a cellmate, whom the prisons authorities knew to be both racist and violent. **Article 2** required that there should be a full, independent, investigation into his death, with legal representation funded for the family: *R (JL) v Secretary of State for Justice* [2009] 2 All ER 521.

The three detainees would clearly seem to have suffered human rights infringements and so would be 'victims' of an unlawful act and able to bring a case against a 'public authority' under ss. 6 and 7 HRA 1998.[5] The Act does not define a public authority, but the Home Secretary clearly is, as seen by the cases against him mentioned earlier in this essay. The private security company that runs the camp might also be a public authority, because in *Yarl's Wood Immigration Ltd v Bedfordshire Police* [2009] 2 All ER 886 the court decided that a private company, operating an immigration detention centre under a contract with the Home Office, was a public authority, as it exercised the coercive power of the state.

[5] Many students get confused between Article numbers of the **ECHR** and section numbers of the **HRA 1988**. Do not make that mistake.

The company running the detention centre in our problem also does this, so Karen, Dougie's widow, and Paul can bring their case. They could seek a judicial review of the decision to detain and not release them and compensation for the harm that they have suffered under *R (Greenfield) v Secretary of State for the Home Department* [2005] 2 All ER 240.

[6] Parliamentary supremacy is a key constitutional principle and the **HRA 1998** maintains that principle.

According to **s. 6(2) HRA 1998,**[6] the court cannot overturn an Act of Parliament, even if it is contrary to human rights, but has to enforce it: *Doherty v Birmingham City Council* [2008] 3 WLR 636. So the court would have to consider making a 'statement of incompatibility' under **s. 4** of the Act, as they did in a similar case where the Home Secretary had the statutory power to detain without trial: *A v Home Secretary (No. 1)* [2005] 2 AC 68. There seems little likelihood that the Hunting Act 2009 could be interpreted in a human-rights-friendly way, as courts are required to do by **s. 3 HRA 1998.**

[7] Last impressions are important if you want to gain extra marks, so try to come to a clear, reasoned conclusion to your answer.

So Karen, Paul, and Sharon might well be granted a declaration of incompatibility[7] by the courts; then it would be up to Parliament to amend or repeal the Hunting Act 2009. If Parliament decides not to do so, or delays excessively, there is nothing to stop the three applying to the European Court of Human Rights itself. In light of the gross human rights abuses detailed in this answer, that Court would rule in their favour. The UK government might be ordered to pay compensation to the three and would come under pressure, from the Council of Europe, to remedy these breaches of human rights.

LOOKING FOR EXTRA MARKS?

- A useful tactic to adopt is to look out for new cases, which often make the headlines in the ordinary media, not just legal journals, and show that you are up to date by including them in your answer.

- A deep analysis of the law is required. Closely compare the Articles and cases to the facts of the problem.

- The reasons why you came to your conclusion are more important than the conclusion itself.

TAKING THINGS FURTHER

- Allan T.R.S., 'Judicial deference and judicial review: doctrine and legal theory' (2011) 127 LQR 96.

  This article argues that there should be no 'closed areas' that the courts cannot look at, such as national security. Judges can be trusted to protect national security and it all depends on the facts of the case.

- Black-Branch J.L., 'Parliamentary Supremacy or political expediency? The constitutional position of the Human Rights Act under British law' (2002) 23 Statute Law Review 59.

  *This explains the way that the **HRA 1998** operates and the political choices that were made to draft the Act in that particular way.*

- Clayton R., 'The empire strikes back: common law rights and the Human Rights Act' [2015] Public Law 3.

  *In some recent Supreme Court cases, their lordships have recognized the existence of common law rights. These rights will still exist, even if the **HRA 1998** is repealed or amended.*

- Edwards R., 'Judicial deference under the Human Rights Act' (2002) 65 MLR 859.

  The writer considers the dividing line between what judges should decide and what should be decided by the democratically elected Parliament.

- Feldman D., 'Proportionality and discrimination in anti-terrorism legislation' (2005) 64 Cambridge Law Journal 271.

  *This article considers the important case of **A v Home Secretary (No. 1) [2005] 2 AC 68**, where foreign nationals were detained without trial.*

- Commission on a Bill of Rights, 'A UK Bill of Rights? The choice before us' (2012), <http://webarchive.nationalarchives.gov.uk/20130206065653/https://www.justice.gov.uk/downloads/about/cbr/uk-bill-rights-vol-1.pdf>.

  *Proposals to repeal the **HRA 1998** and to replace it with a British bill of rights.*

- Tickell A., 'More "efficient" justice at the European Court of Human Rights: but at whose expense?' [2015] Public Law 206.

  ***Protocol 15** makes some reforms to the way that applications are made to the **ECHR**. Will this make it harder for deserving cases to be heard?*

- Welch J. and Chakrabarti S., 'The war on terror without the Human Rights Act: what differences has it made?' (2010) 6 EHRLR 593.

  *How the **HRA 1998** has been used to challenge legislation and government decisions made during the 'war on terror'. There is a particular focus on detention without trial and control orders.*

Online Resources

www.oup.com/uk/qanda/

Go online for extra essay and problem questions, a glossary of key terms, online versions of all the answer plans and audio commentary on how selected ones were put together and a range of podcasts which include advice on exam and coursework technique and advice for other assessment methods.

8 Freedom to protest and police powers

ARE YOU READY?

The questions in this chapter concern the law relating to public order and police powers of arrest, entry, and search and seizure. In order to attempt these questions, you need to have covered all of these topics in your work over the year or semester and your revision:

- the **Public Order Act 1986** and the case law interpreting the provisions of this Act;
- obstruction of the highway;
- breach of the peace;
- the **Criminal Justice and Public Order Act 1994** and the case law interpreting the provisions of this Act;
- the **Police and Criminal Evidence Act 1984** and the case law interpreting the provisions of this Act;
- the **European Convention on Human Rights**, particularly **Articles 11** and **10**.

 KEY DEBATES

Debate: The Complexity of the Law

The **Public Order Act 1986** and the **Criminal Justice and Public Order Act 1994** are two major Acts of Parliament governing this area of law. There are also offences such as obstruction of the highway, the concept of breach of the peace, and the **European Convention on Human Rights**. Many of these provisions overlap, making the law complex enough for a law lecturer to interpret, let alone a police officer or protester.

(▶)

Debate: Public Order or Freedom to Protest

The **Public Order Act 1986** increased police powers to deal with public protest, which has been the general tendency of most modern legislation. The **Criminal Justice and Public Order Act 1994** was targeted at the activities of certain groups of whom Parliament disapproved. It criminalized some types of trespass and increased police powers to deal with public assemblies. Is there an increased danger to the public from processions or demonstrations or are we just less tolerant of disruptions to our daily lives?

Debate: The Police and Criminal Evidence Act 1984

The **Police and Criminal Evidence Act 1984** was generally seen as a good modernization of the law, bringing together different statutes, case law, and codes of practice into one place. Is it, however, unnecessarily complex and bureaucratic, making it difficult to understand for both police and suspect?

QUESTION   1

Twelve members of the 'No Abortion Campaign' are protesting on the pavement outside an abortion clinic on Eastby High Street. They are displaying placards with the words 'No to abortion' and speaking to each woman who enters the clinic, asking her to consider whether she is 'doing the right thing'.

The owner of the abortion clinic summons the police and PC Kent arrives. She stands on the pavement observing the 'No Abortion Campaign' members, but takes no action.

Then 12 members of a group in favour of abortion, 'Women's Choice', arrive and start shouting at the 'No Abortion Campaign' members, using insulting words. Three of the members of 'Women's Choice' throw stones, breaking the windows of the clinic.

PC Kent asks the 'No Abortion Campaign' members to leave, which they unwillingly do. They slowly walk the half a mile down the High Street to the railway station.

PC Kent, together with other police officers who have joined her, arrest the 12 members of the 'No Abortion Campaign'.

Advise the 'No Abortion Campaign' on whether they have committed any public order offences and whether the police actions are legal.

CAUTION!

- There are a lot of public order offences; concentrate on those actually raised by the facts of the question.
- In a problem like this there may also be breaches of the ordinary criminal law; concentrate on public order law.
- There are statutes that regulate this area, but do not forget to use case law as well.

○ **DIAGRAM ANSWER PLAN**

Identify the issues	■ Identify the legal issues: Is the 'No Abortion Campaign' committing any public order offences? Is 'Women's Choice' committing any public order offences? What powers do the police have to maintain public order?
Relevant law	■ Outline the relevant law: statutory, general principles and case law, in particular: the **Public Order Act 1986**; the **European Convention on Human Rights**, in particular Article 11; breach of the peace; and obstruction of the highway
Apply the law	■ Have the 'No Abortion Campaign' obstructed the highway or used threatening, abusive, or insulting words? ■ Have 'Women's Choice' committed riot or violent disorder? ■ From the police point of view, is this a breach of the peace, public assembly, or procession?
Conclude	■ Have public offences been committed? ■ What does this allow the police to do? ■ What should the police do?

Ⓐ **SUGGESTED ANSWER**

[1] A brief introduction, setting out what the answer is going to look at, can be enough.

There are a number of public order offences that could have been committed by both the 'No Abortion Campaign' and 'Women's Choice' and also a number of powers that PC Kent could have used to control the developing situation, which can be found in both public order legislation and common law.[1]

A gathering on the pavement has been held to be obstruction of the highway in *Arrowsmith v Jenkins* **[1963] 2 QB 561**. It is still the offence of wilful obstruction, even if there was no intention to obstruct and even if no one was actually obstructed. The highway can only be used for passage and repassage and purposes incidental to that movement. However, the European Court of Human Rights has ruled, in *Plattform Ärzte für das Leben* **(1988) 13 EHRR 204**, that there is a right to hold meetings in a public place. Another case more favourable to the 'No Abortion Campaign' is *DPP v Jones (Margaret)*

[1999] 2 AC 240, where the House of Lords held that a small protest on a roadside verge near Stonehenge was not an obstruction of the highway, as there is a right of peaceful assembly. The protest by the 'No Abortion Campaign' is certainly peaceful and quite small in number, so it is probably not obstruction of the highway.[2]

[2] The preceding paragraph compares different cases, from the English courts and the **ECHR**, applies them to the facts, and comes to a conclusion.

They also do not seem to be committing any offences under the **Public Order Act 1986**. They are not using 'threatening, abusive or insulting words or behaviour', nor are their signs 'threatening, abusive or insulting', and there are no threats of violence, so there is no offence under **s. 4** of the Act. Even the lesser offence in **s. 5**, where it is enough for 'disorderly behaviour' to be likely to cause 'harassment, alarm or distress', is not committed. *DPP v Clarke, Lewis, O'Connell & O'Keefe* [1992] Crim LR 60 also involved a protest outside an abortion clinic,[3] but the protesters had no intent to be threatening, abusive, or insulting. All that the defendants did in that case was to show pictures of an aborted foetus to police officers and one passerby. To commit an offence under **s. 5** the protest needs to be more vigorous, as in *DPP v Fidler and Moran* [1992] 1 WLR 91, where there were also shouts and threats against those attending the clinic, in addition to the display of photographs and models of dead foetuses. *Percy v DPP* (2002) 166 JP 93 confirms that the 'No Abortion Campaign' is unlikely to have committed an offence. Even if behaviour is held to be insulting, this must be balanced against the right to freedom of expression under **Article 10 of the European Convention on Human Rights**.[4]

[3] There are many cases on the meaning of **s. 5**. I happened to know of some about abortion clinics, which feature in this problem, but you could easily use other **s. 5** cases instead.

[4] Under the **Human Rights Act 1998** we must attempt to interpret English law to conform to the **ECHR**.

'Women's Choice' appears to have committed criminal offences.[5] Unlike the 'No Abortion Campaign', they are using insulting words, which seem intended or likely to cause their opponents to fear immediate personal violence: *R v Horseferry Road Magistrate ex parte Siadatan* [1991] 1 All ER 324.

[5] Remember, there are two opposing groups in this problem, doing different things and committing different offences.

There is also a lesser offence under **s. 5 of the Public Order Act 1986**. It seems likely that the 'No Abortion Campaign' would experience harassment, alarm, or distress, unless the courts decide that by their frequent protesting they will have become used to insulting, threatening, and abusive words or behaviour, rather like the police officers in *DPP v Orum* [1988] 3 All ER 449.

It is possible that more serious offences have been committed. **Section 1 of the Public Order Act 1986** defines riot as '12 or more persons who are present together use or threaten violence for a common purpose . . . as would cause a person of reasonable firmness present at the scene to fear for his personal safety'. There are over 12 members of 'Women's Choice' and according to **s. 7** 'violence' can include violence towards property, not just people, and would include the throwing of missiles: *Mitsui Sumitomo Insurance v Mayor's*

[6] Riot is a very technical offence. All the elements must be proved.

Office for Policing [2014] EWCA Civ 682. It would have to be proved, though, that at least twelve of them had a common purpose to violently attack the clinic or their opponents:[6] *Mitsui Sumitomo Insurance v Mayor's Office for Policing*. This could prove difficult, so **s. 2**, which makes violent disorder an offence, is more likely. This is similar to riot, but only requires three participants and does not require a common purpose. The three window breakers would have committed this offence as the 'No Abortion Campaign', those inside the clinic, bystanders, and even the police officer would have been put in fear.

Section 14 of the Public Order Act 1986 allows the senior police officer on the spot to impose conditions on a public assembly, if he reasonably believes that it may result in serious public disorder, serious damage to property, intimidation, or serious disruption to the life of the community. A public assembly used to require a minimum number of 20 persons, but this was reduced to two by the **Anti-social Behaviour Act 2003**. PC Kent could give directions as to the place, number of people, and duration of the assembly. This would seem to allow her to act against either 'Women's Choice' or the 'No Abortion Campaign'. In addition to these powers, she also has common law and other statutory powers to disperse assemblies.[7]

[7] A feature of public order law is that the police have a number of overlapping powers, which they can choose to use.

PC Kent has a common law power to take reasonable measures to prevent a breach of the peace. The accepted definition today of a breach of the peace is an act or threat of violence against a person or their property in their presence, which puts someone in fear of violence: *R v Howell (Erroll)* [1982] 2 QB 416 and *Percy v DPP* [1995] 3 All ER 124. This power has been used to disperse meetings as in *Duncan v Jones* [1963] 1 KB 218 and to refuse to obey the reasonable instructions of a police constable is the offence of obstruction of a police officer in the execution of his duty: *Duncan v Jones*.

On the facts, it seems reasonable for PC Kent to assume that violence might break out, but has she acted against the wrong group? The old case of *Beatty v Gillbanks* (1882) 9 QBD 308 held that the Salvation Army should not be forbidden from marching through Weston-super-Mare, just because they might be violently opposed by the rival Skeleton Army. In *Plattform Ärzte für das Leben*, the European Court of Human Rights has ruled that this is the correct approach and that, in certain circumstances, the state has a duty to protect peaceful protesters from those who would oppose them with violence. In *Redmond-Bate v DPP* [2000] **HRLR 249**, the defendants were women preaching from the steps of Wakefield Cathedral but, as the listening crowd was becoming hostile, the police stopped the women. Sedley LJ said at 259 that the police were wrong to do this and that 'the common law should seek compatibility with the values of the **European Convention on Human Rights**'. 'The question

[8] The preceding paragraph is looking at case law, ancient and modern, English and European, analysing it, and coming to a conclusion.

[9] To write a good answer on this problem, you do need a detailed knowledge of what the Act actually says.

for the police officer was whether there was a real threat of violence and if so, from whom it was coming.' So PC Kent should really have taken action against the troublemakers, 'Women's Choice'. [8]

Processions and marches are well regulated by law and under [9] **s. 11 of the Public Order Act 1986,** the organizers must give the police six days' written notice 'unless it is not reasonably practicable to give any advance notice of the procession' or 'the procession is one commonly or customarily held in the police area'. There is no definition of a procession in the Act and even a mass cycle ride held as a protest in London was held to be a procession: *R (Kay) v Commissioner of Police of the Metropolis* **[2008] 1 WLR 2723.** So, possibly, walking back to the station could be a procession if they were still continuing their protest. It is surely arguable here that it is not reasonable to expect the 'No Abortion Campaign' to notify the police in advance as their march has, in effect, been caused by the police. The law, in the **Public Order Act 1986,** makes a clear distinction between assemblies and processions; for instance, there has never been a minimum number for processions, and assemblies do not have to be notified to the police in advance. The facts of this problem illustrate that there may not be a clear-cut distinction between assemblies and processions, as was shown in *DPP v Jones* **[2002] EWHC 110 (Admin).**

According to *R v Chief Constable of Devon and Cornwall ex parte The Central Electricity Generating Board* **[1982] QB 458,** the police have discretion on how they use their public order control powers. They are not obliged to arrest for crimes or to use their powers to disperse protesters. The police also have a duty to protect the human rights of those affected by protesters. As long as the police act reasonably and do not show any bias for one side or the other, the courts will not interfere with police discretion: *Re E (a child)* **[2009] 1 All ER 467.**

[10] I have come to a strong conclusion. It is perfectly possible to analyse the law in a different way and come to a different conclusion.

In conclusion, PC Kent took legal action against the wrong people, [10] the 'No Abortion Campaign' group, who were merely exercising their peaceful right of protest, a right that PC Kent should have protected. She should have taken action against the violent and threatening 'Women's Choice'.

 ## LOOKING FOR EXTRA MARKS?

- Public order law is capable of many different interpretations. Show that you are aware of this.

- For example, the suggested answer takes a 'liberal' line, that protest should be permitted.

- Your answer could take a different approach; for example, it is imperative to support the police in maintaining public order. See *R (Moos) v Commissioner of Police* **[2012] EWCA Civ 12.**

- You could make more use of European Court of Human Rights decisions on public order law.

Q QUESTION **2**

Margaret and her friends oppose the use of British and US service personnel in Syria and Iraq. They travel from London to protest outside RAF Blackham, an airfield where both British and US aircraft are based.

She and ten of her friends set up an encampment on the roadside just outside the main gates of RAF Blackham. This attracts a lot of attention from passing motorists, many of whom slow down, causing a delay to other traffic.

Two of the group, Janet and Steve, climb over the perimeter wall into Blackham and enter a hangar, where they damage an aircraft by hitting it with hammers. Janet also burns the US flag, the 'Stars and Stripes', which distresses the US service personnel standing nearby.

The police arrive, arrest Janet and Steve and the nine others, dismantle their camp, and take them all back to London, which takes six hours.

All the protesters say that they have not broken the law. They claim that they have a legal right to protest and that they were trying to prevent the aircraft being used in Syria and Iraq, which would be an illegal use of force in international law.

Advise them on the law relating to their case.

! CAUTION!

■ Relevance is everything in this kind of problem. What areas of public order law are actually raised by the facts of this problem?

■ This problem is designed to focus on the **Criminal Justice and Public Order Act 1994**, not the **Public Order Act 1986**.

DIAGRAM ANSWER PLAN

Identify the issues	■ Identify the legal issues: What public order offences have Margaret, Janet, and Steve committed? What powers do the police have to control protests and demonstrations?
Relevant law	■ Outline the relevant law: statutory, general principles and case law, in particular: the **Criminal Justice and Public Order Act 1994**; obstruction of the highway, **s. 5**; **Public Order Act 1986**; case law on breach of the peace, **Articles 10** and **11 of the European Convention on Human Rights**
Apply the law	■ Have Margaret, Jane, and Steve committed the following offences: criminal trespass; obstruction of the highway; aggravated trespass; or insulting words or behaviour? ■ What powers do the police have to control a trespassory assembly or a breach of the peace?
Conclude	■ Have any offences been committed? ■ Were the police actions lawful?

SUGGESTED ANSWER

[1] Problem answers can be introduced in different ways. Rather than starting with the facts of the problem, I have chosen to start with the general issue of lawful public protest.

[2] The **Human Rights Act 1998** requires us to interpret English law to conform to the **ECHR**.

Article 11 of the European Convention on Human Rights (ECHR) guarantees that 'Everyone has the right to freedom of peaceful assembly and to freedom of association with others . . .'.[1] Freedom of expression is also guaranteed by **Article 10**. Irrespective of this, English common law has long recognized that people are allowed to protest and to hold public meetings, even if this is opposed by others, as illustrated by the case of *Beatty v Gillbanks* (1882) **9 QBD 308**.

Protest can become unlawful though. This is recognized both by English common law and by **Article 11(2) ECHR**,[2] which states that the right to freedom of assembly can be restricted 'for the prevention of disorder and crime' . . . 'or for the protection of the rights and freedoms of others'. As long as a protest is peaceful, the law should not forbid it: *Steel v UK* (1999) **28 EHRR 603**. Let us examine whether Margaret's protest is peaceful.

[3] We are concentrating on public order law, not the civil law of tort.

The encampment by the roadside may be trespass, but that is usually only a civil matter that does not involve the police.[3] The **Criminal Justice and Public Order Act 1994** criminalized certain forms of trespass. Under **s. 60** there is a power to remove trespassers, but this was aimed at 'travellers' who are trespassing and requires there to be at least one caravan and one vehicle present. None of this seems to be the case here.

Obstruction of the highway is an offence under **s. 137 of the Highways Act 1980** and can be used by the police to disperse peaceful, non-violent protest. The offence is committed 'if a person without lawful authority or excuse in any way wilfully obstructs the free passage along a highway'. Pavements and grass verges are part of the highway and a person can even be off the highway and yet cause an obstruction on it, as shown by *Nagy v Weston* **[1965] 1 All ER 78**, where a hot dog van in a lay-by caused the obstruction on the highway. *DPP v Jones* **[1999] 2 AC 240** moderates this strict approach. This consisted of a peaceful, non-obstructive assembly of 21 people, including Margaret Jones, on the verge of a road. Lord Chancellor Irvine said that, in addition to the **Article 11** right, there was a common law right of peaceful assembly on the highway.

The right to protest does not justify a major and permanent obstruction of the highway or trespass on someone else's land, as the Occupy Movement camp outside St Paul's Cathedral, in London, found in *City of London v Samede* **[2012] 2 All ER 2017.** Margaret and her friends, however, are only causing minor inconvenience to motorists and are probably acting lawfully.[4]

[4] The preceding two paragraphs look at how the law has developed over the years and notes that the interpretation has changed.

[5] A detailed knowledge of the Act is required here, which needs to be applied to the facts of the case.

The **Public Order Act 1986** gives the police powers to control a public assembly,[5] which was defined in **s. 16** as 'an assembly of 2 or more persons in a public place which is wholly or partly open to the air'. So Margaret's gathering would meet the definition, particularly where a 'public place' includes a highway. By **s. 14**, a senior police officer may impose conditions on a public assembly such as the place it is held, its maximum duration, or the maximum number of persons. Ignoring police directions is a criminal offence. It is important to note that the police may only impose conditions if they reasonably believe the assembly may result in serious public disorder, serious disruption to the life of the community, intimidation to others, or serious damage to property. The 'attack' on the aircraft could be damage or intimidation, so this probably gives the police power to act under this section. However, the 1986 Act gives the police no power to ban or forbid a public assembly of this kind. This can only be done if the protest is moving and therefore becomes a 'procession' or if it is a 'trespassory assembly' under the **Criminal Justice and Public Order Act 1994**. A trespassory assembly has to cause serious disruption to the life of the community or damage to some sort of historical monument. Neither seems to be the case here.

The actions of Janet and Steve in entering the air base and damaging an aeroplane could be aggravated trespass under **ss. 68** and **69 of the Criminal Justice and Public Order Act 1994**. They have trespassed on land. Even entering the aircraft hangar is included, because although the offence originally only covered land in the open air, this was changed by the **Anti-social Behaviour Act 2003** to include all land: *DPP v Chivers* **[2011] 1 All ER 367**. They have obstructed or disrupted 'lawful activity': the activities of the military. These issues were discussed, by the House of Lords, in *R v Jones* **[2006] 2 WLR 772**.[6] Jones (the same Jones as in *DPP v Jones*) and others had entered RAF Fairford and carried out or planned to carry out various acts of damage to military property. They argued that they could not have committed aggravated trespass, because the military were not engaged in 'lawful activity'. The war against Iraq was a crime of aggression under international law and the military were preparing for it. Their lordships accepted that 'aggressive war' was a recognized crime in international law, but it had never been made a crime in the domestic law of the UK. Anyway, this crime could only be committed by the leaders of a state, not by low-ranking service personnel. So it does not seem likely that Janet and Steve have any defence to the charge of aggravated trespass.

Janet destroyed the 'Stars and Stripes', but it is not a crime to destroy a flag, even the flag of the UK. In *Percy v DPP* **[2003] EWHC 1564 (Admin)**, Ms Percy performed a similar action and five US service personnel gave evidence that this caused them distress, so Percy was charged under **s. 5 of the Public Order Act 1986**. The offence is that she used insulting words and behaviour likely to cause harassment, alarm, or distress. On appeal, the court held that her right to freedom of expression, under **Article 10 ECHR**,[7] outweighed any distress she might have caused. Janet could use a similar argument.

The police could use the ancient common law power to control a breach of the peace to justify their dispersal of the demonstration. In another case involving Ms Percy, *Percy v DPP* **[1995] 1 WLR 1382**, breach of the peace had to involve violence or a threat of violence. This could include provoking others to violence, or, as the court put it, where violence from some third party was a natural consequence of her action. In that case, Percy had repeatedly trespassed on a military base, but she had not committed a breach of the peace, as highly trained military personnel were unlikely to respond to an unarmed trespasser with violence. So, applying this case, it does not look like Janet has committed a breach of the peace.

[6] House of Lords and Supreme Court cases are generally important and deserve more detailed attention than the decisions of lower courts.

[7] As in 2, we see the effect of the ECHR.

According to older cases such as *Moss v McLachlan* [1985] **IRLR 76**, if a police officer honestly and reasonably considers that there is a real risk of a breach of the peace in close proximity, both in place and time, then the officer may take reasonable measures to prevent the breach of the peace. This permitted a police roadblock in *Moss*. In *R (Laporte) v Chief Constable of Gloucestershire Constabulary* [2007] 2 AC 105,[8] the police prevented three coachloads of demonstrators from joining an anti-Iraq War demonstration outside RAF Fairford in Gloucestershire. They were stopped at some distance from RAF Fairford and then conducted non-stop back to London. The House of Lords did not think that the police could reasonably apprehend that a breach of the peace was imminent. The protesters were nowhere near the protest site and there were plenty of police at Fairford to deal with any breach of the peace. This can be contrasted with the later Court of Appeal case, *Austin v Metropolitan Police Commissioner* [2008] 1 All ER 564,[9] where there was a large May Day demonstration in London. The police confined around 3,000 people, not all of whom were protesters, in Oxford Circus for seven hours. This practice is known as 'kettling'. It was held that a breach of the peace was imminent and that these were extreme and exceptional circumstances, as violence had occurred at previous May Day demonstrations. On appeal to the House of Lords, [2009] 3 All ER 455, it was argued that the police action infringed **Article 5**, the right to liberty. It was held that other rights had to be considered, such as the right to life of those threatened by mob violence. The police decision took into account the interests of the whole community, was taken in good faith, and was proportionate and therefore not unlawful. The European Court of Human Rights agreed in *Austin v UK* (2012) **55 EHRR 14**.

So, in conclusion, the police are probably justified in moving Janet and Steve away.[10] They have committed the crime of aggravated trespass, and breach of the peace does include violence against property, not just people: *R v Howell (Erroll)* [1982] QB 416. Janet and Steve are inside the perimeter fence and can be easily separated from Margaret and the other protesters, which was not the case in *Austin v Metropolitan Police Commissioner* [2008] 1 All ER 564. Following *R (Laporte) v Chief Constable of Gloucestershire Constabulary* [2007] 2 AC 105, Margaret and the other demonstrators should be allowed to continue their peaceful protest.

[8] Here we have two court decisions with contrasting approaches to the law. Compare them and assess which of them you consider is most applicable to the facts of the problem.

[9] Again, we have two House of Lords decisions with contrasting approaches to the law. Compare them and assess which of them you consider is most applicable to the facts of the problem.

[10] The conclusion is not afraid to give a definite answer to this legal problem.

LOOKING FOR EXTRA MARKS?

- The **Criminal Justice and Public Order Act 1994** was a highly controversial piece of legislation. It is acceptable to criticize it.

- 'Kettling' is a controversial police tactic. There are several other cases on its use, for example *R (Castle) v Commissioner of Police for the Metropolis* [2012] 1 All ER 953, *Mengesha v Commissioner of Police of the Metropolis* [2013] EWHC 1695 (Admin).

- Occupation of someone else's land in order to protest has also been considered in several cases, for example *Manchester Ship Canal v Persons Unknown* [2014] EWHC 645 (Ch), *Barda v Mayor of London* [2017] EWCA Civ 2114.

Q QUESTION 3

Article 11 of the European Convention on Human Rights refers to the right to freedom of peaceful assembly, subject to the imposition of lawful restraints on the exercise of that right.

Consider whether citizens of the UK enjoy the right to peacefully assemble or whether the lawful restraints mean that such right exists only so far as the police in the exercise of their discretion allow it.

! CAUTION!

- This is not a general essay about the **European Convention on Human Rights (ECHR)**.

- Concentrate on the specific issue raised: how does **Article 11 ECHR** affect English public order law?

- You need to know about **ECHR** cases, as well as English ones.

- The purpose of this essay is to make a comparison.

☐ DIAGRAM ANSWER PLAN

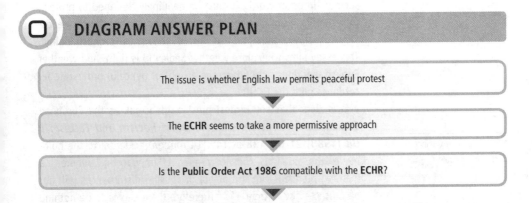

The issue is whether English law permits peaceful protest

⬇

The **ECHR** seems to take a more permissive approach

⬇

Is the **Public Order Act 1986** compatible with the **ECHR**?

⬇

> Is the common law power to control a breach of the peace compatible with the **ECHR**?
>
> ▼
>
> Is obstruction of the highway compatible with the **ECHR**?
>
> ▼
>
> Is the state required to actively permit and protect peaceful protest?
>
> ▼
>
> Conclusion—does English law permit peaceful protest and does it conform to the **ECHR**?

(A) SUGGESTED ANSWER

[1] The introduction gets straight to the point by describing the traditional common law approach.

[2] It might be possible to remember short quotations for exam purposes.

[3] The question specifically asks about the **ECHR**, so you need to know what is says.

[4] The quotation explained this far better than I could.

Some have suggested that English law unduly hinders peaceful protest.[1] The traditional approach can be found in *Duncan v Jones* **[1936] 1 KB 218** at 222 that 'English law does not recognize any special right of public meeting for political or other purposes'.[2] Even in the current century, Lord Bingham, in *R (Laporte) v Chief Constable of Gloucestershire Constabulary* **[2007] 2 AC 105** observed that the common law had still not fully recognized freedom of expression and assembly.

The **Human Rights Act 1998**, giving effect to **Articles 10** and **11 ECHR**,[3] represented what Sedley LJ in *Redmond-Bate v DPP* **[2000] HRLR 249** at 256 aptly called a 'constitutional shift'. **Article 11(1) ECHR** states that: 'Everyone has the right to freedom of peaceful assembly . . .'. **Article 11(2)** allows this right to be restricted, but the restrictions must be 'prescribed by law' and must meet at least one of the legitimate aims listed there, such as 'national security', 'public safety', 'the prevention of disorder or crime', or 'the protection of the rights and freedoms of others'. The restriction on the right to protest must also be justified as 'necessary in a democratic society'. In other words, it must be genuinely designed to protect, for example, 'public safety', but must go no further than is necessary to achieve that purpose. This is known as 'proportionality'. This essay aims to explore whether Sedley LJ is right, and whether English law does now guarantee a right of peaceful protest in accordance with the **ECHR**.

It is clear that any protest must be peaceful, as the European Commission held in *Christians against Racism and Fascism v UK* **(1980) 21 DR 138** at 148: 'Disruption incidental to the holding of the assembly will not render it "unpeaceful," whereas a meeting planned with the object of causing disturbances will not be protected by **Article 11**.'[4] Therefore there seems to be nothing objectionable to the offences in the **Public Order Act 1986**, for an essential element of riot, violent disorder, and affray is that violence or threats of violence are used, so, by definition, they are not 'peaceful' actions. Even the 'threatening, abusive or insulting words or behaviour' in **s. 4** must carry with them a threat of violence or at least provoke violence. **Section 5**, which merely requires the 'threatening, abusive or insulting words', etc. to be likely to cause 'harassment, alarm or distress' seems more suspect, as violence is not a constituent of the offence. In *Chorherr v Austria* **(1993) 17 EHRR 358**, however, the European Court of Human Rights held that a protest that caused annoyance or agitation was not protected by **Article 11**. Hence, **s. 5 of the Public Order Act 1986** might well be acceptable. Some have argued that it is an undue interference with public protest to prohibit processions under what is now **s. 13 of the Public Order Act 1986**. This has, however, been considered acceptable under the **ECHR** if there is a likelihood of violence in the area: *Christians against Racism and Fascism v UK and Rai v UK* **(1995) 82 ADR 134**.[5]

[5] For this question, cases from the European Court of Human Rights (ECtHR) are more important than English cases.

Turning aside from the statutory provisions of the **Public Order Act 1986**, the ancient common law power to control a breach of the peace has often caused concern amongst civil libertarians. According to Lord Denning in *R v Chief Constable of Devon and Cornwall ex parte the Central Electricity Generating Board* **[1982] QB 458**, at 471: 'There was a breach of the peace whenever a person who was lawfully carrying out his work was unlawfully and physically prevented by another from doing it.' Other cases have preferred a tighter definition, which involves threats of harm or violence. This was expressed in *R v Howell (Erroll)* **[1982] 2 QB 416** as 'an act done or threatened to be done which actually harms a person, or in his presence his property, or is likely to cause such harm or which puts someone in fear of such harm being done'. This was further explained in *Percy v DPP* **[1995] 3 All ER 124**, that to be conduct that was a breach of the peace it had to involve violence, a threat of violence, or carry a real risk that it would provoke violence in others.[6]

[6] This paragraph looks at the evidence from the cases, analyses it, and comes to a conclusion.

The use of breach of the peace has been questioned in the European Court of Human Rights. Each time, the Court has been satisfied that the restriction that breach of the peace makes upon the right to protest is 'prescribed by law'. In other words, it is sufficiently well defined for someone to be able to understand what it is they are forbidden to do. The Court has, however, preferred the definition in *Howell* and *Percy*, which stresses the need for violence to make the conduct unlawful, for 'peaceful assembly' is a right. On the facts though, the Court has disapproved of the use of breach of the peace in some circumstances. In *Steel v UK* **(1999) 28 EHRR 603**, acts that might provoke violence were not considered peaceful protest.

In *McLeod v UK* **(1999) 27 EHRR 493**, the police had been present when Mr McLeod entered and removed items from his ex-wife's house, because they claimed that they feared a breach of the peace. The Court held that this was unjustified, as there was in fact little or no risk of disorder or crime occurring, as Mrs McLeod was not there at the time.

Finally, in *Hashman and Harrup v UK* **(2000) 30 EHRR 241**, the European Court of Human Rights objected to hunt saboteurs being bound over to be of 'good behaviour' to keep the peace. The Court found this to be unacceptable because it did not tell the protesters what it was they were forbidden to do. Restrictions on the right to protest must be 'prescribed by law' and this lacked any clear definition.

The English courts have been moving tentatively towards accepting a right of peaceful protest on the public highway. Completely peaceful assemblies, protests, and demonstrations have often fallen foul of **s. 137 of the Highway Act 1980**, because it is a criminal offence to obstruct the highway. Cases such as *Arrowsmith v Jenkins* **[1963] 2 QB 561**, have held that the only lawful use of the highway is for passage and repassage, so a public meeting in the street was an obstruction. Other cases, such as *Hirst v Chief Constable of West Yorkshire* **(1987) 85 Cr App R 143**, have taken a slightly more lenient line, that very minor protests, which cause no real obstruction, can be tolerated. Some judges have been willing to go further and find that a right of peaceful assembly on the highway might exist. The Lord Chancellor, Lord Irvine, and Lord Hutton, gave tentative support for such an idea in *DPP v Jones (Margaret)* **[1999] 2 All ER 257** and felt that, if necessary, the common law should develop in order to conform to **Article 11**. The English courts seem to be gradually getting into line with the rulings of the European Commission, in *Rassemblement Jurassien et unite Jurassiene v Switzerland* **(1979) 17 DR 93** and the European Court of Human Rights, in *Plattform Ärzte für das Leben* **(1988) 13 EHRR 204**, where it was held that there is a *right* to hold meetings in public places. However, a permanent protest encampment outside St Paul's Cathedral in London by the Occupy Movement was not a proportionate use of the right to protest. It interfered with the property rights of others and blocked the highway: *City of London v Samede* **[2012] EWCA Civ 160** at para. 49. The right to protest has to be respected, but it does not override the rights of others to use the land on which the protest is held.[7]

[7] The preceding paragraph compares the case law of the EtCHR and the English courts.

The *Plattform Ärzte für das Leben* case also made clear that the state does not merely have a duty to permit peaceful protest; in certain circumstances there may be a duty to protect peaceful protesters from those who would oppose them with violence. Even the English courts have occasionally endorsed this approach and asserted that the authorities should not merely take the easy way out and prevent those with an unpopular message from speaking for fear of the possible reaction: *Beatty v Gillbanks* (1882) **9 QBD 308** and *Redmond-Bate v DPP* [2000] **HRLR 249**.[8]

[8] Again, the essay compares EtCHR and English cases.

It might be apparent from the contrasting cases given that the police have many difficult decisions to make.[9] Do they permit free speech or step in to prevent a possible outbreak of public disorder? The English courts have usually been most unwilling to interfere with police discretion. In *R v Chief Constable of Devon and Cornwall ex parte Central Electricity Generating Board* [1982] **QB 458**, even though the Court of Appeal seemed confident that criminal offences were occurring, they were unwilling to instruct the police to act. Similarly, in *Re E (a child)* [2009] **1 All ER 467** the police were not obliged to stop a Protestant protest that was menacing Roman Catholic schoolchildren. **Article 11 ECHR** explicitly allows for the balancing of conflicting interests and, indeed, the decisions of the European Court of Human Rights in this area do not seem any more willing to 'overrule' the decisions of the police than the English courts. Perhaps all the English courts need to do is to try and be a little more consistent and not forget the basic principle that peaceful protest should be permitted.

[9] To make the conclusion more interesting, it looks at this area from a slightly different perspective: the police, rather than protester, point of view.

✚ LOOKING FOR EXTRA MARKS?

■ New cases are common in this area. Look out for them.

■ The conclusion of the suggested answer is that English and **ECHR** law are not so different and are gradually coming together.

■ You do not have to come to that conclusion, but back your argument with evidence, for example case law or academic opinion.

Q

Jennifer has been arrested for allegedly committing an armed robbery. While being taken to the police station, she escapes from police custody and is pursued. She flees into Brian's house, where she has a room. Brian refuses to let the police enter his house, but the police overcome his slight resistance and enter anyway. Jennifer is seized by the police in Brian's living room. The police search Jennifer and the living room but do not find anything.

Brian is asked by the police whether they can search Jennifer's rented room and he consents, even though Jennifer objects. While searching her room, the police find documents that seem to indicate her involvement in a financial fraud. The police ask Jennifer about these documents and she explains that her solicitor, Peter, deals with her business affairs and that they will have to ask him about the documents.

The police go to Peter's office with Jennifer. Peter insists that they need a search warrant, but the police say that they do not, as they have just arrested Jennifer. The police search the office and remove all the files relating to Jennifer's business affairs.

Jennifer, Brian, and Peter seek your advice on the legality of the police conduct.

Advise Jennifer, Brian, and Peter.

! **CAUTION!**

- The **Police and Criminal Evidence Act 1984** is a lengthy Act, but we are only looking at arrest, entry, and search of premises in this problem.
- Do not just recite the provisions of the Act. The case law is equally, if not more, important.

DIAGRAM ANSWER PLAN

Identify the issues	■ Identify the legal issues: Jennifer has been arrested, her home has been searched, and the premises of her solicitor have been searched ■ Are the actions of the police legal?
Relevant law	■ Outline the relevant law: statutory, general principles and case law, in particular: the **Police and Criminal Evidence Act 1984** and case law interpreting the meaning of its provisions
Apply the law	■ Powers of arrest ■ Powers of entry to premises ■ Powers to search premises, upon arrest, with consent and with a warrant ■ Powers of seizure
Conclude	■ Conclusion—have the police used their powers in a lawful manner?

A SUGGESTED ANSWER

[1] This is a problem question. The introduction sets out the two main issues.

We must first consider whether Jennifer has been lawfully arrested and then go on to consider the various powers that the police have to enter private premises and to search those premises. Most of those powers of entry and search depend on whether a person has been arrested, so the first question to ask is whether Jennifer has been lawfully arrested.[1]

No warrant has been issued for the arrest of Jennifer, so we must consider the powers that the police possess to arrest without a warrant. Under **s. 24 of the Police and Criminal Evidence Act 1984 (PACE 1984)**, a police constable may arrest anyone who is guilty of an offence or anyone whom he has reasonable grounds to suspect of being guilty of an offence, if it is necessary for the effective investigation of the offence or to prevent the disappearance of the offender: *Hayes v Chief Constable of the Merseyside Police* **[2012] 1 WLR 517**. 'Suspicion' was defined by Lord Devlin in *Shaaban Bin Hussien v Chong Fook Kam* **[1970] AC 942**, at 948 as 'a state of conjecture or surmise where proof is lacking . . . I suspect but I cannot prove'. It would seem that the police have reasonable grounds for suspecting Jennifer, for she has escaped from police custody, which is a crime, and allegedly committed armed robbery, for which they could re-arrest her.[2]

[2] The law is applied to the facts and a conclusion is reached.

Blackstone defined arrest as 'the apprehending or restraining of one's person in order to be forthcoming to answer an alleged or suspected crime' (Blackstone's *Commentaries*, p. 289). The old case of *Genner v Sparks* **(1705) 6 Mod Rep 173**, which also involved the recapture of a fugitive, requires that there must be some touching or seizure of the person. This seems to have occurred. The police must also tell the person that they are under arrest and the reasons for the arrest: **s. 28 PACE 1984** and *Christie v Leachinsky* **[1947] AC 573**. The explanation must be in simple, non-technical language that the arrested person can understand, as explained in *Taylor v Thames Valley Chief Constable* **[2004] 3 All ER 503**. It appears that Jennifer has been told nothing, but the case law allows her to be told later. This might be because it was impracticable to tell her at the time, say if she was resisting arrest or trying to escape again: *DPP v Hawkins* **[1988] 3 All ER 673**. Even if there was no particular reason to delay, if she is told the reasons, for example when she is taken to the police station, then the failure to inform her when first arrested will not make the subsequent police actions unlawful: *Lewis v Chief Constable of South Wales* **[1991] 1 All ER 206**.[3]

[3] Even though **PACE 1984** codifies the law, you still need to know the case law.

A more contentious issue is that the police appear to have forced entry to Brian's house, without a warrant and without his permission. **Section 17(1)(d) PACE 1984** allows a constable to enter and search for the purpose 'of recapturing a person who is unlawfully at large and whom he is pursuing'.[4] There must be a genuine and continuous pursuit: *D'Souza v DPP* **[1992] 4 All ER 545**. The police here seem to be in pursuit of Jennifer and it does not matter that it is not her house: *Kynaston v DPP* **(1987) 84 Cr App R 200**. According to **s. 117 PACE 1984** the police may use 'reasonable force, if necessary' when exercising their powers under the Act; so pushing their way past Brian, if that is what they did, is not unlawful.

[4] To answer a problem on **PACE 1984** you do need to know exactly what the Act says.

Once they have gained entry, the police commence to search the house. Under **s. 17(4) PACE 1984** the police may only search 'to the extent that is reasonably required for the purpose for which the power of entry is exercised'. In other words, they can search for Jennifer, but for nothing else under this section. They have, however, already found her, so does Brian's consent make their further searching lawful? This is not dealt with in the sections of **PACE 1984** because it has been clear, at least since the great case of *Entick v Carrington* **(1765) 19 St Tr 1030**, at 1066, that if the owner or occupier consents to another entering, it cannot be unlawful.

[5] The Codes of Practice under **PACE 1984** are as important as the Act itself.

Under the Codes of Practice that accompany **PACE 1984**,[5] the police should obtain Brian's consent in writing. Again, according to the Codes, Brian is unable to consent to the search of a room that is occupied by Jennifer, not him. The fact that the provisions of the Codes have been infringed does not necessarily render the search unlawful. Under **s. 67(11)** of the Act, breach of the Codes of Practice is just something that 'shall be taken into account' in any subsequent proceedings.

[6] Sections 18 and 32 PACE 1984 appear similar, but they grant different powers to the police.

Even if there are doubts about the validity of the consent of Brian, the police have other powers to search under **PACE 1984**. Section 32 allows a constable to search the arrested person, but it also allows the police to use **s. 32(2)(b)** and 'to enter and search any premises in which he was when arrested or immediately before he was arrested for evidence relating to the offence for which he was arrested'.[6] There is some doubt about whether the police can use this power to arrest a person and then, later, return and search the site of arrest (*McLorie v Oxford* [1982] QB 1290), but here the search is contemporaneous. It would seem reasonable for the police to assume that there could be further evidence of an armed robbery at the suspect's home. The permitted search is not unlimited, because **s. 32(3)** of the Act only allows 'search to the extent that is reasonably required for the purpose of discovering . . . any such evidence'.

[7] Sections 18 and 32 PACE 1984 appear similar, but they grant different powers to the police.

In addition, the police have powers to search the 'premises occupied and controlled' by a person that they have arrested, under **s. 18 PACE 1984**: *Khan v Commissioner of Police of the Metropolis* [2008] EWCA Civ 723.[7] They can either search when they arrest the person or return later. Entry and search is permitted if the constable 'has reasonable grounds for suspecting that there is on the premises evidence' of that offence or a connected or similar offence. In *Jeffrey v Black* [1978] QB 490, the defendant was arrested for the theft of a sandwich from a public house, but the police searched his house and found illegal drugs. This was an unlawful search, as there were no reasonable grounds for the police to suspect that there would be evidence of further sandwich theft at his home. It would seem reasonable, however, to suspect that there could be further evidence of Jennifer's armed robbery at her home.

[8] Searching for evidence and seizing that evidence is not the same thing, so they are governed by different legal powers.

The police find documents that they suspect indicate involvement in a financial fraud while they are searching for something else, evidence of an armed robbery. It is legal to seize evidence of a crime when the police are lawfully on the premises, according to Lord Denning in *Ghani v Jones* [1970] 1 QB 693. This is confirmed by **s. 19 PACE 1984**, the 'General power of seizure'.[8] When a constable is lawfully on any premises he may seize anything that he has reasonable grounds for believing is evidence of any offence. It does not have to be evidence of the offence that he is investigating. If the police suspicions are reasonable, they may take Jennifer's documents.

[9] In order to add variety to the answer, the conclusion is stated first. Then the evidence is examined.

The search of the solicitor's office is illegal.[9] The police should have obtained a search warrant under **s. 8 PACE 1984**. As indicated by the case of **Redknapp v Commissioner of the City of London Police [2009] 1 All ER 229**, the police must follow the correct procedure to apply for the warrant, including practical details such as including the correct address. The police must produce some evidence of why they needed the court order, and the judge must clearly state his reasons for granting it: **R (S and others) v Chief Constable of the British Transport Police [2013] EWHC 2189 (Admin)**. Jennifer's business records would be held in confidence by the solicitor, so they would be regarded as 'special procedure material' under **s. 14** of the Act. The police should apply to a circuit judge, who could issue a Production Order to the solicitor if the judge agreed that it was likely to be evidence of substantial value to the investigation. A search warrant would only be issued as a last resort, if it seemed that Peter was not likely to comply.

The police are not permitted to search for legally privileged material. This is defined in **s. 10 PACE 1984** as legal advice to a client or material connected with legal proceedings. Jennifer's business documents do not seem to be legally privileged and are not protected from search (**R v Crown Court at Northampton ex parte DPP (1991) 93 Cr App R 376**), but the police do need a warrant, which they have not got.

So, in conclusion, Jennifer has little to complain about. Her arrest was probably lawful which, in turn, gives the police the legal power to search under **ss. 18** and **32**. The search of Peter's office was unlawful, as the police needed a search warrant or Peter's permission, which they did not obtain. Peter could make an official complaint about the police or sue them for trespass.

➕ LOOKING FOR EXTRA MARKS?

- The facts of this problem are very specific, so you cannot do anything particularly original here.
- Instead, show that you have analysed the facts in detail.
- Show that you have a detailed and accurate knowledge of **PACE 1984**.
- Carefully compare the facts of our problem with the facts of reported cases and come to a reasoned conclusion.

TAKING THINGS FURTHER

■ Allen M.J. and Cooper S., 'Howard's Way: a farewell to freedom?' (1995) 58 Modern Law Review 364. (The public order parts of this Act are considered on pp. 378–89.)

*The **Criminal Justice and Public Order Act 1994** is still in force, with a few amendments. The authors criticize the public order parts of this Act as the deliberate criminalization of the activities of certain groups in society such as travellers, gypsies, those who attend free pop festivals and raves, and environmental protesters.*

■ Austin R., 'The new powers of arrest: plus ça change: more of the same or major change?' [2007] Crim LR 459.

*Powers of arrest contained in **PACE 1984** were changed by the **Serious Organised Crime and Police Act 2005**. The author considers that this might make it more difficult to arrest and might render **Holgate-Mohammed v Duke [1984] AC 437** out of date.*

■ Bailey S.H., Harris D.J., and Jones B.L., 'Policing and Police Powers' in *Civil Liberties: Cases and Materials* (6th edn, OUP 2009) ch. 4.

This is a very good and detailed account of police powers and the sections on arrest and entry, search, and seizure are particularly relevant.

■ Bonner D. and Stone R., 'The Public Order Act 1986: steps in the wrong direction?' [1987] Public Law 202.

*This is a detailed explanation and critique of the, then new, **Public Order Act 1986**, most of which is still in force. The codification of old common law offences, such as riot, is deemed a helpful modernization of the law, but the extension of police powers to control processions and public assemblies is criticized as a restraint on free speech.*

■ Fenwick H., 'Marginalising human rights: breach of the peace, 'kettling,' the Human Rights Act and public protest' [2009] Public Law 737.

*The police have wide discretionary powers to control an imminent breach of the peace. Using these powers, the police have developed the tactic of 'kettling', confining a crowd to a particular space. This article considers the two leading cases of **R (Laporte) v Chief Constable of Gloucestershire [2007] 2 AC 105** and **Austin v Metropolitan Police Commissioner [2008] 1 All ER 564**.*

■ Geddis A., 'Free speech martyrs or unreasonable threats to social peace? "Insulting expression" s.5 of the Public Order Act 1986' [2004] Public Law 853.

*The courts have taken contrasting approaches to whether what a person says or does is insulting or reasonable free expression. This article considers three cases, including **Percy v DPP [2003] EWHC 1564 (Admin)**.*

■ Nicolson D. and Reid K., 'Arrest for breach of the peace and the European Convention on Human Rights' [1996] Crim LR 764.

*The police duty to maintain public order and deal with breaches of the peace is one of the most ancient parts of common law. This article looks at some of the case law and assesses whether English law conforms to the requirements of the **ECHR**.*

Online Resources

www.oup.com/uk/qanda/

Go online for extra essay and problem questions, a glossary of key terms, online versions of all the answer plans and audio commentary on how selected ones were put together, and a range of podcasts which include advice on exam and coursework technique and advice for other assessment methods.

Freedom of expression

9

ARE YOU READY?

The questions in this chapter are a problem question on obscenity and contempt of court, a problem question on the **Official Secrets Act** and breach of confidence, an essay on freedom of information, and a problem question on the right of privacy. To be able to answer these questions, you need to have covered all of the following topics in your work and revision:

● understanding the **Obscene Publications Act 1959** and the case law interpreting that Act;

● understanding the **Contempt of Court Act 1981** and the case law on contempt of court;

● understanding the **Official Secrets Acts 1911** and **1989** and the case law interpreting those Acts;

● understanding the **Freedom of Information Act 2000** and the case law interpreting that Act;

● understanding how breach of confidence developed into a right of privacy.

KEY DEBATES

Debate: Freedom of Speech

Freedom of speech is the most important right in a democratic society. It allows discussions of alternative policies. Most people would accept that there should be some restrictions on this right, in order to protect the rights of others, but does English law have the correct balance, with its criminalization of obscenity, contempt of court, and official secrets?

◀

Debate: A Right of Privacy

English law has no Act of Parliament specifically guaranteeing a right of privacy, yet the courts have developed such a right, using a combination of the ancient equitable doctrine of breach of confidence and **Article 8 of the European Convention on Human Rights**. Has the right balance between freedom of expression and the individual's right to privacy been secured?

Q | **QUESTION** | **1**

Humbert, who lives in Alphaville, is interested in computing and child pornography. He obtains from his computer images of young children engaged in sexual activity. He shares and exchanges these pictures with his friends. He also exchanges DVD recordings dealing with similar subject matter. He is arrested by the police and prosecuted.

In his defence, he wishes to argue that his sexual desires are incurable and that looking at such pictures is beneficial in that it satisfies those desires. He also wishes to argue that some of the computer images are of artistic merit. Eminent psychiatrists and art experts are willing to give evidence on his behalf.

Two days before his trial the local newspaper, *The Alphaville Record*, publishes an article under the headline, 'Hanging Is Too Good for Humbert' and reveals that he has previously been convicted for sexual offences. The editor defends publication as in the public interest.

Advise Humbert and the editor of *The Alphaville Record*.

! | **CAUTION!**

- A number of amendments have been made to the **Obscene Publications Act 1959**. Pay attention to the case law, which gives meaning to the Act.
- The laws on contempt of court are very strict in England and Wales and have only partly been moderated by the **Human Rights Act 1998**.

DIAGRAM ANSWER PLAN

Identify the issues	▪ Identify the legal issues: Has Humbert published an obscene article? Does Humbert possess an indecent photograph? Has Humbert committed any other offences? Has the newspaper committed contempt of court?

Relevant law	▪ Outline the relevant law: statutory and case law, in particular: the **Obscene Publications Act 1959**; the **Criminal Justice and Public Order Act 1994**; the **Video Recordings Act 2010**; the **Human Rights Act 1998**; and the **Contempt of Court Act 1981**

Apply the law	▪ Does the material that Humbert publishes have a tendency to deprave and corrupt? ▪ Is the material that he publishes for the public good? ▪ Are his photographs indecent? ▪ Is Humbert's human right of free expression infringed? ▪ What is contempt of court and are there any defences available?

Conclude	▪ Would Humbert be convicted of the offences? ▪ Is the newspaper in contempt of court?

A   SUGGESTED ANSWER

The first offence that springs to mind is that Humbert might have contravened the **Obscene Publications Act 1959. Section 1** makes it an offence to publish an obscene article.

[1]'Publication' is the first element of this offence. This paragraph looks at the case law in order to decide whether there has been publication.

Publishing includes any form of distribution.[1] It is not necessary to show that Humbert did this for gain; distributing or circulating is enough according to the Act. Even if this was not the case, an 'exchange' might well be held to be for gain. Whether obscene material stored on a computer was an 'article' was open to doubt until the **Criminal Justice and Public Order Act 1994 (s. 168 and Schedule 9, para. 3)** made it clear that the transmission of electronically stored data was covered by the 1959 Act. Electronic transmission to just one person would be enough to constitute the offence: *R v Smith (Gavin)* **[2012] 1 WLR 3368.**

The test for obscenity is set out in **s. 1 of the Obscene Publications Act 1959**. It holds that the article is obscene 'if its effect . . . is, if taken as a whole, such as to tend to deprave and corrupt persons who are likely, having regard to all relevant circumstances, to read, hear or see' it. This test has eluded precise definition. *R v Secker and Warburg* **[1954] 2 All ER 683** stated that the material being merely shocking and disgusting was not enough. The famous, though unreported, case concerning the book Lady Chatterley's Lover in 1960 suggested that it meant 'to make morally bad, to pervert, debase or corrupt morally'. The old case *R v Hicklin* **(1868) LR 3 QB 360** mentioned 'exciting impure or libidinous thoughts'. It is not necessary to show that anyone was actually depraved or corrupted, merely that the material has that tendency.[2]

[2] A clear conclusion on how obscenity is legally defined.

The statutory definition also demands that the likely audience is taken into account. If it is children, obscenity is more likely to be proved: *DPP v A & BC Chewing Gum* **[1968] 1 QB 519** and *R v Anderson* **[1972] 1 QB 304**. Here though, although the material concerns children, they are most unlikely to be the 'target' audience. This is likely to be adults. Humbert cannot argue that they are likely already to be paedophiles and so incapable of further corruption. The argument that the 'audience' for pornography is already corrupt has not succeeded: *R v Anderson* **[1972] 1 QB 304**; *DPP v Whyte* **[1972] AC 849**.

The vague definition of obscenity may not be a problem. The jury will decide. Expert evidence is not permitted to help them on this issue unless the type of obscene material is outside the normal experience of adults. Expert evidence was allowed on the effects of cocaine in *R v Skirving* **[1985] QB 819** and the effects of horrific pictures on children in *DPP v A & BC Chewing Gum*. There seems no justification for this type of expert evidence in this case, as the 'target audience' for the material is adults.[3]

[3] This is the conclusion to the arguments put forward in the previous two paragraphs.

Section 4 of the 1959 Act does, however, permit expert evidence on 'artistic merit' (*R v Anderson*; Lady Chatterley). If the material can be shown to be for the 'public good' it is not obscene. The jury decide first whether material is obscene and then, if it is, whether considerations of public good outweigh this and if publication is desirable. More general arguments and evidence that pornographic material has therapeutic effects has never been permitted: *DPP v Jordan* **[1977] AC 699** and *Attorney-General's Reference (No. 3 of 1977)* **[1978] 3 All ER 1166**. So Humbert's art experts could give evidence, but not his psychiatrists. On balance, it seems that Humbert's computer images and DVDs will be judged to be obscene.[4]

[4] An overall conclusion can be reached.

If this is not so, there are other offences that could be considered. Humbert's pictures are unlikely to be regarded as 'extreme pornographic images' under **s. 63 of the Criminal Justice and Immigration Act 2008** as they would have to be 'grossly offensive, disgusting or otherwise of an obscene character' and involve certain specified activities such as violence, corpses, or animals, not just children. Mere possession of an 'indecent' photograph is an offence under the **Protection of Children Act 1978**. The prosecution must prove that Humbert had 'knowledge' of what he possesses, but on the facts here that does not seem too difficult: *Atkins v DPP* **[2000] 2 All ER 425**. **Section 84 of the Criminal Justice and Public Order Act 1994** makes very clear that 'photographs' include both electronic data and the printout. Even if Humbert had deleted the images from his computer, if he had the necessary skill to recover them he would still be guilty: *R v Porter* **[2006] 1 WLR 2633**. There is no defence of the public good for this offence, nor for the common law offences of 'conspiracy to corrupt public morals' (*Shaw v DPP* **[1962] AC 220**) or conspiracy to outrage public decency (*Knuller v DPP* **[1973] AC 435**). Paedophile 'rings' have been dealt with under these offences.[5] Finally, it is highly unlikely that Humbert's DVDs have been given a classification under the **Video Recordings Act 2010** by the British Board of Film Classification. This is particularly so, since the board was urged to have 'special regard' to DVDs dealing with 'human sexual activity' in **s. 90 of the Criminal Justice and Public Order Act 1994**. It is a criminal offence merely to supply such a video, punishable by imprisonment. The **Video Recordings Act 1984** had to be re-enacted in 2010, because the original Act had never complied with European Community law, but even if Humbert's offence was committed before 2010, he will have no defence: *R v Budimir* **[2010] 2 Cr App R 29**.

The **Human Rights Act 1998** may not help him very much. The European Court of Human Rights has consistently allowed contracting states a 'margin of appreciation' in the area of obscenity law, because they cannot find an agreed European standard of morals in the domestic law of these states. So the Court refused to say that obscenity laws infringed the **Article 10** right to freedom of expression in both *Handyside v UK* **(1976) 1 EHRR 737** and *Muller v Switzerland* **(1991) 13 EHRR 212**. The UK House of Lords[6] has taken these cases into account and shown no signs of any desire to use freedom of expression to liberalize the laws restricting the sale of pornography: *Belfast City Council v Miss Behavin' Ltd* **[2007] 1 WLR 1420**.

The Alphaville Record is almost certainly guilty of contempt of court.[7] Under **s. 2(2) of the Contempt of Court Act 1981** there needs to be a 'substantial risk that the course of justice will be seriously impeded or prejudiced'. The publication of previous convictions has long been held to be contempt: *R v Odhams Press* **[1957] 1 QB**

---

[5] A really good answer would consider other possible offences.

[6] A House of Lords/Supreme Court decision is a binding precedent and should be chosen in preference to a decision of the European Court of Human Rights, which only has to be 'taken into account'.

[7] Look closely at a problem question; it may involve more than one area of law.

73. The proceedings are clearly 'active' because Humbert has been arrested (**s. 2(3)**).

There is a defence under **s. 5** that the risk of prejudice is purely incidental to 'a discussion in good faith of public affairs'. A passing mention in a newspaper article about a forthcoming trial might benefit from this section: *Attorney-General v English* **[1983] 1 AC 116**. Here, though, the main purpose of the article seems to be to discuss Humbert, his trial, and his previous convictions. It is a clear contempt. The **Contempt of Court Act 1981** was enacted to bring English law into line with the **European Convention on Human Rights**, following Britain's defeat in *Sunday Times v UK* **(1979) 2 EHRR 245**. *R v Sherwood ex parte The Telegraph Group* **[2001] 1 WLR 1983** confirms that contempt laws are necessary to guarantee a fair trial under **Article 6**.

Indeed, it could be argued that the editor obviously knows about the trial and is deliberately trying to interfere with the administration of justice. This intentional contempt is not covered by the Act (**s. 6**) but remains as a common law offence: *Attorney-General v Hislop* **[1991] 2 WLR 219**. The Attorney General could bring a prosecution. The Record should have postponed their report until the trial was over. Reporting a trial is neither contempt nor a breach of confidence: *Khuja v Times* **[2017] UKSC 49**.

[8]The final paragraph can be brief, if you have given some of your conclusions earlier in the answer.

In conclusion, both Humbert and the editor face conviction.[8] In a strange way, the contempt might help Humbert. If convicted, he might be able to appeal successfully on the ground that the contempt meant that he did not receive a fair trial: *R v Taylor* **(1993) 98 Cr App R 361**.

LOOKING FOR EXTRA MARKS?

- There is a considerable debate on whether the **Obscene Publications Act 1959** is too strict and hampers artistic freedom or is so weak that it permits pornography. Even in a problem question these criticisms can be brought into the answer.

- Contempt of court is a neglected area of law, but has plenty of interesting case law.

QUESTION | 2

Jane is a civil servant working for the Ministry of Defence. Because of the nature of her work she signed the **Official Secrets Act** on commencing her employment. During the course of her work, Jane comes across a document indicating that a British company is selling artillery shells to the government of Fantasia. She knows that this is contrary to British law and contrary to the stated

⊙

policy of Her Majesty's Government. Jane asks a more senior civil servant what she should do. He tells her that the Secretary of State for Defence knows all about it but the matter is to be kept secret.

Jane is still concerned that the law is being broken, so she hands over a copy of the document to a journalist who works for the Sentinel newspaper. That journalist discovers that there is a Defence Advisory Notice relating to arms sales to Fantasia. He and his editor decide to publish the document anyway.

The government learns about the proposed publication and wants to stop it. It also wishes to punish the parties responsible.

Advise the government.

(!) CAUTION!

■ At first glance it is difficult to see what this question is about. It could, just conceivably, be about ministerial responsibility.

■ Read the last part of the problem. The government wants to 'punish' the people responsible. That means the criminal law, ie the **Official Secrets Acts**.

■ Read the last part of the problem. The government wants to stop publication. That means the civil law and remedies such as injunctions, ie breach of confidence.

DIAGRAM ANSWER PLAN

Identify the issues	▪ Identify the legal issues: Has Jane committed offences under the **Official Secrets Acts 1911** and **1939**? Does a 'whistle-blower' like Jane have any defence? Can the government restrain a breach of confidence?
Relevant law	▪ Outline the relevant law: statutory and case law, in particular: the **Official Secrets Act 1911**; the **Official Secrets Act 1989**; **Article 10 of the European Convention of Human Rights**; and *Attorney-General v The Observer, The Times (Spycatcher)* **[1990] AC 109**
Apply the law	▪ Has Jane acted against the safety and interests of the state? ▪ Has Jane damaged the UK's defence interests? ▪ Has Jane any public interest defence? ▪ How is the public interest determined in a breach of confidence action? ▪ Does the right to freedom of expression in the **Human Rights Act 1998** protect Jane?
Conclude	▪ Would Jane be convicted of offences under the **Official Secrets Acts**? ▪ Would the government be granted remedies to restrain a breach of confidence?

A SUGGESTED ANSWER

[1] The opening paragraph is short, but very to the point.

The most obvious avenues for the government to explore are the **Official Secrets Acts 1911** and **1989** (**OSA 1911** and **1989**), but there are other possibilities. A civil action, for breach of confidence, might also be possible.[1]

Jane has signed the **Official Secrets Act**. This is a common procedure, but has no legal effect. All it does is warn her that she is in the sort of job that may be subject to the Act. Despite the reforms of 1989, **s. 1 OSA 1911** remains in force. Breach of this is a serious offence and can be committed by communicating to an enemy information that may be 'prejudicial to the safety and interests of the State'. Jane might well argue that she has not communicated to an enemy and that her actions are not 'prejudicial to the safety and interests of the State'. *Chandler v DPP* **[1964] AC 763** indicates that only the government can decide what is in the interests of the state. In *R v Ponting* **[1985] Crim LR 318**, Clive Ponting, another civil servant, tried to argue that he was helping the state by revealing to an MP information that ministers were hiding from Parliament. This is the 'whistle-blower' argument: he had a duty to expose wrongdoing. In *Ponting*, the court ruled that this argument was unacceptable, for, as in *Chandler*, only the government of the day could rule on what was 'in the interests of the State'. Despite the ruling, the jury acquitted Ponting.[2] For this reason, it is unlikely that the government would use **s. 1** against Jane or the journalist, who would also be liable.

The old s. 2 of the 1911 Act was replaced by the **OSA 1989**. The Act is meant to focus only on those areas where the Crown is genuinely concerned with the revelation of official information. **Section 1** warns Crown servants, such as Jane, that she must not reveal information acquired during her work if it relates to the security or intelligence services. Her revelation would not seem to affect security or intelligence, but it might affect defence. Under **s. 2** it is an offence to disclose 'defence' information. 'Defence', as defined in **s. 2(4)(b)**, includes 'weapons' but only those used by the Armed Forces of the Crown. Foreign Armed Forces are not included. Maybe it is possible that foreign weapon sales come under **subs. (d)**, the more general 'defence policy'. The prosecution must also prove that disclosure of information is 'damaging' to British defence. It is difficult to see how this could be so. Damage to British interests abroad is also mentioned in **s. 2** and might be easier to prove on our facts. There is also a 'did not know' defence in **s. 2(3)** of the Act, together with a similar defence in **s. 3(4)**. Read literally, the subsections seem to reverse the burden of proof and require Jane to prove that she did not know that it was defence information and did not know that it was damaging to reveal it. The Court of Appeal held, in *R v Keogh* **[2007] 1 WLR 1500**, that this was incompatible with the presumption of innocence in **Article 6 of the European Convention on Human Rights**.[3] It would be up to the prosecution to prove that Jane knew that it was defence information and that it would be damaging to reveal it. Another government possibility is **s. 3** of the Act, which protects information relating to 'international relations' in a similar way. Conceivably, arms sales to a foreign country might well be connected to foreign policy matters. Again, the prosecution would have to prove that Jane knew that the information was damaging to international relations.

Chandler v DPP suggests that the courts would accept the government's view on what was 'defence', 'international relations', or 'the interests of the United Kingdom abroad'. It was hoped that the

[2] Occasionally a jury will defy a judge's direction on the law and decide what they think is right.

[3] The **Human Rights Act 1998** requires courts to interpret Acts of Parliament in a way that is compatible with human rights.

courts would take a more liberal line under the 1989 Act and allow defendants, such as Jane, to put forward their own evidence on what was damaging to the country's defence or international relations. In *R v Shayler* [2003] 1 AC 247, however, the defendant claimed that he had tried to reveal the wrongdoings of the security services and that this was in the public and national interest. He also argued that the **OSA 1989** was incompatible with **Article 10 of the European Convention of Human Rights**, because it infringed his right to freedom of expression. The House of Lords did not agree. It followed decisions of the European Court of Human Rights,[4] where the needs of 'national security' were deemed to outweigh freedom of expression: *Engel v Netherlands (No. 1)* (1976) 1 EHRR 647 and *Klass v Germany* (1978) 2 EHRR 214.

[4] If both the House of Lords and the European Court of Human Rights agree on the interpretation of the law, this forms a very strong argument.

Shayler's 'whistle-blower' argument also fell on stony ground. *R v Ponting* [1985] **Crim LR 318** had stated that a civil servant, concerned about wrongdoing, should report their worries to their superiors, not the press. The House of Lords suggested that Shayler should have told his Secretary of State. It seems, on these precedents, that Jane's best hope would be to use *R v Keogh* [2007] **1 WLR 1500** and argue in defence that she did not know that the information that she revealed would be damaging, but instead hoped that her revelation of wrongdoing would be for the benefit of the country.[5]

[5] It is permissible to put forward your own ideas on how the law should be interpreted.

The journalist also commits an offence if he knowingly receives the information and knowingly passes it on (**s. 5**). This, the Sentinel newspaper seems determined to do. It is necessary, however, for the information to contravene the foregoing provisions of the Act for this to be an offence. As we have seen, it is by no means clear that it is 'defence' or 'international relations' information. The journalist also has a 'not damaging' defence.

Under **s. 8**, it is a specific offence for a Crown servant like Jane to retain the actual document 'contrary to her official duty'. Again, though, for the offence to be committed it has to relate to 'defence' or 'international relations'.

The government has other measures that it could utilize against Jane. The 'Defence Advisory Notice'[6] is a non-statutory warning issued by a committee of members of the media, civil servants, and the military, known as the Defence, Press and Broadcasting Advisory Committee. It advises journalists not to publish information relating to certain military and intelligence matters. It is not an offence to ignore the notice, but it acts as a warning that publication might infringe the law.

[6] Knowing about little-known areas of law might impress the examiners.

The most flexible remedy that the government has is to seek an injunction for breach of confidence. It is clear that Jane has an obligation of confidence as a civil servant. The government would need to show that it was in the public interest to prevent disclosure: *Attorney-General v The Observer, The Times (Spycatcher)* [1990] 1 AC 109.

Damage to the security services was the reason for non-disclosure in that case. Here, though, Jane wishes to reveal breaches of the law. It is permissible to reveal criminal wrongdoing, even if it is a breach of confidence: *Cork v McVicar* **(1984) The Times, 31 October**. The court did not extend this approach to the revelation of government wrongdoing in *Attorney-General v The Observer, The Times (Spycatcher)* **[1990] AC 109** and advised civil servants, such as Jane, to report their worries to their superiors and not the press.[7] If the newspaper paid her, the fee could be recovered as damages for breach of confidence, according to *Attorney-General v Blake* **[2001] 1 AC 268**.

It is possible though that the entry into force of the **Human Rights Act 1998** might help Jane. Decisions of the European Court of Human Rights have emphasized the importance of freedom of expression. Although the Court found the law on breach of confidence acceptable in *Observer v UK* **(1991) 14 EHRR 153**, they thought that the 'Spycatcher' injunction should have been lifted earlier, as the material was already in the public domain. Now, under **s. 12 of the Human Rights Act 1998**, the courts of the UK must have special regard to freedom of expression. In *Attorney-General v The Times* **[2001] 1 WLR 885**, the newspaper was about to publish extracts from a book by Tomlinson, a former MI6 officer. The court allowed this, as the material had already been published elsewhere. It was up to the government to prove that there was a need to restrict freedom of expression 'in the interests of national security'. The newspaper did not have to prove that the material was already in the public domain, the government had to prove that it was not.

Jane's problem is that her material is not already in the public domain. I would suggest that the court is more likely to follow the approach in *Shayler* and issue an injunction to protect national security. The Sentinel would also be injuncted and all other newspapers that could reasonably be expected to know about the injunction would also be bound, as happened when Punch magazine published some of the *Shayler* material in *Attorney-General v Punch Ltd [2003] 1 All ER 289*. So, in conclusion, Jane risks conviction under the **OSA 1989**, damages for breach of confidence and an injunction forbidding her disclosures. The **Human Rights Act 1998** does not seem to have allayed the courts' fears about endangering national security.[8]

[7] A major criticism of the **OSA 1989** was that it contained no public interest defence for whistle blowers. Examiners like to introduce controversial areas of law into questions.

[8] For once, the **Human Rights Act 1998** makes little difference to UK law.

✚ LOOKING FOR EXTRA MARKS?

■ This is a legal question and requires an answer with legal material, rather than just opinion on the rightness or wrongness of government actions.

■ Concentrate on a careful analysis of the main cases on official secrets and breach of confidence.

Holders of public office should be as open as possible about all the decisions and actions that they take. They should give reasons for their decisions and restrict information only when the wider public interest clearly demands.

(The Fifth 'Nolan Principle', Committee on Standards in Public Life Cm 2850-I)

Consider whether a Freedom of Information Act would give people more information about the workings of government.

! **CAUTION!**

- The **Freedom of Information Act 2000** can seem a rather dry and uninteresting topic, but the Act sets out what must be revealed and what can be withheld in an organized and schematic way. It can be mastered with patience.
- New case law from the Supreme Court, *R (Evans) v Attorney General* and *Kennedy v Charity Commission* may be about to revolutionize this area of law. Look out for new cases!

O **DIAGRAM ANSWER PLAN'**

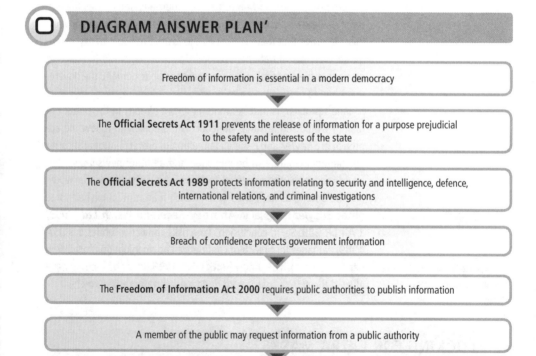

Freedom of information is essential in a modern democracy

The **Official Secrets Act 1911** prevents the release of information for a purpose prejudicial to the safety and interests of the state

The **Official Secrets Act 1989** protects information relating to security and intelligence, defence, international relations, and criminal investigations

Breach of confidence protects government information

The **Freedom of Information Act 2000** requires public authorities to publish information

A member of the public may request information from a public authority

But there are many exemptions controlled by the government

There is an appeal to the Information Commissioner and then the courts

Conclusion—the courts have tried to reduce the exemptions

(A)

SUGGESTED ANSWER

The Home Office's 1999 consultation paper on freedom of information starts by stating that:

Freedom of information is an essential component of the government's programme to modernise British politics. This programme of constitutional reform aims to involve people more closely in the decisions which affect their lives.

While this may be true, the government did not plan to repeal the laws that successive governments had used to control the release of government information.

[1] The **Official Secrets Acts** are worth mentioning so that you can show that you appreciate the context within which the **Freedom of Information Act** operates.

The **Official Secrets Act 1911** [1] can always be used in a serious case, as **s. 1** remains and makes it an offence to obtain or communicate any document or information 'for a purpose prejudicial to the safety or interests of the State'. *R v Ponting* [1985] **Crim LR 318** held, in the case of a whistle-blowing civil servant who wanted to reveal documents about a controversial military act to an MP, that only the government could decide what was in 'the safety or interests of the State'. The **Official Secrets Act 1989** was a reform, but the crucial areas of information that a government would wish to keep secret are still protected by criminal sanction. These are security and intelligence, defence, international relations, and criminal investigations. The Defence Advisory Notice, which warns journalists not to investigate certain areas, for fear of prosecution, also still exists, as does the practice of 'signing' the **Official Secrets Act**, which serves a similar warning function for individuals.

[2] Similarly, to get the whole picture, breach of confidence is also relevant.

Failing this, a government could always use the civil remedy of breach of confidence [2] to restrain, by injunction, government employees, ex-employees, and those they pass the information to, such as newspapers and publishers, from betraying confidences. The most spectacular example of this was the protracted litigation against the ex-security agent Peter Wright's book Spycatcher in the late 1980s and early 1990s, culminating in the House of Lords' decision *Attorney-General v Guardian Newspapers (No. 2)* [1990] **1 AC 109**, where the injunctions were only lifted because the information was, by now, so well-known that to continue them would be pointless. Governments have not tired of pursuing such actions; in

Attorney-General v Blake **[2001] 1 AC 268** an ex-member of the Secret Intelligence Service had been sued for breaching his contractual obligation not to reveal what he had learnt from his employment. The House of Lords decided that Blake would have to account (ie restore) the profits made from the book that he published about his career.

[3] In an essay, it is a good idea to refer back to the question itself.

The Nolan Committee reported in 1995 urging more openness in government[3] and in response, the **Freedom of Information Act 2000** was enacted. The government wanted to promote a 'change of culture within the public sector' and encouraged all 'public authorities' to voluntarily publish far more information. Public authority is broadly defined to mean any body or office exercising a public function and includes those providing services of that nature to the public authority. There is a list of over 400 public authorities in the **Freedom of Information Act 2000** and all must draw up a publication scheme. This includes things like schools admission criteria and how priorities on hospital waiting lists are determined, which are matters of concern to the general public, not just to those interested in politics.

Otherwise, any person can request information from a public authority. The public authority has a duty to confirm or deny whether they hold the information or not. If they do, they must provide it, although a small fee may be charged. The applicant may even express a preference about whether they want the information to be provided as a copy of a document, a digest, or summary, or whether they just want to inspect it. There are a number of grounds on which the public authority can refuse to supply the information, such as that it is already available, about to be published, would be too expensive, or the request is 'vexatious'; for example, the applicant has made repeated requests for the same information.

The main criticism of the Act is that there are a large number of exempted categories of information where there is no duty to disclose. Apart from this obvious criticism, the different exemptions are

[4] To answer a question like this, you do need to master the intricacies of the Act.

differently defined,[4] which may cause confusion amongst the public. There are categories of information that are absolutely exempt from disclosure, such as those relating to security organizations, court records, personal data, information obtained in confidence, and information whose disclosure is forbidden by statute, EU obligation, or would be in contempt of court. There is a longer list of information categories where it has to be decided whether the public interest requires disclosure or withholding of the information. Defence, international relations, the economy, public investigations, law enforcement, the formulation of government policy, the award of honours, and communications with the Queen are just some of the 'public interest' exempt categories.

Another problem is the strong government role in these exemptions, when the government is the very organization that may be trying to conceal information. Government ministers certificate whether information has been supplied by a security or intelligence agency and whether it is a threat to national security. Communications between government ministers, Cabinet communications, and advice from civil servants on policy formulation are all exempted information. What is more, a government minister can also give an opinion that information should be withheld because it could prejudice the convention of collective responsibility, or inhibit the free and frank provision of advice, or prejudice public affairs. The courts of Scotland have held, in *Scottish Ministers v Scottish Information Commission* [2007] **SC 330**, that this does not allow ministers to say that all documents containing advice to ministers should be withheld.[5] The Information Commissioner was entitled to examine individual documents to assess whether they could safely be released. A ministerial diary, which listed with whom the Secretary of State for Health had met, was also released in *Department of Health v Information Commissioner and Simon Lewis* [2017] **EWCA Civ 374**. The Information Tribunal can and does order the revelation of minutes of Cabinet meetings. *Cabinet Office v Information Commissioner EA/2008/0024* and *EA/2008/0029* ordered the release of minutes relating to the decision to invade Iraq, which contained the controversial advice from the Attorney-General on the legality of military action. Most controversially, under **s. 53 of the Freedom of Information Act 2000** a Secretary of State can add to the list of exempt information, merely by using delegated legislation. Parliament has to agree to this delegated legislation, as the Act requires the affirmative resolution procedure and Parliament did agree in the case of the 'Iraq minutes'.

This process was repeated in 2013 to prevent the disclosure of communications sent by the Prince of Wales to government departments. This time, the Supreme Court disagreed and ordered the Prince's letter to be disclosed in *R (Evans) v Attorney-General* [2015] **UKSC 21**.[6] **Section 53** required the Secretary of State to have 'reasonable grounds' to overrule the decision of the Upper Tribunal. His disagreement with their decision was not enough; he would need something like evidence unknown to the tribunal to justify overruling them. The courts have found other ways of outflanking some of the exemptions in the Act. In *Kennedy v Charity Commission* [2014] **UKSC 20**, a journalist wanted information uncovered by a Charity Commission inquiry into the alleged misuse of funds by the Mariam Appeal. Documents created for an inquiry are exempt from disclosure under **s. 32(2)** of the Act, but the Supreme Court advised the Charity Commission to fulfil its common law duty of openness and transparency and disclose this information in the public interest.[7]

The **Freedom of Information Act 2000** comes complete with a fairly robust enforcement system. First, the public authority needs to provide an internal complaint procedure. Then the applicant can apply to the 'Information Commissioner', an independent official created by the Act. Either the applicant or the public authority has an appeal to the unified tribunal system, with further appeals on a point of law to the High Court and then upwards to the Court of Appeal and Supreme Court, if necessary. The courts ordered the disclosure of MPs' expenses in *Corporate Officer of the House of Commons v Information Commissioner* **[2009] 3 All ER 403**, which provoked a huge public scandal and the retirement of many MPs.[8] The Information Commissioner also has fairly impressive enforcement powers and he will be able to investigate, obtain search warrants, and order the release of information. The penalty for defying him or lying to him could be proceedings in the High Court for contempt of court.

[8] More evidence of the courts supporting freedom of information.

The **Freedom of Information Act** does seem to have rather a lot of exemptions and they are rather widely drawn. The government also seems to have undue power to widen the scope of these exemptions. A strong Information Commissioner would help to counteract this, and it seems that the courts are now willing to help with their rediscovery of the common law principle of open justice, as seen in *Kennedy v Charity Commission* **[2014] UKSC 20** and *R (Evans) v Attorney-General* **[2015] UKSC 21**.[9]

[9] The evidence deployed earlier in the essay supports the final conclusion.

LOOKING FOR EXTRA MARKS?

- This is a highly complex area of law, but a hard-working student can master the detail and impress the examiner.

- Look out for the latest controversies sparked by government attempts to refuse information.

QUESTION | 4

Bob is a professional footballer, who plays in the English Premier League. He is captain of both his football club and of the England football team. When interviewed by the media, he has always said that he is happily married to Chantelle and has two children whom he adores.

Bob is photographed leaving a hotel with a woman, Dolores, who is not his wife. *The Daily Snitch* publishes the photograph, together with a story from Dolores, telling of her passionate love affair with Bob. The photograph and the story also appear on *The Daily Snitch* website.

Bob does not welcome this publicity, but admits that what Dolores says is true.

Advise Bob.

CAUTION!

- There is no Act of Parliament detailing what the right of privacy involves. It is determined by case law.

- Do not confuse the right of privacy with defamation. A libel or slander has to be untrue.

- This is a new area of law, which is still developing, so expect to encounter some contradictions and uncertainty in the case law.

DIAGRAM ANSWER PLAN

Identify the issues
- Identify the legal issues: Is there a breach of confidence? Does Bob have a right of privacy? What is the public interest in Bob's case?

Relevant law
- Outline the relevant law: statutory and case law, in particular: *Attorney-General v Guardian Newspapers (Spycatcher) (No. 2); Campbell v Mirror Group Newspapers; Von Hannover v Germany; Rio Ferdinand v MGN Ltd; European Convention on Human Rights*, in particular **Articles 8 and 10**

Apply the law
- Has there been a libel?
- Does Bob have a confidential relationship that can be breached?
- Does Bob have a right of privacy that extends to the newspaper revelations about him?
- Does the public interest justify keeping these matters confidential or publicizing them?

Conclude
- Would the court try to prevent further revelations or allow publication?

We need to consider whether Bob has any legal rights to prevent The Daily Snitch intruding into his private life. In order to do so, we need to look at two areas of law, defamation and breach of confidence.[1]

[1] The first paragraph pinpoints the two areas that we need to consider.

Historically, no right of privacy was recognized in English law, unlike the situation in other European countries such as France or Germany, where the protection of privacy is a recognized part of the law. In England, privacy did not become accepted as a recognized tort, nor has there been legislation on the subject.

Libel is defamation in a permanent form, such as writing or a photograph. It is defined as the publication of something that is untrue, which lowers the victim's reputation in the eyes of 'right thinking members of society generally': *Sim v Stretch* **[1936] 2 All ER 1237**. The newspaper story might be damaging to Bob's reputation, but it cannot be libel because it is true. *The Daily Snitch* could prove that their story was 'substantially true', which would be a complete defence under **s. 2(1) of the Defamation Act 2013**.[2]

[2] There is no need to go into great detail about defamation, because it obviously does not apply.

A better argument for Bob to use would be the old equitable doctrine of breach of confidence. The Court of Chancery decided in *Prince Albert v Strange* **(1849) 1 Mac & G 25**, that Strange could not publish etchings that Prince Albert had made of members of his immediate family. Prince Albert had not given permission for any publication and so to publish them would be a breach of confidence. In Bob's case, photographs could be regarded as a more modern form of portraiture than etching. Many years later, *Strange* was followed in the notorious case of *Argyll v Argyll* **[1967] Ch 302**, where the Duke and Duchess of Argyll were divorcing and the Duke sold a story, with intimate details of their married life, to the *People* newspaper. Publication could be restrained because this was information from a confidential relationship, marriage.

The concept of the confidential relationship was developed in *Attorney-General v Guardian Newspapers (No. 2)* **[1990] 1 AC 109**, where Peter Wright, a retired intelligence services officer, published a book, *Spycatcher*, revealing what he had allegedly done during his working life. The government tried to stop publication of the book and newspaper reports of what it contained by suing for breach of confidence. Lord Keith, at 255, held that: 'The law has long recognised that an obligation of confidence can arise out of particular relationships.'[3]

[3] Short quotations can be remembered and can be useful, if they are a clear statement of the law.

He gave examples such as doctor and patient, priest and penitent, solicitor and client, and banker and customer. There does not have to be a contract between the parties to give rise to a duty of confidence. Third parties, such as journalists, outside the relationship of confidence, could also be restrained from revealing the confidential information. The public interest also had to be taken into account, which enables the court to consider many factors. Here it was not in the public interest for government secrets to be revealed, particularly as it might encourage other intelligence officers to follow Wright's example.

[4] A few cases have had to be examined, but we can finally conclude that Bob does not have a confidential relationship to protect.

Unfortunately for Bob, he is not seeking to protect information from a confidential relationship.[4] In *A v B plc and another* [2003] **QB 195**, a married professional footballer was having sexual relationships with two other women, who had sold their stories to a national newspaper. He wanted to stop publication, but failed on the grounds that the court set great store in protecting the confidentiality of marriage and other permanent relationships, but far less value in protecting the confidentiality of this sort of liaison. By the date of this case, the **Human Rights Act 1998** had introduced a right to a private life, which was protected by **Article 8**, but also the right to freedom of

[5] The old law has had to be adapted to take into account the rights introduced by the **Human Rights Act 1998**.

expression, which was guaranteed by **Article 10**. This balancing of interests was familiar from the equitable origins of breach of confidence, as Lord Woolf CJ explained at 202:[5]

The court is able to achieve this by absorbing the rights which **articles 8** and **10** protect into the long-established action for breach of confidence.

An important case in Bob's favour followed shortly afterwards. Naomi Campbell gained a partial victory in *Campbell v Mirror Group Newspapers* [2004] **2 AC 457**, where a newspaper had revealed that she was receiving treatment for drug addiction. This was acceptable because she had previously denied that she took drugs, so the newspaper was entitled to set the record straight. Publishing photographs of her leaving the place of treatment was not, as medical treatment is private. Lord Nicholls had some important things to say about the development of the right of privacy. Although **s. 6 of the Human Rights Act** says only that 'public authorities' can be sued for breaching human rights, this type of action could be brought between individuals and between individuals and a non-governmental body such as a newspaper. He also wanted to abandon the use of the term 'duty of confidence' and the insistence that only 'confidential' information could be protected. He preferred to refer to it as 'private'

[6] This paragraph describes an important shift in the law from protecting confidential relationships to a right of privacy.

information and stated at 465: 'The essence of the tort is better encapsulated now as misuse of private information.' The right of privacy does not now depend upon the existence of a confidential relationship. So Bob could argue that his sexual relationships are private.[6]

Under both the old law of breach of confidence and the newer human rights law, the court must consider all the factors that go to make up the public interest. The 'public interest' is not at all the same thing as the public being interested in something. Just because Bob is well known, it does not mean that the public is entitled to know everything about him. Prince Charles is an internationally known public figure, but that did not entitle a newspaper to publish the contents of his private diaries: *HRH Prince of Wales v Associated Newspapers Ltd* [2008] Ch 57.

The publication of unauthorized photographs is a particularly sensitive issue. According to the European Court of Human Rights, it is not permissible to publish photographs of the private life of a public figure unless it contributes to political debate: *Von Hannover v Germany* (2005) 40 EHRR 1. Princess Caroline of Monaco successfully complained that German newspapers should not publish photographs of her with her husband and children when engaged in their private life. The state has an obligation to protect the private life of individuals from other individuals. This case has been further developed in decisions of the UK courts. In *Murray v Express Group Newspapers* [2008] HRLR 33, the Court of Appeal suggested that taking a photograph, without permission, of the young child of J.K. Rowling on an Edinburgh street was a breach of the child's 'reasonable expectation of privacy'. Ms Murray (J.K. Rowling) had not courted publicity in the past for her child, nor has Bob, for his extramarital relationship. Private sexual relationships received the protection of the courts in *Mosley v News Group Newspapers* [2012] EMLR 1, where the News of the World was condemned for publishing a story, photographs, and a video of the head of motor racing's Formula 1 engaged in an orgy with five prostitutes. He was a public figure, but his sexual preferences were private and did not relate to his work. Max Mosley received compensation for the intrusion into his private life.[7]

[7] There is a strong argument that a person's sex life is private.

Unfortunately for Bob, there could be a strong counter-argument; that it is in the public interest to reveal the wrongdoings of public figures. The Court of Appeal ruled that there was 'no confidence in iniquity' in *Woodward v Hutchins* [1971] 1 WLR 760, where the Daily Mirror published details of the private life of the singer Tom Jones. Jones had courted publicity in the past, portraying a more wholesome image, so he could not complain about unwelcome publicity now. We can see the same kind of thinking in *Campbell v Mirror Group Newspapers* [2004] 2 AC 457: if the celebrity is misleading the public, the media are entitled to reveal the truth. This is particularly the case if the complainant is holding themselves out as some kind of role model, say for the young. In *Rio Ferdinand v MGN Ltd* [2011] EWHC 2454 (QB), the media were allowed to reveal the existence of

[8]There is also a strong argument that it is in the public interest to reveal wrongdoing.

a very famous, married footballer's extramarital affair. He had publicly held himself out to be a 'family man' and, as captain of Manchester United and England, he was admired by many, who needed to know the truth about him.[8]

So there does now seem to be a right of privacy, but the granting of this right is highly discretionary and depends upon many factors. It may depend on how explicit the revelations are. Revelations about the private sexual live of a famous person were not allowed in *Mosley v News Group Newspapers* [2012] EMLR 1. The reason might be that the revelations about Mosley included material of a very private nature, a video of an orgy taking place. The Supreme Court took a similar line in *PJS v News Group Newspapers* [2016] UKSC 26, where the Sun on Sunday was not allowed to publish a detailed account of alleged sexual encounters between PJS, a well-known figure in the entertainment business, and others. Just to report, in print, that such an event took place, as in *Rio Ferdinand v MGN Ltd* [2011] EWHC 2454 (QB), might be more permissible. Bob's success depends on the extent to which the court accepts that the role model argument justifies the need, in the public interest, to reveal his wrongdoing.[9]

[9]The *PJS* case rather conflicts with the exposure of wrongdoing cases, so it is acceptable to come to a tentative conclusion.

LOOKING FOR EXTRA MARKS?

■ There is steady stream of new case law as 'celebrities' sue in order to protect their privacy.

■ Do not be afraid to argue for your own point of view, backed up by the evidence, the case law.

■ It is perfectly possible to come to the opposite conclusion, that Bob has a good case for damages and an injunction preventing further publication, depending on how you choose to interpret the case law.

TAKING THINGS FURTHER

■ Birkinshaw P., 'Regulating Information' in J. Jowell, C. Oliver, and C. O'Cinneide (eds) The Changing Constitution (8th edn, OUP 2015) 378.
*This chapter considers not only the **Freedom of Information Act 2000**, but also official secrets legislation, European Union requirements, and the **Data Protection Act 1998**.*

■ Childs R., 'Outraging public decency: the offence of offensiveness' [1991] Public Law 20.
The offence of conspiracy to outrage public decency was used in **R v Gibson** *[1990] 2 QB 619. Should being offensive, rather than obscene, be a crime?*

■ McGlynn C. and Rackley E., 'Criminalising extreme pornography: a lost opportunity' [2009] Crim LR 245.

The authors discuss the criminalizing of 'extreme pornography' in the **Criminal Justice and Immigration Act 2008**. *First, they consider the law in the* **Obscene Publications Act 1959** *and then assess the changes made in the more recent Act. Their view is that the law fails to distinguish what is merely offensive from harmful sexual violence.*

■ Miller C.J., 'The Contempt of Court Act 1981' [1982] Crim LR 71.

The author gives a detailed account of the then new Act and explains how it was passed partly to deal with the liberalization of contempt law by the European Court of Human Rights in **Sunday Times v UK (1979)** *2 EHRR 245. In the same volume, there is also a case note on* **Attorney-General v English** *[1983] 1 AC 116 at 744.*

■ Moreham N.A., 'Privacy in the common law: a doctrinal and theoretical approach' (2005) 121 LQR 628.

This article looks at **Campbell v Mirror Group Newspapers** *[2004] 2 AC 457, which developed the idea of an actionable right of privacy. The author considers what has to be proved and how effective the remedy is.*

■ Palmer S., 'Tightening secrecy law' [1990] Public Law 243.

This is an overview of the **Official Secrets Act 1989**, *which looks at the categories of information protected by the Act, what the prosecution must prove, and the lack of a public interest defence. The Act was passed partly as a reaction to the* **Spycatcher** *cases, so this article explains how the Act tries to prevent members of the Secret Services from revealing information.*

■ Thomas R., 'The British Official Secrets Acts 1911-1939 and the Ponting case'. [1986] Crim LR 491.

This article considers the fate of Clive Ponting and other 'whistle-blowers' under official secrets legislation and how the interests of the state are defined.

 ## Online Resources   www.oup.com/uk/qanda/

Go online for extra essay and problem questions, a glossary of key terms, online versions of all the answer plans and audio commentary on how selected ones were put together, and a range of podcasts which include advice on exam and coursework technique and advice for other assessment methods.

Administrative law: judicial review

10

ARE YOU READY?

The questions in this chapter are an essay on the development of administrative law, a problem on procedural *ultra vires*, a problem on breach of natural justice, a problem on substantive *ultra vires*, and an essay on the procedure to apply for judicial review. In order to attempt these questions, you need to have covered all of the following topics in your work and your revision:

● understanding how judicial review developed out of the ancient prerogative writs system and the remedies that a court may award in a judicial review;

● understanding the procedure by which an applicant applies to court for a judicial review;

● understanding the different bases of judicial review, which can be summarized under the next four bullet points, as suggested in *Council of Civil Service Unions v Minister for Civil Service* [1985] AC 374 (GCHQ case);

● understanding 'illegality', which includes substantive *ultra vires*, the fettering of discretion, and misuse of powers;

● understanding 'irrationality', which includes the older concept of '*Wednesbury* unreasonableness';

● understanding 'procedural impropriety', which includes procedural *ultra vires*, breach of natural justice, and breach of legitimate expectation;

● understanding 'proportionality' and breaches of the **Human Rights Act 1998**.

KEY DEBATES

Debate: Executive versus the Judiciary

There has been a considerable expansion in the use of judicial review to challenge government decisions, particularly since the **Senior Courts Act 1981** and the **Human Rights Act 1998**. Are unelected judges now taking the sort of economic, social, and political decisions that should be taken by the elected House of Commons? The government thinks that too many frivolous applications for judicial review are being brought and has attempted to limit this in the **Criminal Justice and Courts Act 2015**. Is this really an attempt to stifle legitimate claims?

Debate: The Expansion of Judicial Review

Traditional concepts of judicial review, such as *Wednesbury* reasonableness, have been expanded. The same could be said for the ancient concept of breach of natural justice. This has been extended to include a right to be consulted and a duty to give reasons for decisions. New concepts have been developed in judicial review, such as breach of legitimate expectation, proportionality, and mistake of fact.

QUESTION | 1

The twentieth century saw both the decline of administrative law to virtual extinction, and its revival and development to unprecedented heights.

Why has the development of administrative law been so erratic?

CAUTION!

- Judicial review is not like an ordinary civil court case, where a claimant sues a defendant to gain compensation (damages).

- The claimant is trying to prove that a public body has exceeded its legal powers and to get the court to order the public body to stop doing this.

- The idea of administrative law is not just to provide a remedy for the claimant, but to provide better government, by restraining public bodies.

- The courts did not want to do this in the first half of the twentieth century, but have since changed their minds. Treat older case law with caution.

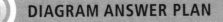

DIAGRAM ANSWER PLAN

Historical development; the prerogative remedies

▼

The development of *ultra vires* and breach of natural justice in the nineteenth century

▼

The revival of judicial review in the 1960s: concern for individual rights

▼

The **Senior Courts Act 1981** and judicial review

▼

The **Human Rights Act 1998**

Conclusion—the **Criminal Justice and Courts Act 2015** and the future

SUGGESTED ANSWER

The history of English administrative law can be traced back through many centuries. The prerogative writs of certiorari, prohibition, and mandamus were originally developed in the Middle Ages, but first came to prominence with the growth of a more effective administrative system under the Tudors. The seventeenth century sees the first precedents concerning the rules of natural justice (**Baggs case (1615) 11 Co Rep 93b**) and the doctrine of *ultra vires* (**Hetley v Boyer (1614) Cro Jac 336**).

It was during the nineteenth century that something approaching a system of administrative law was established, in the wake of the Victorian reforms of central and local government, and official intervention in such areas as health, factory conditions, and sanitation. The courts were able to use the old prerogative remedies against the new administrative authorities, and to develop and refine the concepts of natural justice and *ultra vires*, in cases like **Cooper v Wandsworth Board of Works (1863) 14 CB (NS) 180**. Maitland pointed out in 1888 that half the reported cases in the Queen's Bench Division dealt with aspects of administrative law. New remedies also became available; in **Dyson v Attorney-General [1911] 1 KB 410**, the Court of Appeal confirmed that a declaration could be granted to a person who wished to establish the unlawfulness of administrative action.

[1] A concise summary of 100 years of legal development.

By the beginning of the twentieth century, it seemed that English law was well on the way to developing a comprehensive and effective system of administrative law.[1]

But during the next 50 years this promising development was halted; in some respects the law went into reverse. One of the main factors was a conceptual problem about judicial and administrative decisions. Until the nineteenth-century reforms, much local administration was conducted through the justices of the peace, and it was natural to describe their power as judicial and their decisions as judicial, whether they were convicting a thief or allocating poor relief. The availability of the prerogative remedies of certiorari and prohibition were also described as being dependent on the decision challenged being judicial. This presented no problems as long as the courts were willing to define decisions as judicial whenever they affected individual rights. But, during the 1920s and 1930s the courts started to distinguish between judicial and administrative decisions more strictly, confining the definition of judicial decisions to those where Parliament had imposed some kind of judicialized procedure.

[2] Administrative law changes. Be careful with old cases.

As a consequence, the rules of natural justice were no longer applied to decisions affecting individual rights where these were classified as administrative: see *R v Metropolitan Police Commissioner ex parte Parker* [1953] 1WLR 1150.[2]

Over the same period, the courts showed some antipathy to the very idea of administrative law, perhaps under the influence of A.V. Dicey, who was critical of the French idea of a special body of rules governing the conduct of the administration, assuming that it would give them too much protection. The term *'droit administratif'* was used almost as a term of abuse! Perhaps as a further effect of this, academic lawyers paid little heed to the subject, and it was not taught except as a minor part of constitutional law.

What was perhaps most unfortunate in these developments was that the courts abdicated their responsibility for protecting the rights of the individual at the very time when the government's activities put those rights most at risk. A notorious example is the case of *Liversidge v Anderson* [1942] AC 206, where the Secretary of State had the power to detain persons without trial if he had reasonable cause to believe them to be of hostile origin or associations, a power justifiable enough in wartime. But the House of Lords, with the honourable exception of Lord Atkin, held that the reasonableness of the Secretary of State's belief was not reviewable, turning an objective power into a wholly subjective one.

[3] *Liversidge* and *Duncan* are famous cases supporting the argument in this paragraph.

A similarly unfortunate ruling was made in *Duncan v Cammell Laird* [1942] AC 624, when the House of Lords held that the Crown had an absolute and unreviewable privilege to withhold documents in litigation if ministers felt it was in the public interest to do so.[3]

The courts' attitude was not surprising in wartime, but even after the war the courts remained very reluctant to interfere in the work of the administration in any way. In *Franklin v Minister of Town and Country Planning* [1948] AC 87, the House of Lords refused to apply the rule against bias to an administrative decision taken by a minister, even where Parliament had imposed a quasi-judicial process. In *Smith v East Elloe RDC* [1956] AC 736, the House of Lords accepted as effective a clause excluding judicial review, even where bad faith was alleged. A rare exception was *R v Northumberland Compensation Appeal Tribunal ex parte Shaw* [1952] 1 KB 338, where the Court of Appeal revived the doctrine of error of law on the face of the record after a century of disuse, as a means of controlling the increasing numbers of statutory tribunals.[4]

[4] Further case law evidence builds up the argument.

Overall, anyone surveying the condition of administrative law in the early 1960s would have found a depressing sight. Natural justice was restricted, discretionary power not subject to judicial control, and remedies constrained by ancient rules and obscurities. As a consequence, few applicants considered the risks of litigation to be worthwhile, causing the law to fall yet further into decline.

To the surprise of many, the English courts showed themselves to be capable of reviving this moribund area of law. In *Ridge v Baldwin* [1964] AC 40, the House of Lords attacked the dichotomy of judicial and administrative decisions, restoring the rule that decisions affecting the rights of subjects were subject to natural justice, even if Parliament was silent on the need for a hearing. This was followed by a stream of cases, extending the right to a fair hearing even into areas that had always been characterized as administrative. Other precedents were reversed. In *Conway v Rimmer* [1968] AC 910, the House of Lords removed the Crown's power to withhold documents in litigation, replacing it with the power of the court to grant public interest immunity. In *Anisminic v Foreign Compensation Commission* [1969] 2 AC 147, the House of Lords found a way of defeating the express exclusion clause that had been held effective in *Smith v East Elloe RDC*, and in so doing extended the courts' powers to review errors of law. In *Padfield v Minister of Agriculture* [1968] AC 997, the House of Lords rejected the idea of the unfettered and unreviewable administrative discretion.[5]

[5] Another line of cases is used to support the opposite argument.

Why did the courts change the law so radically and so unexpectedly? One important factor was certainly a change in judicial personnel, with judges used to Diceyan orthodoxy being replaced by others with a less restricted outlook. One of the most influential was Lord Reid, who came to the House of Lords from Scotland, where administrative law had never fallen to such a low ebb. Lord Denning also played a significant part, as he did in so many branches of the law. Throughout the 1970s, administrative law continued to develop. Within a few years, a new body of precedents had been built up, and cases decided between 1910 and 1960 are almost always viewed with suspicion. To consolidate this new law, procedural reforms were introduced on the advice of the Law Commission and the process was given the now well-known name of judicial review in 1977: see **s. 31 of the Senior Courts Act 1981**. This gave the courts further impetus to develop the law and a couple of landmark decisions followed. The House of Lords declared in *O'Reilly v Mackman* [1983] **2 AC 237** that the judicial review procedure must be used for matters of public law. Then the Lords attempted to summarize the main bases of judicial review in *Council for Civil Service Unions v Minister for the Civil Service* [1985] AC 374 as illegality, irrationality, and procedural impropriety, and also foretold that proportionality would one day be added as a ground of judicial review.[6]

[6] These two cases are really important, even today.

Proportionality came to be accepted after the **Human Rights Act 1998** added breach of human rights as another way in which judicial review could be obtained. As explained by Lord Hoffmann in *Secretary for the Home Department v Nasseri* [2010] 1 AC I, judicial review now extends beyond merely considering whether the decision-making process was correct, to whether the decision itself was right or wrong.[7]

[7] Contrasting the old approach with the new.

This has proved controversial and sometimes brought the courts into conflict with government. There has been a huge increase in the number of applications for judicial review, from 160 in 1974 to 15,700 in 2013. It is fair to say, though, that the success rate is quite low. Only a couple of hundred applications each year would actually succeed.[8] The government considers this a waste of public money, hence, the **Criminal Justice and Courts Act 2015** makes it more expensive to apply for judicial review. The courts, however, do not take kindly to attempts to make access to justice too expensive. In *R (Unison) v Lord Chancellor* [2017] UKSC 51, it was held that a large increase in fees to use employment tribunals was unlawful.

[8] Statistics can be used in a law essay.

These 'reforms' were vigorously opposed by most lawyers and judges, who considered that the government was really motivated by a desire to protect itself from legal challenge. The 2015 Act has not had much effect and the courts have continued to develop judicial review to protect individual rights.[9]

[9] A speculative conclusion is acceptable in an essay like this.

➕ LOOKING FOR EXTRA MARKS?

- If you know anything about foreign systems of administrative law include them for comparison; for example, the essay mentions the French system of *'droit administratif'*.

- Lord Denning played a key role in developing the modern system of administrative law. Look for some of his cases.

- As you can see from the final paragraphs, this area of law is still developing. Keep up to date.

Q ▸ QUESTION | 2

Under the (imaginary) Radiation Protection Act 1993, any person wishing to use radioactive materials must obtain a licence from the Radiation Protection Agency (RPA). On receipt of an application, the RPA must consult any organization that it considers to be representative of those affected, and must publish notice of the application in the national and local press, and in any other way it considers desirable. The RPA must allow three months for the submission of comments and objections, which should include the name and address of the sender. After considering all representations submitted to it, and giving the applicant a hearing, the RPA may grant or refuse a licence.

Sulphurous Chemical plc applied for a licence to use radioactive materials in its factory in Coketown. The RPA published notice of the application in three national and two local newspapers, and put up a small notice in the Coketown public library. The RPA wrote to the Coketown Borough Council and the Cokeshire County Council asking for comments. It received a reply only from the Coketown Borough Council. The RPA made no attempt to consult the National Union of Chemical Workers, which represented the majority of Sulphurous Chemical's employees.

The RPA received many objections, including several from an unknown and unidentified group calling itself the Green Anti-Nuclear Faction; the RPA threw these away. A petition signed by 25,000 inhabitants of Coketown was presented the day after the three-month submission period had expired, but the RPA refused to accept it.

After completing its consideration and giving Sulphurous Chemical a hearing, the RPA granted the licence.

Consider the validity of the licence.

! ▸ CAUTION!

- Usually problem questions on judicial review focus on a particular area of judicial review, so do not just describe the whole of judicial review.

- The theme of this question is procedural *ultra vires*, in particular, consultation requirements. Concentrate on that.

- Concentrate on substantive law, rather than court procedure.

DIAGRAM ANSWER PLAN

Identify the issues	■ Identify the legal issues: Is the consultation requirement mandatory or directory? What does proper consultation require? What remedy might be awarded?
Relevant law	■ Outline the relevant law: statutory, general principles and case law, in particular: *O'Reilly v Mackman; Agricultural, Horticultural and Forestry Training Board v Aylesbury Mushrooms Ltd; R v Secretary of State for the Environment ex parte Greenpeace; R v Inland Revenue Commissioners ex parte National Federation of Self-employed & Small Businesses*; s. 31 of the Senior Courts Act 1981
Apply the law	■ Consultation is mandatory ■ There has not been adequate consultation ■ Applicants have *locus standi*
Conclude	■ A successful application for judicial review is likely ■ Conclusion—quashing order or declaration

A SUGGESTED ANSWER

The validity of this licence can be challenged by judicial review, because, as laid down in *O'Reilly v Mackman* **[1983] 2 AC 237**, it concerns the activities of a public body in matters relating to public law. The grounds of challenge mostly concern procedural defects in the way the RPA dealt with the application.[1]

In dealing with procedural defects, the courts have to balance the need to ensure that statutory procedural safeguards are carefully observed against the risk that trivial procedural defects are used as a pretext by objectors seeking to halt or delay an unpopular scheme. To do this, the courts have generally drawn a distinction between mandatory and directory procedural requirements. A mandatory requirement is one that is regarded as so essential that failure to observe it justifies treating the decision reached as invalid. A directory requirement is one whose non-observance will not invalidate the decision. In *London & Clydeside Estates v Aberdeen District Council* **[1980] 1WLR 182**, Lord Hailsham LC suggested that these two categories should not be

[1] A concise introduction.

regarded as the only two alternatives, but as the extremes of a range of possibilities. An example of a more subtle approach can be found in *Coney v Choyce* [1975] 1WLR 422, where various detailed publication requirements were only partially complied with. The court held that it was mandatory for there to be substantial compliance with the requirement of publication, but that the exact details were merely directory.It is possible for statute to specify the precise consequences of failure to comply with procedural requirements, but in practice this rarely occurs. It is therefore left to the courts to decide retrospectively whether the failure has invalidated the decision. This area of the law is criticized as uncertain, but some guidance may be obtained from decided cases.[2]

[2] A lengthy comparison of mandatory/directory follows. It is the core of the answer.

The RPA is required by the Act to publish notice of the application 'in the national and local press'. They published it in three national and two local newspapers. In *Bradbury v Enfield London Borough Council* [1967] 1WLR 1311, the court held that giving notice was to be construed as a mandatory requirement as it was essential for the protection of the rights of the individual citizen. But in that case there was a complete failure to give notice. In *Coney v Choyce*, substantial compliance was held to be sufficient. It could be argued here that there has been substantial compliance. The size of the petition is evidence that there was widespread awareness of the application. In *Coney v Choyce*, it was considered material that all those affected had become aware of the proposal in spite of the defects in the publication. The RPA is given discretion to publicize the application 'in any other way it considers desirable'. It could be argued that one small notice in the library is not sufficient. But any challenge would have to be on the ground of '*Wednesbury*' unreasonableness: see *Associated Provincial Picture Houses v Wednesbury Corporation* [1948] 1 KB 223. It is unlikely that the courts would consider this to be beyond the limits of a reasonable exercise of discretion.[3]

[3] *Coney v Choyce* is applied to the facts and a conclusion is reached.

The RPA is required to consult 'organisations that it considers to be representative of those affected'. Consultation is generally held to be a mandatory requirement, as it is a means of protecting the interests of those affected: see *R v Secretary of State for the Environment ex parte Association of Metropolitan Authorities* [1986] 1 WLR 1. The consultation of the Coketown Borough Council seems to have been satisfactory. But in *Agricultural, Horticultural and Forestry Training Board v Aylesbury Mushrooms Ltd* [1972] 1 WLR 190, sending a letter that went astray, and failing to make further inquiries was held not to amount to adequate consultation. If the RPA has made no attempt to follow up its letter to the Cokeshire County Council and check that it indeed has no comment to make, it will be considered to have broken a mandatory requirement.[4] As this is a

[4] *Aylesbury Mushrooms* is applied to the facts and a conclusion is reached.

licence application to use radioactive materials, in fairness the RPA should disclose the scientific information on which their decision is based to the groups consulted: *R v Health Secretary ex parte US Tobacco International Inc* [1992] QB 353 and *R (Eisai) v National Institute for Health and Clinical Excellence* [2008] EWCA Civ 438.

The Supreme Court reminded us in *R (Moseley) v London Borough of Haringey* [2014] UKSC 56 that a consultation must be genuine. It is not acceptable to pretend to consult when the decision has already been made. The RPA must show that it had not already decided to award the licence, but was willing to listen to the views of those who wanted the application rejected.

The RPA's failure to consult the National Union of Chemical Workers could be challenged as an unreasonable use of discretion, as in *Secretary of State for Education v Metropolitan Borough of Tameside* [1977] AC 1014; no reasonable authority could have failed to consider the union representative of those affected.[5]

[5] Steadily, case law builds up a strong case for the applicants.

The RPA is required to consider 'all representations submitted to it', but it throws away the objections from the Green Anti-Nuclear Faction. The only possible justification for this is the provision in the Act that objections should include the name and address of the sender. This requirement could be classed as mandatory if it is essential for the conduct of the administration. In *Chapman v Earl* [1968] 1 WLR 1315, the failure of a tenant to indicate the proposed rent in an application to a rent tribunal was held to be a breach of a mandatory requirement. However, requirements imposed merely for the convenience of the administration are likely to be classified as directory only. In *Jackson Developments v Hall* [1951] 2 KB 488, the requirement that the tenant supply the landlord's name to a rent tribunal was held to be directory. In this problem, the objectors' failure to identify themselves hardly seems of sufficient importance to be treated as breach of a mandatory requirement. Their objections should therefore have been considered.[6]

[6] Another conclusion is reached.

The petition is rejected because it is submitted one day late. Time limits will be held to be mandatory where they are essential in establishing legal rights and obligations. In *Howard v Secretary of State for the Environment* [1975] QB 235, the statutory time limit of 42 days for appealing against an enforcement notice was held to be mandatory because it determined the legal powers of the local authority. But if no such compelling reasons exist, time limits will be treated as directory. In *James v Minister of Housing and Local Government* [1966] 1 WLR 135, a local authority was held to be entitled to make a planning decision after three months, though regulations imposed

[7] Another conclusion.

a limit of two months. In this problem, as the RPA will be spending some time considering the application, there seems no reason to treat the time limit for receipt of representations as mandatory.[7]

An application for judicial review to challenge the validity of the licence under **s. 31 of the Senior Courts Act 1981** and **Part 54 of the Civil Procedure Rules** could be made by any person with *locus standi*, that is, with a sufficient interest in the matter. Cokeshire County Council and the National Union of Chemical Workers would clearly have a sufficient interest, as would members of the Green Anti-Nuclear Faction, if willing to identify themselves.[8] In *R v Secretary of State for the Environment ex parte Greenpeace* **[1994] 4 All ER 352**, Greenpeace was held to have *locus standi*, as a pressure group with local members, to challenge the licensing of the THORP nuclear plant. It could further be argued that any of the inhabitants of Coketown who had signed the petition would have *locus standi*. In *R v Inland Revenue Commissioners ex parte National Federation of Self-employed & Small Businesses* **[1982] AC 617**, Lord Diplock referred to the desirability of 'a single public-spirited taxpayer' being able to challenge the validity of unlawful administrative action.

[8] The inhabitants and GA-NF are mentioned in the facts. This is a clue to consider 'sufficient interest'.

[9] A concise conclusion.

The most appropriate remedies in this case would be a quashing order to quash the licence, or a declaration that it was invalid.[9] It would, however, be open to Sulphurous Chemical plc to make a further application for a licence.

LOOKING FOR EXTRA MARKS?

- There is a very large number of cases on judicial review. You could answer this question using a completely different set of cases.

- Unlike in other areas of law—for example, Contract—the facts of these cases are unlikely to be similar to the facts of our problem.

- You need to extract the general principle from a case, try to understand it, and apply it to the facts of our problem.

QUESTION   3

Under the (imaginary) Social Services Act 2000, all residential homes for the elderly must be licensed by the local authority. Unsatisfactory homes will be refused a licence and closed down, but there is a right to appeal against the refusal of a licence to an Appeal Tribunal.

⊙

Mrs Danvers applied to the Cokeshire County Council for a licence for the Manderley Home. The application was referred to the Social Services Committee, which instructed Rebecca, one of its employees, to investigate the suitability of the Home. Rebecca visited the Home, posing as someone looking for accommodation for an elderly relative. After completing her researches, Rebecca produced a report recommending that a licence be refused because the kitchens and bathrooms were not cleaned properly and few of the staff had the appropriate professional qualifications.

The Committee considered the report and then invited Mrs Danvers to a meeting to discuss her application. She came to the meeting accompanied by her husband, a solicitor, but he was asked to wait outside. At the meeting, she was handed a copy of Rebecca's report and asked to comment on it. She asked for an adjournment so that she could consult her husband, but the Committee refused. She denied the allegations in the report and invited the members of the Committee to visit the Home and to talk to the residents. The Committee declined to do so and, after deliberating in private, refused the licence.

Mrs Danvers appealed to the Tribunal, which gave her a hearing, but refused to hear evidence from the staff of the Home or allow her to cross-examine Rebecca, who gave evidence in person. The Tribunal confirmed the original decision. Mrs Danvers has now discovered that the wife of the Chair of the Committee is a member of the board of a charity that campaigns for better care for the elderly.

Advise Mrs Danvers.

! CAUTION!

- Identify the area of judicial review that this problem is based upon, ie breach of natural justice.
- Concentrate on breach of natural justice. Other areas of judicial review—for example, illegality and irrationality—are irrelevant.
- There are two parts of breach of natural justice. Those are the right to a fair trial and the right to an unbiased judge. Cover them both.
- Do not be put off by the length of the question. Concentrate on identifying the legal issues.

DIAGRAM ANSWER PLAN

Identify the issues	■ Identify the legal issues: the right to a fair hearing
Relevant law	■ Outline the relevant law: statutory, general principles and case law, in particular: *Ridge v Baldwin; R (Osborn) v Parole Board; R (G) v Governors of X School; R v Hull Prison Visitors ex parte St Germain; Porter v Magill*
Apply the law	■ Does natural justice apply to this type of decision? ■ Has Mrs Danvers been notified of the charges? ■ Should she be entitled to legal representation? ■ Is there a real possibility that the Tribunal was biased?
Conclude	■ Conclusion—will Mrs Danvers be able to quash the decision of the Tribunal?

A   SUGGESTED ANSWER

As Mrs Danvers has exhausted the statutory procedure, she will have to use judicial review if she wishes to challenge the refusal of a licence. Both the Council Committee and Tribunal are clearly public bodies and her grounds of challenge derive from public law, making judicial review the appropriate procedure to use. She must apply to the Administrative Court *ex parte* for permission to make an application for judicial review promptly, and in any event within three months of the Tribunal's decision. As the person directly affected by the decision, she has *locus standi*.[1]

It appears that Mrs Danvers will have grounds for arguing that there has been a breach of the rules of natural justice, but she must first establish that she was entitled to a fair hearing. In ***Ridge v Baldwin* [1964] AC 40**, it was held that natural justice applied whenever a decision affected the rights of the individual, and it was made clear in *Re HK* **[1967] 2 QB 617** that this applied even if the decision was of an administrative nature. By imposing a requirement that a licence must be obtained for an activity that could previously have been carried on without restriction, the law is affecting individual rights and so

[1] Procedural issues are dealt with swiftly. Concentrate on the substantive law.

[2] A conclusion can be reached: natural justice applies here.

a fair hearing must be given. This was applied in *R v Gaming Board ex parte Benaim* [1970] 2 QB 417 to the grant of gaming licences and is clearly applicable here.[2]

At what stage in the procedure is Mrs Danvers entitled to be heard? There is no general right to be heard during preliminary investigative or preparatory processes. In *Pearlberg v Varty* [1972] 1 WLR 534, it was held that there was no right to a hearing by the Inland Revenue as they prepared a taxpayer's assessment; he would be heard at the proper time before the relevant tribunal. It is therefore acceptable for Cokeshire County Council to conduct a covert investigation. Nor is there an objection to the matter being referred to a committee, as the **Local Government Act 1972** specifically authorizes this form of delegation. But, before any decision is made about the licence, Mrs Danvers must be given an opportunity to state her case. For this, it is necessary that she be informed of the matters that are causing concern, otherwise she cannot offer an effective defence. In *Fairmount Investments v Secretary of State for the Environment* [1976] 1 WLR 1255, a compulsory purchase decision was held to be invalid because the inspector had based his decision on defects in the building that he had noticed but had not mentioned to the parties. Here Mrs Danvers is not shown Rebecca's report in advance, or even informed of its contents. The Committee could argue that she was shown the report at the hearing, but this did not allow her any time to prepare a defence. In *R v Thames Magistrates' Court ex parte Polemis* [1974] 1 WLR 1371, it was held that it was a breach of the rules of natural justice to serve a summons on a defendant in the morning and try him that afternoon as he had no chance to prepare a

[3] A detailed analysis of the case law leads to the conclusion that there has been a breach of natural justice.

defence. It therefore appears that there has been a breach of the rules of natural justice.[3]

Mrs Danvers was refused permission to be accompanied by or to consult her husband, who was presumably also her legal adviser. The traditional rules of natural justice do not lay down any hard-and-fast rules on what is required for a fair hearing; it all depends on the circumstances. The Supreme Court stressed the need for procedural fairness, which would often require an oral hearing with the ability to question witnesses in *R (Osborn) v Parole Board* [2013] UKSC 61. This would be necessary where important facts were in dispute and should not be denied because it would save the Council time, trouble, and expense.

In *R (G) v Governors of X School* [2012] 1AC 167, a teaching assistant was dismissed by the disciplinary committee of his school, who did not allow him to be represented by his solicitor. The decision on whether he could continue teaching would be taken by the Independent Safeguarding Authority (ISA), where he could be represented. The Supreme Court said that the question was whether the first disciplinary hearing would determine the result of the ISA hearing, or at least have 'a major influence on the outcome'. The answer in G's case was no, as the ISA would give him a complete rehearing looking at all the available evidence, listening to representations, and coming to their own decision, irrespective of what was decided by the disciplinary committee of the school governors. Even though Mrs Danvers had two hearings, it does not look as though she received a fair hearing. At the Committee hearing she is not allowed legal representation, but neither the Committee nor the Tribunal is willing to hear all the evidence by listening to the witnesses. The Committee is obliged to hear all relevant evidence: see *R v Hull Prison Visitors ex parte St Germain (No. 2)* [1979] 1 WLR 1401. As to Rebecca's evidence at the Tribunal, there is no absolute right to cross-examine, as is made clear by *R (G) v Governors of X School* [2012] 1AC 167. However, if the allegation has serious consequences for the accused person, as it does for Mrs Danvers, and, in effect, Rebecca is giving evidence against her, the right to cross-examine is appropriate: *R v Hull Prison Visitors ex parte St Germain (No. 2)* [1979] 1 WLR 1401. We need to consider the cumulative effect of the two hearings, as neither seem decisive, but, taken together, the two hearings do not seem to be fair: *Lloyd v McMahon* [1987] AC 625.[4]

[4] The case law here must be closely analysed.

The final substantive issue is the allegation that one member of the Tribunal was biased. It is clear that the presence of one biased person is enough to invalidate a decision. A breach of natural justice could involve several forms of bias, which are conveniently subdivided into 'actual bias' and 'apparent bias', according to the House of Lords in *R v Abdroikov* [2008] 1 All ER 315. Actual bias leads to automatic disqualification and includes: a financial interest in the decision, as in *Dimes v Grand Junction Canal Co* (1852) 3 HLC 759; the decision-makers have already decided the matter before the hearing, as in *Eszias v North Glamorgan NHS Trust* [2007] 4 All ER 940; or direct association with a party to the case, as in *Ex parte Pinochet* [1999] 1 All ER 577. The last two seem the more likely on the facts here, but neither seem strong enough to invalidate the decision of the Tribunal.[5] For other, more indirect, forms of 'apparent bias', the courts have formulated various tests, such as looking for a 'real likelihood' or 'reasonable suspicion' of bias. In *Porter v Magill* [2002] 1 All ER 465, the House of Lords formulated a general test for bias as follows:

[5] Not all the case law helps Mrs Danvers.

whether the fair-minded and informed observer, having considered the facts, would conclude that there was a real possibility that the Tribunal was biased.

This was confirmed as the correct approach in the Privy Council case of *Yiacoub v The Queen* [2014] UKPC 22.

[6] The 'judge' does not seem to be biased.

Can it be argued that there is such a real possibility here? It is doubtful; the Tribunal's very existence is in order to improve the care of the elderly, and there is nothing in the background of the Chair of the Tribunal to indicate any connection with or prejudice against Mrs Danvers.[6]

[7] But Mrs Danvers has not had a fair hearing.

Nevertheless, Mrs Danvers was not allowed to properly argue her case, so she should succeed on the first aspect of natural justice and be successful in her judicial review application.[7] The most appropriate remedy would be a quashing order to quash the decisions of the Committee and Tribunal, though a declaration would also be a possibility. She could, in addition, ask for a mandatory order to compel them to reconsider her application. The award of remedies is at the discretion of the court, but there seems no reason why the court should decline

[8] An important point on how judicial review works.

to give redress. However, the court's decision will not necessarily mean that Mrs Danvers will obtain the licence that she seeks.[8] That decision will be made by the Committee and the Tribunal and will be based, as it should be, on the suitability of the home that she runs.

LOOKING FOR EXTRA MARKS?

- There are new breach of natural justice cases all the time. Look out for them.

- Natural justice is not as simple as it looks. What is a fair hearing depends a lot on the circumstances. The same goes for the right to an unbiased judge.

- Identify the cases most relevant to these facts and try to analyse what those cases are really saying.

Q   **QUESTION   4**

As a result of local elections, the Radical Party has taken control of the Coketown District Council. It has implemented the following changes and wishes to know whether there could be any legal challenge to them. It also wishes to know who could make such a challenge and by what legal process.

a   to revoke, with immediate effect, the licences given to Able (A), Baker (B), and Charlie (C) to sell ice-cream from their vans in council-owned parks;

b   to refuse to give any more discretionary grants for the insulation of homes;

c   to save money by closing the three old people's homes that it runs and instead paying privately run old people's homes to house these old people;

d   to licence no more taxis in Coketown, because 300 taxis are too many. (In fact, there are only 250 taxis in Coketown.)

Advise.

! CAUTION!

- In a multi-part problem, make sure that you answer all the parts.
- Concentrate on which part of judicial review is being asked about in each section.
- Part (a) is about breach of natural justice and proportionality.
- Part (b) is about fettering of discretion.
- Part (c) is about legitimate expectation.
- Part (d) is about irrationality or reasonableness and mistake of fact.

O DIAGRAM ANSWER PLAN

Identify the issues
- Identify the legal issues: breach of natural justice and proportionality; fettering of discretion; legitimate expectation; irrationality; and mistake of fact

Relevant law
- Outline the relevant law: statutory, general principles and case law, in particular: *Ridge v Baldwin; R (Daly) v Home Secretary; Attorney-General ex rel Tilley v Wansdworth; British Oxygen v Board of Trade; R v North Devon Health Authority ex parte Coughlan; Mandalia v Secretary of State for the Home Department; Associated Provincial Picture Houses v Wednesbury; R v Home Secretary ex parte Doody; R v Criminal Injuries Compensation Board ex parte Lain*

Apply the law
- The right to a hearing and proportionality
- A policy may be adopted, but individual applications must be considered
- When should a public body consult those affected by its decisions?
- The obligation to give reasons for a decision and decisions based on incorrect facts

Conclude
- Conclusion—the applicants in (a), (b), and (d) are likely to succeed, but not in (c)

Because the Council is a public body, its decisions can be challenged by way of judicial review. Any person who has a sufficient interest will be able to bring a case on the grounds characterized by Lord Diplock as illegality, irrationality, and procedural impropriety: *Council for Civil Service Unions v Minister for the Civil Service* **[1985] AC 374 (GCHQ case)**. Such a person must apply to the Administrative Court for permission to make an application for judicial review within the three-month time limit. If permission is granted, the case will proceed to a full hearing.[1]

[1]In a multi-part question, deal with common issues first.

(a) No information is given about the grounds on which the Council has acted, but it is clear from the facts given that the way the decision was made is open to challenge. A, B, and C, as licence holders, have rights, and under the general principle laid down in *Ridge v Baldwin* **[1964] AC 40** decisions affecting the rights of individuals must be made in accordance with the rules of natural justice. Indeed, it was specifically held in *R v Wear Valley DC ex parte Binks* **[1985] 2 All ER 699** that contractual as well as statutory licences were protected. It therefore appears that if the revocation of the licences was not preceded by an opportunity for A, B, and C to state their cases, it can be challenged. It has been held, however, that in situations of extreme urgency a decision can be made before any hearing is given. In *R v Secretary of State for Transport ex parte Pegasus* **[1989] 2 All ER 481**, it was held that an air charter company's licence could be revoked with immediate effect because of fears over public safety. If the Council's decision in this problem was provoked by, for example, fears that the ice-cream posed a threat to public health, there would be no breach of natural justice, provided a proper hearing was given at a later stage.[2]

[2]A conclusion can be reached.

Nowadays, the court might also consider the issue of proportionality when a person's livelihood is at stake. 'Proportionality' has been defined in *R (Daly) v Home Secretary* **[2001] 3 All ER 433** as that there has to be a lawful reason to restrict the fundamental right and the means used are no more than necessary to achieve the objective. So Coketown District Council would have to prove that there really was a public health problem and that there was no other way of dealing with it, short of shutting down the businesses of A, B, and C. In an early case, *R v Barnsley MBC ex parte Hook* **[1976] 1 WLR 1052**, Lord Denning MR quashed the council's decision to revoke the licence of a market trader who had urinated in the street. The punishment was out of all proportion to the crime. A, B, and C clearly have *locus standi* as the persons directly affected by the decision and are likely to seek

[3]This summarizes A, B, and C's case.

either a quashing order to quash the Council's decision or a declaration that it is invalid.[3]

(b) The Council appears to have a discretion to make these grants. It is entitled to adopt general policies to guide it in allocating such grants, but that does not permit it to adopt a rule and refuse to depart from it. In *R v London County Council ex parte Corrie* **[1918] 1 KB 68**, the Council was held to have acted *ultra vires* in adopting a rule against the sale of pamphlets in parks and refusing even to consider making an exception to it.[4] In *Attorney-General ex rel Tilley v Wandsworth LBC* **[1981] 1 WLR 854**, the court declared invalid a council's decision never to use a statutory power to rehouse homeless families with children.

[4]This may be an old case, but it is still relevant.

There is, however, nothing unlawful in the adoption of a policy, provided that consideration is given to each individual case. In *British Oxygen v Board of Trade* **[1971] AC 610**, a decision to refuse the applicant an investment grant, in accordance with a stated policy, was held to be valid, because consideration had been given to the individual application. The easiest way to demonstrate that individual cases are considered is to offer applicants an opportunity to state their case either orally or in writing. The Council would therefore be well advised to adopt a procedure that shows its willingness to consider applications; it can then lawfully reject any applications that it does not feel justify a departure from its policy.

If the Council does not do so, its decision could be challenged by anyone who has applied for a grant and been rejected. Such an applicant could ask for a declaration that the Council was acting unlawfully or a mandatory order to compel them to consider the application again.[5] It will remain within the Council's discretion, however, whether any particular grant is made or not.

[5]A conclusion for part (b).

(c) This situation seems to resemble *R v North Devon Health Authority ex parte Coughlan* **[2001] QB 213**. In 1993, North Devon moved Coughlan and other geriatric patients into a new home and assured them that this could be their home for life. However, in 1998, North Devon decided to close the home and move the residents into local authority care. The court held that North Devon could not go back on its promise to the residents, as they now had a 'legitimate expectation' that they could stay and it would be an abuse of power to break the promise. This case seems to do justice, but as a precedent it has caused problems for public authorities, who often need to change their policies, particularly if the financial situation changes. *R (Bibi) v Newham Borough Council* **[2002] 1 WLR 237** is a comparable case, where Newham had told some refugees that it would place them in permanent, secure accommodation, because Newham had thought that they were under a legal obligation to do so. This turned out not to be the case, but the court still ruled that a legitimate expectation had been raised. The law has been further developed in *Mandalia v Home Secretary* [2015] UKSC 59. There need no longer be any promises made to individuals. Instead, a public authority should not depart from a published policy, unless it can prove that there is good reason to do so. Our facts do not reveal that Coketown District Council have made any specific promises to any of the residents of the old people's homes or published any policy that the homes will remain open. In conclusion, if there was a challenge to the closure by one or more of the residents, it is likely that it would fail.[6]

[6] The conclusion can be that the claimants have no case.

(d) This final decision could be challenged on three grounds. First, it is based on facts that are clearly incorrect, so it could be suggested that the decision is unreasonable or irrational, within the strict test laid down by Lord Greene in *Associated Provincial Picture Houses v Wednesbury Corporation* [1948] 1KB 223, at 229: 'something so absurd that no sensible person could ever dream that it lay within the powers of the authority'.[7]

[7] There are three distinct arguments here. Clearly identify each of them; this is argument 1.

Secondly, there is a breach of natural justice. Although there is no general duty in administrative law to give reasons for a decision, fairness would probably require that the Council gave some kind of explanation for their decision to the local taxi drivers: *R v Home Secretary ex parte Doody* [1994] 1 AC 531. The taxi drivers should be given an opportunity to respond and make their own representations before a final decision is taken: *Re Liverpool Taxi Fleet Operators' Association* [1972] 2 QB 299.[8]

[8] This is argument 2.

Thirdly, although judicial review is not an appeal against a finding of fact and usually only involves legal mistakes made by public bodies, a new head of challenge has recently emerged, that of mistake of fact. A decision cannot be based on facts that can be shown to be incorrect, are material to the decision, and cause unfairness. It is the Council that is mistaken about the number of taxis and there is no error or misleading on the part of the taxi drivers themselves.[9] These principles were laid down by the House of Lords in *R v Criminal Injuries Compensation Board ex parte A* [1999] 2 AC 330, where the Board did not see a vital doctor's report. Mistake of fact was further developed in *E v Secretary of State for the Home Department* [2004] QB 1044, where a tribunal did not consider relevant new evidence, and was upheld in *R (March) v Secretary of State for Health* [2010] Med LR 271, where the government minister was mistaken as to the true facts of the case.

[9] This is argument 3.

The taxi drivers have a good case. The Council decision could be

[10]Conclusion for part (d).

held unlawful by a declaration. Then Coketown would have to take their decision again, based on the correct number of taxis and giving the taxi drivers the opportunity to make representations.[10]

+ LOOKING FOR EXTRA MARKS?

- Each part of the question focuses on different aspects of judicial review.
- Clearly identify that area and show the depth of your legal analysis.
- A detailed knowledge of the principles laid down by the case law is essential.
- Look for new cases in developing areas such as proportionality, breach of legitimate expectation, and mistake of fact.

Q QUESTION | 5

What are the main procedural difficulties facing someone who wishes to make an application for judicial review? Should any of the rules in this area be reformed?

! CAUTION!

- Read the question carefully. This is about the *procedure* to apply for judicial review, not the substance of the claim (the different types of *ultra vires*).
- This question is not about the court rules, but the legal tests an applicant must meet.
- So key cases are still important.

☐ DIAGRAM ANSWER PLAN

Historical origins of judicial review

▼

Only public bodies may be judicially reviewed

▼

It is no longer always necessary to use the judicial review procedure

▼

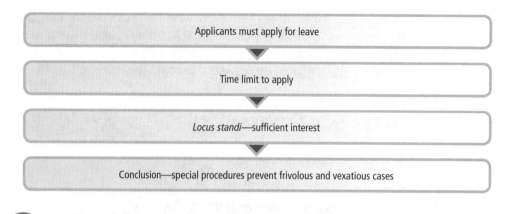

Applicants must apply for leave

Time limit to apply

Locus standi—sufficient interest

Conclusion—special procedures prevent frivolous and vexatious cases

A SUGGESTED ANSWER

From the earliest times when the courts developed the prerogative writs, there have been special procedures for obtaining judicial review, which have differed from those used in ordinary civil proceedings. Generally, such procedures have made it more difficult to seek judicial review, because they have been imposed to protect public authorities. Whether the retention of special procedures can be justified has been widely debated.[1] Some changes to the rules have been made, but other aspects remain problematic.

An applicant who is thinking of seeking judicial review must first of all be sure that judicial review is the appropriate procedure to use. The defendant must be a public body, not a private body. But because the conceptual difference between public and private is not a traditional part of English law, this rule may be difficult to apply, and litigants have failed through using the wrong procedure. The courts have little difficulty in identifying as private those bodies whose legal authority derives only from contract, such as trade unions and sporting bodies: see *R v Disciplinary Committee of the Jockey Club ex parte Aga Khan* **[1993] 1 WLR 909**. But where bodies of uncertain status perform a public function the courts tend to classify them as public, in order to subject them to judicial review, as in *R v Panel on Takeovers and Mergers ex parte Datafin* **[1987] QB 815**. The Panel had been established by the London Stock Market to regulate company takeovers and mergers. It was not created by Act of Parliament. The view of the court was that the Panel was performing a vital public function and if it did not exist a statutory body would have had to have been created to take its place. Other non-statutory bodies, such as the Advertising Standards Authority, LAUTRO, and university visitors, have also been confirmed as public bodies and therefore subject to judicial review. If this was not so, it would be difficult to subject the decisions of these bodies to legal control.[2]

[1] The theme of the essay is introduced: can the special procedures be justified?

[2] All these propositions come from cases, but in an exam, memory and time does not permit naming them all.

In the early days of the new judicial review procedure, the courts were strict in insisting that if the case involved a public law matter the judicial review procedure must be used: *O'Reilly v Mackman* **[1983] 2 AC 237**. The claimant could not use ordinary High Court procedure to challenge the decision of a public body. However, since the reform of High Court procedure in 1998, the courts are much more relaxed about this, because even if a case is begun by writ in the High Court, it can be transferred to the judicial review procedure: *Clark v University of Lincolnshire and Humberside* **[2000] 1 WLR 1988**. Judicial review is not, however, suitable to decide 'potentially complex disputes of fact', particularly where these events may have happened some time ago. So the claimants in *Sher v Chief Constable of Greater Manchester* **[2011] 2 All ER 364** had to seek remedies in tort for their alleged unlawful arrest, detention, and search.[3]

[3] Judicial review is not always appropriate.

Having decided to use judicial review, applicants are faced with one of the main procedural hurdles: they cannot commence proceedings as of right, but must apply for permission (formerly leave). The defendant public authority will be informed, and then a judge in chambers will consider the papers and decide whether to grant permission. If the judge is minded to refuse, the request will be considered in open court. Why is permission needed? The justification offered is that attempts are made to seek judicial review in cases that are plainly hopeless, sometimes as a publicity stunt or as a last desperate throw of the dice. There would be a great waste of resources if public authorities had to defend all such cases at a full hearing. It should be understood that the courts regard judicial review as a last resort and would far rather the parties settle their differences without going to court, by, say, using internal or statutory complaint or disciplinary procedures, mediation, etc.: *R (Cowl) v Plymouth Council* **[2002] 1 WLR 803**. In any event, the success rate in judicial review is quite low; in a year there might be 2,500 applications, of which 1,000 would be granted leave, but less than 200 would actually succeed.[4] So **s. 50 of the Criminal Justice and Courts Act 2015** introduced a tougher test for granting leave. Leave must be refused 'if it appears to the court to be highly likely that the outcome for the applicant would not have been substantially different if the conduct complained of had not occurred'.

[4] Statistics may be used in a law essay.

Sections 88 and **89** of the same Act also increase the financial risk in applying, by reducing the use of protected costs orders, in order to discourage frivolous applications.[5]

[5] Keeping up to date impresses examiners.

The next problem for the applicant is the time limit. Application must be made promptly, and in any event within three months of the decision being challenged. This is a much shorter time limit than applies in normal civil proceedings, but it is justified by the need for the legal position of public authorities to be firmly settled at the earliest opportunity. The courts do have the power to extend the period for a good reason; in *R v Stratford on Avon DC ex parte Jackson* [1985] 1 WLR 1319, the applicant justified his delay by showing that he was waiting for a decision from the Legal Aid Board. But the court will not allow a belated application if this would cause administrative difficulties. In *R v Dairy Produce Quota Tribunal ex parte Caswell* [1990] 2 AC 738, it was too late to challenge the award of milk quotas two years after they had been allocated. The three months started to run from the beginning of a consultation process in *R (Nash) v Barnet LBC* [2013] EWCA Civ 1004. If the judicial review involves EU law, there is a fixed time limit of three months, as the European Court of Justice has rejected 'promptly' as too vague: see, for example, *R (Buglife) v Medway Council* [2011] 3 CMLR 39. Further complexity is added by the time limit for actions alleging breach of human rights being one year in s. 7(5) of the **Human Rights Act 1998**.[6]

The final issue that may cause problems for applicants is *locus standi*. When the Application for Judicial Review was introduced, *locus standi* was deliberately described in words without a previous legal meaning as a 'sufficient interest' in the matter. The meaning of this expression was discussed by the House of Lords in *R v Inland Revenue Commissioners ex parte National Federation of Self-employed and Small Businesses* [1982] AC 617. The applicants wished to challenge the validity of an agreement between the Inland Revenue Commission and Fleet Street casual workers about past and future payments of tax. Although the challenge failed on the facts, the House of Lords felt that only 'busybodies, cranks and other mischief makers' should be regarded as not having *locus standi* to seek judicial review of the actions of public authorities. Pressure groups and even 'a single public-spirited taxpayer' should be allowed to bring such cases, in order to ensure that the rule of law applies.

The effect of this decision was a general liberalization of the rules of *locus standi*. The 'single public-spirited taxpayer' has brought actions for judicial review. In *R v HM Treasury ex parte Smedley* [1985] 1 QB 657, a taxpayer challenged, albeit unsuccessfully, the UK's payment of certain sums to the European Community. The *locus standi* of pressure groups has been generally accepted, though in *R v Secretary of State for the Environment ex parte Rose Theatre Trust* [1990] 1 QB 504 the judge refused to allow a pressure group formed specifically for the purpose of saving the Rose Theatre to challenge the government's decision. Other cases have been more generous. Most striking was the decision in *R v Foreign Secretary ex parte World Development Movement* [1995] 1 WLR 386. The applicants were a respected voluntary organization whose interest in challenging the use of UK aid to fund the Pergau Dam in Malaysia was purely moral. But,

[6] Differing time limits complicate the procedure.

as the court said, if the World Development Movement did not have *locus standi*, no one would be able to challenge the decision, except people living in a remote area of Malaysia whose opportunity to take legal action in the English High Court is limited. It seems therefore that *locus standi* will not cause a problem to genuine applicants and no change to the law on this point is needed.[7]

[7] Two paragraphs are devoted to *locus standi*, but it is an important part of this essay.

In conclusion, it can be argued that although there are practical problems in bringing any type of legal action, the special rules relating to judicial review do not act as too great a hindrance to litigants. The need to obtain permission is the most contentious issue, but even this can be defended. It would be a great problem for those seeking judicial review if frivolous or vexatious cases filled the courts and caused delay to genuine applicants.[8]

[8] Conclusion—the special procedures can be justified.

LOOKING FOR EXTRA MARKS?

- Show that you understand the more difficult legal issues in this question.
- Explain the difference between a public and a private body.
- Give the meaning of sufficient interest.
- Keep up to date with the courts' reaction to the reforms of judicial review in the **Criminal Justice and Courts Act 2015**.

TAKING THINGS FURTHER

- Ahmed F. and Perry A., 'The coherence of the doctrine of legitimate expectations' (2014) 73 Cambridge Law Journal 61.
  The doctrine of legitimate expectations has been criticized as 'incoherent', but this article argues that: 'According to our rule-based account, a legitimate expectation arises when a public body binds itself with a non-legal and goal-dependent rule.' Cases that are mentioned in this chapter, such as **CCSU v Minister for the Civil Service (GCHQ)** *and* **R v North Devon Health Authority ex parte Coughlan** *are assessed.*

- Craig P., 'Judicial review, appeal and factual error' [2004] Public Law 788.
  This is one of the newer areas of judicial review and this article considers cases on this subject, including **R v Criminal Injuries Compensation Board ex parte A** *and* **E v Secretary of State for the Home Department**.

- Craig P., 'The nature of reasonableness' (2013) 66 CLP 131.
  This article also considers how far judicial review can go in reconsidering the decisions taken by public bodies. It traces the evolution of the concept of reasonableness from **Associated Picture House v Wednesbury**, *through* **CCSU v Minister for the Civil Service** *to the* **Bancoult** *cases. It attempts to provide clarification for this elusive concept.*

- Hickman J.R., 'The substance and structure of proportionality' [2008] Public Law 694.

  CCSU v Minister for the Civil Service (GCHQ) *recognized the concept of proportionality, which is well known in European law. It is argued that proportionality should be considered in a structured way and leading cases from this chapter such as* **R (Daly) v Secretary of State for the Home Department** *are considered.*

- Hilson C., 'Judicial review policies and the fettering of discretion' [2002] Public Law 111.

  Old cases, such as **Attorney-General ex rel Tilley v Wandsworth** *and* **British Oxygen v Board of Trade***, which both feature in this chapter, and new cases on this area are considered and the effect of the* **Human Rights Act 1998** *on this area is assessed.*

- Lever A., 'Is judicial review undemocratic?' [2007] Public Law 280.

  Some argue that with the expansion of judicial review the courts are taking political and social decisions that should be taken by Parliament. This paper argues that this is not so. Judicial review tends to focus on claims that may not be popular and get ignored by parliamentary democracy.

 Online Resources www.oup.com/uk/qanda/

Go online for extra essay and problem questions, a glossary of key terms, online versions of all the answer plans and audio commentary on how selected ones were put together, and a range of podcasts which include advice on exam and coursework technique and advice for other assessment methods.

Administrative law: ombudsmen, tribunals, and delegated legislation

11

ARE YOU READY?

The questions in this chapter are an essay on the work of the Parliamentary Commissioner for Administration, a problem question on the work of tribunals, and a problem question on judicial review of a statutory instrument.

KEY DEBATES

Debate: The Parliamentary Commissioner for Administration and the MP Filter

The Parliamentary Commissioner for Administration was introduced as long ago as 1967 to provide an alternative remedy to the courts or a complaint to their MP for aggrieved citizens. By all accounts it has worked quite well, and similar mechanisms have been extended to the Health Service and local government, among others. To further improve the ombudsman remedy, the Commissioner should be given the powers to investigate without the need for a reference from an MP and to enforce his/her rulings.

Debate: Improving the Tribunal System

Tribunals are the poor relations of the justice system. Few people know much about how they work and not so much is written about them, but they decide the vast majority of legal cases in this country. The problem has been how to improve the standard of justice that tribunals dispense, while not making them too expensive for the government to run or for litigants to use.

Debate: Judicial Control of Delegated Legislation

Most of the law in this country is delegated legislation, rather than Act of Parliament. Some of it is passed hurriedly with a lack of attention to detail, which might cause injustice. The courts are willing to intervene and overturn delegated legislation in a judicial review application, something the courts could not do to an Act of Parliament.

Q

QUESTION | **1**

How effective has the Parliamentary Commissioner for Administration (PCA) been in providing redress for citizens?

!

CAUTION!

- This is a straightforward essay on the jurisdiction powers and practices of the PCA.
- But you will need to be accurate on what the **Parliamentary Commissioner Act 1967** actually says.
- You will also need to know how the PCA fits in with other remedies such as complaint to an MP and judicial review.
- So you will need to know about other areas of the syllabus and how it all fits together into the constitutional system.

○

DIAGRAM ANSWER PLAN

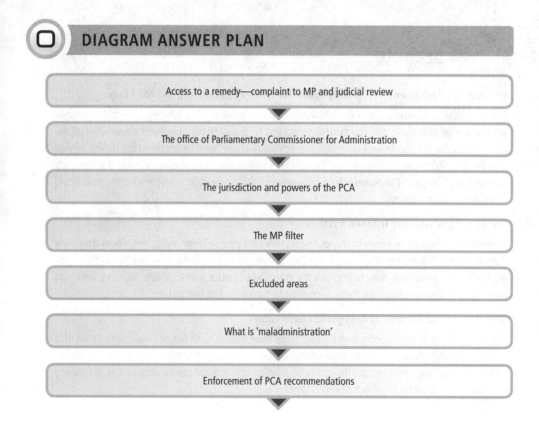

Access to a remedy—complaint to MP and judicial review

▼

The office of Parliamentary Commissioner for Administration

▼

The jurisdiction and powers of the PCA

▼

The MP filter

▼

Excluded areas

▼

What is 'maladministration'

▼

Enforcement of PCA recommendations

▼

Other ombudsmen

Conclusion—ombudsmen and the parliamentary system

A **SUGGESTED ANSWER**

Citizens are often aggrieved by something that the government does to them, but they may not have a convenient remedy. They could complain to their MP, but their MP may not have time to investigate their complaint or may not get much information from the government department or public body complained against. Going to court is expensive and time-consuming and judicial review is only available on the narrow grounds of illegality, unreasonableness, or procedural impropriety: *Council of Civil Service Unions v Minister for the Civil Service* **[1985] AC 374 (GCHQ case)**. Sweden created the office of *Justitieombudsman* in 1809, a representative of the people, who would investigate their grievances against the government. In the twentieth century, other Scandinavian countries followed suit, and then many other countries introduced officials with similar functions. The UK appointed its first 'ombudsman' under the **Parliamentary Commissioner Act 1967 (PCA 1967)**.[1]

[1] The introduction summarizes the main issues.

The Parliamentary Commissioner for Administration (PCA) works for Parliament, but is independent of it, being appointed by the Crown on the advice of the government, following consultation with the Chairman of the House of Common's Select Committee on the Parliamentary Commissioner for Administration. The position has some similarity with that of a judge, being held 'during good health and behaviour', meaning that the incumbent cannot just be removed if they displease Parliament or the government. The office of Parliamentary Commissioner and the office of Health Service Commissioner for England are held by the same person, currently Rob Behrens CBE. The PCA employs a staff and has full investigative powers. He can order the production of documents, including government papers, with the exception of Cabinet documents, and witnesses can be summoned and questioned on oath. The PCA is not restricted by the **Official Secrets Acts**, Crown privilege, or public interest immunity, meaning that his investigations are very thorough and he can discover more than an individual, even an MP, could.[2]

[2] Strong evidence in support of the PCA.

Complaints must be made in writing and must be made within 12 months of the complainant becoming aware of the matter about which they wish to complain. No fee is chargeable and there is no need to use a lawyer. First the complaint must be made to the complainant's constituency MP, who then refers it to the PCA. This system was imposed partly because of fears that the PCA would be overwhelmed by the number of complaints, and partly to preserve the traditional method of redress via the constituent's MP. Parliament did not wish to undermine the traditional doctrine of ministerial responsibility. The so-called 'MP filter' has been criticized as making it difficult and confusing to complain, as long ago as the JUSTICE Report, *Our Fettered Ombudsman* (1977), but the PCA does explain its work to MPs and encourage them to refer complaints to them.[3]

[3] The greatest restriction on the PCA.

There are quite a few excluded areas which cannot be investigated by the PCA. These include the police, nationalized industries, parole board, tribunals, Bank of England, Criminal Injuries Compensation Board, government commercial and contractual transactions, the Cabinet Office, and Prime Minister's Office. Some of these, though, have their own complaints mechanism, like the police. Under **s. 5(2) PCA 1967**, the PCA may not investigate a matter that the aggrieved person could have taken to a court or tribunal, unless it is not reasonable for the complainant to use that remedy. This has been interpreted to mean that if a legal remedy would be too cumbersome, slow, or expensive, the PCA may act. So, occasionally there is both a legal and ombudsman remedy as in the case about the withdrawal of television licences: *Congreve v Home Office* **[1976] QB 629**.[4]

[4] Cases are always relevant evidence in a law essay.

Under **s. 5(1) PCA 1967**, the complainant must claim 'to have sustained injustice in consequence of maladministration'. Under **s. 5(5)**, the Commissioner has discretion whether to investigate and how to investigate.

The PCA's decisions are subject to judicial review, but the courts are reluctant to overrule his decisions: *R v Parliamentary Commissioner for Administration ex parte Dyer* **[1994] 1 All ER 375**.

'Maladministration' is not defined in the Act, but the sponsoring minister, Richard Crossman, gave some examples during the passage of the bill: 'bias, neglect, inattention, delay, incompetence, ineptitude, perversity, turpitude, arbitrariness and so on', which is sometimes known as 'the Crossman Catalogue'. It is important to note that the Commissioner is only allowed to investigate the process by which a decision has been taken, not the merits of the actual decision itself. This would seem like a great hindrance to complainants, but the PCA investigates up to 7,000 complaints a year, 34 per cent of which succeed. To take a recent example: in December 2017 the PCA reported that a woman, married to a British citizen had been told that his working abroad would not affect her immigration status, but when she returned from visiting him, she was ordered to leave the country. Following a complaint to the PCA, she was allowed to stay and UK Visas and Immigration agreed to give her £2,000 compensation.[5] The

[5] Up-to-date examples are always useful.

PCA works with government departments, so that they can improve their complaints procedures. The Home Office is the government department most complained against, followed by the Ministry of Justice, Work and Pensions, and HM Revenue and Customs.

The Parliamentary Commissioner is not a court and so cannot award damages. It can make recommendations, which can include the paying of compensation. If a government department declines to accept the recommendations, then the Commissioner can make another report and involve the Parliamentary Select Committee on Public Administration, to which it reports. HM Treasury declined to follow the recommendations in the PCA report, 'Equitable Life: A Decade of Regulatory Failure' of July 2008. The government did not want to pay compensation to thousands of policy holders with Equitable Life, who had lost their pensions. The courts increased the pressure on the government to pay in *R (Equitable Members Action Group) v HM Treasury* **[2009] EWHC 2495 (Admin)**, by stating that the Secretary of State could not reject the PCA report, just because she (at the time, Dame Julie Mellor DBE) favoured her own view, but had to have 'cogent reasons' to do so.[6] The court did not think that the Secretary of State had good reasons to reject a report, which was based on clear evidence and expert advice.

[6] More useful case law.

Ombudsmen have proved a useful device for dealing with complaints, and since 1967 a number of other Commissioners have been appointed. In 1973, a Health Service Commissioner was introduced to deal with complaints about the National Health Service. Since that date, the office of Parliamentary Commissioner for Administration and the office of Health Service Commissioner have been held by the same person. Arguably, the newer office has more power. There is no equivalent of the MP filter, so complaints can come direct and complaints can be not just about maladministration, but can also be about failure to provide a service. The clinical judgement of medical practitioners can also be questioned.[7]

[7] A comparison with a different ombudsman system.

A year later, the **Local Government Act 1974** established Commissioners for Local Administration to deal with complaints about maladministration and failure to provide a service by local councils. Direct access to these Commissioners was introduced in 1989, which led to a large increase in complaints. About 40 per cent of complaints are about housing and 30 per cent about planning permission. Inadequate provision of school places has also been found to be maladministration.

A Legal Services Commissioner was introduced by the **Courts and Legal Services Act 1990**. This ombudsman can deal with complaints about solicitors and barristers, if the relevant professional body fails to deal with the complaint adequately.

Even the EU has its own ombudsman, introduced by the **Treaty on European Union** in 1992. Citizens of the EU may complain direct or through their Member of the European Parliament about maladministration by any institution of the EU.

The **Freedom of Information Act 2000** introduced the Information Commissioner, who may intervene if the government body's internal inquiry into a refusal to provide information does not satisfy a complainant. Interestingly, the 'MP filter' remains for this type of complaint.[8]

[8] A comparison with another different ombudsman system.

A whole host of private-sector bodies have introduced their own ombudsman to deal with complaints. Examples include the Banking Commissioner, the Pensions Commissioner, Investment Commissioner, Insurance Commissioner, and so on. The attraction seems to be the same as the original reasons for establishing the Parliamentary Commissioner. It is cheaper and easier for both sides than going to court. The Parliamentary Commissioner remains practically unique in still insisting on complaints first going to the constituency MP. MPs jealously preserve their right to investigate their electors' complaints, as they see it as an important part of their job, and publicity for their successes probably does not harm their re-election prospects. Successive Prime Ministers have defended the doctrine of ministerial responsibility, because it gives them authority and control over their government. So they do not want to disturb the traditional system either, where MPs bring complaints to ministers about the departments for which those ministers are responsible. One could say that since its inception, the Parliamentary Commissioner for Administration has been a qualified success.[9]

[9] The evidence is weighed and a conclusion reached.

LOOKING FOR EXTRA MARKS?

- Find some up-to-date examples of the ombudsman's work on the PCA website.
- Have a look at the case law on this. There have been many judicial review challenges to the PCA's investigations and recommendations.
- It would also be possible to write an essay that is critical of the PCA, as there are many limitations on its powers.

QUESTION | 2

Because of global warming, it is considered likely that sea levels around the UK coast will rise, making existing sea defences inadequate. The government has decided that, in certain vulnerable areas, no further attempts will be made to protect them from flooding. Instead, a scheme will be established to pay compensation to property owners as their land becomes unusable. The government seeks your advice on how they should administer the compensation claims.

Advise the government.

! CAUTION!

■ This is really an essay disguised as a problem. You need to describe and comment on the tribunal system.

■ The question does have a theoretical part to it. What is the difference between a judicial and an administrative process? Be clear on this.

■ You do need to know about the reforms in the **Tribunals, Courts and Enforcement Act 2007** in some detail.

O DIAGRAM ANSWER PLAN

Identify the issues	■ Identify the legal issues: the differences between a court and a tribunal
Relevant law	■ Outline the relevant law: statutory, general principles and case law, in particular: **Tribunals, Courts and Enforcement Act 2007**; *R (Unison) v Lord Chancellor*; **Constitutional Reform Act 2005**; *Anisminic v Foreign Compensation Commission; R (Cart) v Upper Tribunal*
Apply the law	■ Tribunals are judicial bodies as are courts ■ They are different from courts in that the tribunal specializes in one type of claim, members of the tribunal are experts on that subject, and they are cheaper and more informal than the courts ■ They link into the court system via the Upper Tribunal and Court of Appeal
Conclude	■ A tribunal would be suitable for this type of claim

A SUGGESTED ANSWER

There are three reasons why the government would find it wise to set up some machinery dealing with this matter. First, there are bound to be disputes about eligibility and allegations of mistakes being made in the initial administrative assessment of such claims. Any attempt to have such disputes dealt with by purely administrative machinery is likely to be unpopular, as the public will not believe that it is impartial. Secondly, at a more theoretical level, any scheme should give people an entitlement to compensation if they fulfil the relevant criteria. This makes disputes about entitlement judicial rather than administrative in nature. The doctrine of separation of powers requires such disputes to be dealt with by a judicial body, whether a court or a tribunal. Thirdly, any failure by the government to set up some specific machinery for these disputes will lead to cases coming to the courts. Dissatisfied claimants may seek judicial review, which is available in respect of any decisions made by public bodies under public law, unless specifically excluded by Parliament. Past attempts to prevent claimants challenging compensation decisions in court have failed, as illustrated by *Anisminic v Foreign Compensation Commission* **[1969] 2 AC 147**, where the courts did not allow the words of an Act of Parliament to prevent a claimant challenging an unjust decision. Because the process of judicial review is slow, inconvenient for both parties, and uncertain in its application, the government would be wise to reduce, though not eliminate, its incidence by providing a specialized means of dealing with these claims.[1]

[1] A detailed introduction, highlighting the main issues.

Should these disputes be dealt with by a tribunal or by the ordinary courts? A tribunal, like a court, can be defined as an independent, impartial body with power to make decisions binding on the parties by the application of legal rules to facts established by evidence. The distinction between courts and tribunals lies in terminology rather than substance. The term 'court' is generally used where the body has a general jurisdiction over a wide range of cases, whereas 'tribunal' refers to body with a limited, often very specific jurisdiction. The Committee on Administrative Tribunals and Enquiries (the Franks Committee, Cmnd 218, 1957) investigated the working of tribunals in 1957 and concluded that they were part of the judicial system, not part of the Executive. Just like the courts, they needed to be 'open, impartial and fair', so that the public would accept their decisions and not just think that they were an arm of government.[2]

[2] Conclusion—tribunals are 'judicial'.

If these disputes were to be referred to an ordinary court, they would have to be dealt with by the ordinary judges, whereas a tribunal could be staffed by persons with specialist expertise. Tribunals often consist of three people, a legally qualified chair and two lay members with appropriate qualifications and experience. A tribunal that compensated property owners would probably require someone who could value land, such as a surveyor. A further advantage would be that the members of the tribunal, by specializing in dealing with this particular type of claim, would develop a particular expertise and experience, which should enable them to deal with cases more quickly and efficiently.[3]

[3] An advantage in using tribunals.

The government's main concern in practice is likely to be the relative cost of using a tribunal or a court. If there are only a few cases, the expense of establishing a tribunal will hardly be justified, but if there are many, it will certainly be cheaper than the High Court or County Court, and there is no need for their expensive and elaborate procedure.

The procedures of tribunals are designed to be as simple, straightforward, and informal as possible. The idea is that many applicants will represent themselves, with maybe only an adviser from, say, the Citizens' Advice Bureau or a trade union, to help them. Particularly nowadays, legal aid is rarely available for tribunal proceedings. The government attempted to make some tribunals self-funding, by raising the fees charged by applicants, but this was held to be unlawful, as it prevented access to justice: *R (Unison) v Lord Chancellor* [2017] UKSC 51. So, a newly established tribunal would not be able to charge high fees, but it is likely that the government would not provide legal aid. Legal aid only remains for really sensitive tribunal cases, such as the detention of patients by the Mental Health Review Tribunal and some immigration issues. Unfortunately for some applicants to a tribunal, they may find themselves, unrepresented, facing a lawyer appearing for the other side, particularly where, as in our suggested flooding tribunal, their opponent is the government. That would place the claimant at some disadvantage.[4]

[4] A disadvantage in using tribunals.

To try to redress this imbalance, tribunals take a more active part in the proceedings than the traditional judge, who remains neutral. The procedure may be a little more inquisitorial than the adversarial courts. For example, a tribunal chair might suggest issues that the applicant and the witnesses might like to talk about. The formal rules of evidence will not be applied and witnesses will be encouraged to tell their story in their own words, rather than being tripped up by awkward questioning.[5]

[5] An advantage in using tribunals.

Getting a case to court can be a slow process, which is not ideal for the sometimes relatively minor disputes dealt with by tribunals. One of the main reasons for establishing tribunals in the first place was to ensure that cases were dealt with promptly. However, such is the growth in legal challenges to government decisions that even tribunals experience considerable delays nowadays.

It used to be that each tribunal was different, with its own composition and own procedural rules, although a body called the Council on Tribunals tried to encourage more standardization. A review, *Tribunals for Users—One System, One Service*, reported in 2001 and recommended a tribunal service that was better organized and clearly independent of government departments. This led to the **Tribunals, Courts and Enforcement Act 2007 (TCEA 2007)**. A new, unified tribunal system was created, run as an executive agency of the Ministry of Justice, which clearly signals that these are independent judicial bodies and not just the complaints departments of government ministries. There are two main tribunals, the First-tier Tribunal and the Upper Tribunal. Both are subdivided into 'chambers'. These are, for the First-tier: the General Regulatory Chamber, Health Education and Social Care Chamber, Immigration and Asylum Chamber, the Property Chamber, Social Entitlement Chamber, Tax Chamber, and War Pensions and Armed Forces Compensation Chamber. A tribunal dealing with compensation for land would fit most easily into the Property Chamber. Some important tribunals, such as the Employment Tribunal, remain outside this chambers system, probably because of the sheer number of cases, but it is unlikely that a flood compensation tribunal would be swamped with claims. Appeals could go to the Upper Tribunal, which has a Lands Chamber, as well as an Administrative Appeals Chamber, an Immigration and Asylum Chamber, and a Tax and Chancery Chamber.[6]

[6] A detailed knowledge of the **TCEA 2007** is required.

Section 1 TCEA 2007 extends the guarantee of judicial independence under **s. 3 of the Constitutional Reform Act 2005** to tribunals. A Senior President of Tribunals heads the whole system and reports to the Lord Chancellor. This President is appointed by the Crown on the recommendation of the Lord Chancellor following consultation with senior judges or the Judicial Appointments Commission. He or she holds office during good behaviour and can only be removed from office by an address of both Houses of Parliament, just like the senior judiciary. Tribunal members are also appointed by the Judicial Appointments Commission.

One of the problems with the old tribunal system was that each tribunal had different procedural rules. Under the new system there is far more standardization, at least within each chamber. There is a guarantee of a hearing, unless both of the parties and the tribunal agree that it is not necessary. Written reasons for a decision are also required. Mediation to solve the dispute is also on offer as an alternative to a full-scale hearing.[7]

[7] Another advantage in using tribunals.

There is a proper appeal mechanism. There is a right of appeal on a point of law from the First-tier to the Upper Tribunal. From there, there is further appeal on a point of law to the Court of Appeal, but the Upper Tribunal or Court of Appeal must grant permission and an important principle of law must be involved. Although the Upper Tribunal holds the power of the High Court, it is still possible to judicially review its decisions, if there is an important point of principle or practice: *R (Cart) v Upper Tribunal* [2012] 1 AC 663.

[8] The evidence is reviewed and a conclusion reached.

In conclusion, it appears that the establishment of a tribunal may be the most satisfactory way of dealing with these flooding compensation cases.[8] The reputation of tribunals has been enhanced by the 2007 reforms and a good standard of service and justice is provided. The only problem might be paying for a lawyer, if the complainant feels the need for one, but with the recent restrictions on legal aid, an applicant might well find themselves in the same position, even if this category of complaint was assigned to, say, the County Court or the High Court.

LOOKING FOR EXTRA MARKS?

- You could answer this question in a different way, by concentrating in detail on, say, one example of a tribunal.

- Then you could contrast and compare with our imaginary scenario and assess whether a tribunal would solve the government's problem.

- Tribunal decisions are quite often judicially reviewed, so you could consider more of these cases, not just *R (Cart) v Upper Tribunal* [2012] 1 AC 663.

QUESTION | 3

The (imaginary) Protection of Airfields Act 2010 empowers the Secretary of State to make regulations, in the form of a statutory instrument, 'in order to protect and maintain the security of airfields used by the Royal Air Force'. The Act provides that before drafting such regulations the Secretary of State 'shall consult organisations and groups appearing to him to be representative of those who may be affected by the regulations'. It is further provided that before the regulations become law the draft statutory instrument must be approved by the House of Commons under the affirmative resolution procedure.

In 2012, the Secretary of State for Defence made SI 1688, the RAF Crookwaters Protection Regulations, under which it is an offence, punishable with a maximum fine of £200, for anyone to go within one mile of the perimeter fence of RAF Crookwaters. The Secretary of State only consults the RAF, and the regulations are not laid before the House of Commons.

Alan is a farmer whose fields border RAF Crookwaters. He has been threatened with prosecution if he enters any of his fields that are within a mile of the airfield. He has never heard of these regulations and nor has the National Farmers Union, as the regulations have not yet been published.

Discuss.

CAUTION!

- This is a problem question. Just describing the procedure to make an SI only answers part of the question.
- You need to know how judicial review works to answer this question.
- There are judicial review cases that specifically relate to delegated legislation. You need them to answer this question.

DIAGRAM ANSWER PLAN

Identify the issues	■ Identify the legal issues: Is **Statutory Instrument 1688** legally valid? How can Alan change it?
Relevant law	■ Outline the relevant law: statutory, general principles and case law, in particular: *Council for Civil Service Unions v Minister for the Civil Service; Agricultural, Horticultural and Forestry Training Board v Aylesbury Mushrooms Ltd; DPP v Hutchinson;* **European Convention on Human Rights**
Apply the law	■ Consider whether there is: ■ procedural impropriety; ■ illegality; ■ irrationality—breach of human rights; ■ non-publication; ■ application to the High Court or defence to prosecution in the magistrates' court
Conclude	■ Conclusion—Alan has a good case on all three grounds of judicial review

SUGGESTED ANSWER

It seems that Alan's livelihood is threatened by the RAF Crookwaters Protection Regulations, yet he faces prosecution for allegedly infringing them. It is not possible for him to challenge the fairness and legality of the Protection of Airfields Act 2010. Due to the doctrine of the supremacy of Parliament, it is not possible for the courts to question the legal authority of an Act of Parliament: *Pickin v BRB* [1974] AC 765.

There is nothing, however, to stop Alan seeking to challenge the legal validity of the statutory instrument. This could be done by seeking a judicial review.[1] The Secretary of State for Defence is a government minister and he has made delegated legislation, so the Secretary of State is clearly a public body exercising a public law power. So, according to *R v City Panel on Takeovers and Mergers ex parte Datafin Ltd* [1987] QB 817, the matter is susceptible to judicial review. All types of delegated legislation can be judicially reviewed under the three main grounds of illegality, irrationality, and procedural impropriety: *Council of Civil Service Unions v Minister for the Civil Service* [1985] AC 374 (GCHQ case).[2] For Alan to succeed in a judicial review on the grounds of procedural impropriety, he would need to show that the Secretary of State for Defence has failed to follow the correct procedure when making the RAF Crookwaters Protection Regulations. The correct procedure is laid down in the parent Act, the Protection of Airfields Act 2010, and requires that before making the regulations, the Secretary of State consults those who may be affected by the regulations. Despite the wording 'appearing to him', which seems to allow the Secretary of State to consult whoever he chooses, the courts have held that a minister does not have complete discretion on this matter. The minister must provide information about the draft scheme, an outline of the realistic alternatives, and the reasons for his choice: *R (Moseley) v Haringey LBC* [2014] UKSC 56. In *Agricultural, Horticultural and Forestry Training Board v Aylesbury Mushrooms Ltd* [1972] 1 WLR 190, the court held that, although the minister had a discretion on whom to consult, he must exercise that discretion reasonably and in good faith. In *Aylesbury Mushrooms* just sending a letter and a copy of the draft regulation, which did not arrive, was not proper consultation. Similarly, allowing insufficient time for the consulted body to study the proposals before replying does not amount to genuine consultation: *R v Secretary of State for Social Services ex parte Association of Metropolitan Authorities* [1986] 1 WLR 1. Here, the Secretary of State for Defence has not consulted at all, except for the RAF, who would presumably agree to the regulations anyway. There may be an expectation of consultation, particularly as Alan is so personally affected by the regulations. The courts have certainly held that where there has been a previous practice of consultation it should continue, and not to consult is a breach of natural justice: *Council of Civil Service Unions v Minister for the Civil Service* [1985]

[1] A statutory instrument can be judicially reviewed, but an Act of Parliament cannot.

[2] This paragraph summarizes two major cases on judicial review.

[3] The law is analysed and applied to the facts.

AC 374. If the court agrees that there is a procedural impropriety, then the regulations are *ultra vires* and of no legal effect.[3]

It also seems, from the facts, that the affirmative resolution by the House of Commons has not taken place. This, too, is a statutory requirement, but there is little case law on the matter. Older cases, such as *Bailey v Williamson* **(1873) LR 8 QB 118**, suggest that this might only be a directory requirement and not mandatory, but where an affirmative resolution is required it would seem logical to argue that the resolution must be granted by Parliament, or the regulations will be null and void and of no effect: *R v Department of Health and Social Security, ex parte Camden LBC* **(1986) The Times, 5 March.** This would seem particularly to be the case nowadays, where the courts are very careful to stop the Executive from exceeding the power granted by Parliament. In *R (Alvi) v Secretary of State for the Home Department* **[2012] 1 WLR 2208**, changes to the **Immigration Rules** were not laid before Parliament, as required by the **Immigration Act 1971**, and so were held to be unenforceable.[4]

[4] Modern cases tend to be more authoritative than older ones.

Illegality, as ground of judicial review, means that the court will closely inspect the wording of the delegated legislation and the parent Act and decide whether the delegated legislation goes beyond what is permitted under the Act. In *R (Reilly) v Secretary of State for Work and Pensions* **[2013] UKSC 68**, unpaid work schemes for those in receipt of Jobseeker's Allowance were ruled unlawful because they were not of a 'prescribed description', as required by the **Jobseekers Act 1995**. If the delegated legislation allows the authorities to charge a fee or levy a fine, this must be clearly permitted under the parent Act: *Attorney-General v Wiltshire United Dairies Ltd* **(1921) 37 TLR 884.** So the Secretary of State for Defence will have to show that the Protection of Airfields Act 2010 does allow fines to be imposed for breach of a statutory instrument.[5]

[5] The case law is analysed, applied to the facts, and a conclusion reached.

However, is a complete ban on anyone approaching within a mile of the airfield reasonable? Judicial review is also permitted on the ground that a measure is irrational: *Council of Civil Service Unions v Minister for the Civil Service* **[1985] AC 374**. It is fairly unusual for the courts to overturn delegated legislation on the ground that it is irrational, unless it breaches human rights: *R (Javed) v Home Secretary* **[2001] 3 WLR 323**. In *Javed*, the Home Secretary had the power to make statutory instruments designating safe countries, to which asylum-seekers could be returned. The Court of Appeal disagreed with the Home Secretary's assessment that Pakistan was a safe country. This was despite the fact that Parliament had actually approved the Order, as required, by affirmative resolution. So Alan's case seems stronger, as there has been no parliamentary approval on the facts, so the court would not fear that they were obstructing the wishes of the democratically elected Parliament. In *R (CJ) v Secretary of State for Justice* **[2009] QB 657**, the Court of Appeal overturned a statutory instrument that allowed for the physical restraint of children held in privately run secure training centres, partly on the grounds that **Articles 3 and 8 of the European Convention on Human Rights** had been infringed. There is nothing in the Protection of Airfields Act 2010 that explicitly authorizes the restriction of movement caused by the one-mile exclusion zone, so Alan's **Article 8** right, respect for his home, is likely to be breached.[6]

[6] Human Rights is relevant throughout public law.

So it seems that Alan would have a good case for a successful judicial review of the RAF Crookwaters Protection Regulations on a number of grounds, but he might not want to take this course of action. Judicial review cases are heard in the High Court in London, and this would make it expensive and maybe inconvenient for Alan. He could, instead, just wait to be prosecuted in his local magistrates' court, where he could use the same arguments of procedural impropriety (*Boddington v British Transport Police* **[1998] 2 All ER 203** or illegality (*DPP v Hutchinson* **[1990] 2 AC 783**) in his defence.[7]

[7] This is unusual. Usually a judicial review goes to the High Court.

There is a defence in **s. 3(2) of the Statutory Instruments Act 1946** to a prosecution for breach of a statutory instrument if it has not been published. This would give Alan a defence to a prosecution, as we are told that the RAF Crookwaters Protection Regulations have not been published: *Simmonds v Newell* **[1953] 1 WLR 826**. This defence will not, however, be available if the government has taken reasonable steps to bring the contents of the statutory instrument to the attention of the public or to the persons affected by it, as seen in *R v Sheer Metalcraft* **[1954] 1 QB 586**. As neither Alan, who is directly affected by them, nor the National Farmers Union, who represent other farmers, have heard of these new regulations it would seem that the non-publication defence is available to Alan.[8]

[8] The case law is analysed, applied to the facts, and a conclusion is reached.

So, in conclusion, this is probably Alan's best option: carry on using his fields, wait to be prosecuted, and then argue that the RAF Crookwaters Protection Regulations are *ultra vires* and were not published.[9]

[9] The overall conclusion is that Alan has a very good case.

➕ LOOKING FOR EXTRA MARKS?

- ■ You need to really understand this case law.
- ■ Make sure that you apply it to the facts and give reasoned conclusions.
- ■ This is a specialist area: there are more cases to find.

TAKING THINGS FURTHER

■ Abraham A., 'The ombudsman as part of the UK constitution: a contested role?' (2008) 61 Parliamentary Affairs 206.

A retired ombudsman, Anne Abraham, writes about her experiences in the role and gives some examples of her work. She stresses the differences between how the Parliamentary Commissioner makes her decisions and the way that a court might decide: 'my findings are not confined by strict judicial precedent; instead I reach conclusions that are just and reasonable'.

■ Carnwath R., 'Tribunal justice: a new start' [2009] Public Law 48.

*This article explains the **Tribunals, Courts and Enforcement Act 2007** in some detail. It welcomes the consolidation of tribunals and hopes that it will lead to greater consistency in tribunal decisions, particularly with the Upper Tribunal being able to lay down guidelines.*

■ Craig P., 'Delegated Legislation' in P. Craig (ed.) *Administrative Law* (7th edn, Sweet & Maxwell 2014) ch. 22.

This chapter gives a much more detailed account of the judicial review of delegated legislation than can be found in Public Law/Constitutional and Administrative Law textbooks.

■ The Parliamentary Commissioner maintains a useful website <https://www.ombudsman.org.uk>.

Not only does this explain the powers of the different ombudsmen, but it also includes reports of the Commissioner's investigations. From this source you can always obtain good examples of the ombudsman's work.

■ Richardson G. and Genn H., 'Tribunals in transition: resolution or adjudication?' [2007] Public Law 116.

This article explains how tribunals are different from courts, in that they provide 'proportionate dispute resolution' appropriate to the type and level of claim. Tribunals also provide valuable feedback to government departments on how they can improve their administration. The desirability of tribunals holding oral hearings is also discussed.

■ Sales P. and Allen R., 'The impact of the Human Rights Act 1998 upon subordinate legislation' [2000] Public Law 358.

*The courts are able to overturn delegated legislation if it is contrary to human rights. This article considers one of the early cases, **R v Lord Chancellor, ex parte Lightfoot [2000] QB 597**, which concerned a challenge to the Lord Chancellor raising court fees.*

Online resources

www.oup.com/uk/qanda/

Go online for extra essay and problem questions, a glossary of key terms, online versions of all the answer plans and audio commentary on how selected ones were put together, and a range of podcasts which include advice on exam and coursework technique and advice for other assessment methods.

Coursework

12

First Steps

With coursework, as compared to examinations, you have a lot more time. There is more time to read and think about what the question means, and of course a lot more time to research it. With an examination, all that you can write is what you remember. Having more time can, though, bring with it its own disadvantages: there can be problems with finding out far more than you would ever need to answer the question and then having difficulty deciding what is strictly relevant to the question.

One useful starting point is to check how much the coursework is worth in terms of marks. If it is only 25 per cent of the final mark for a module it is not worth putting in as much time and effort as for a piece of work worth 50 per cent. You have other modules to study as well. I find that students often overreact and put a disproportionate amount of work into an essay that is not worth that many marks, simply because it is the nearest work deadline that they can see.

The next thing to do is to check what you have been doing in lectures and seminars for that module. Lecturers rarely set coursework at random. It will probably relate to something that interests them, such as a new case, a new academic article, a new book, or even their own research. In public law, it could be something like the latest government scandal or ministerial resignation. Pay attention and look back at what you have been doing in lectures and seminars; you will often find the answer to the question there. Commonly, seminars are used to go over problems and essays that are very similar to the questions that you are going to be asked in coursework and examinations.

Clearly, you need to read the question carefully. If it is a problem question, IRAC can be useful. First note down the *legal issues* raised by the problem, then find the *law relevant* to those issues. The key thing, though, is to show how much you actually understand the law in the way that you *apply* it to the facts. Do not be afraid to come to a *conclusion*.

With an essay question, you still have to show that you understand the law, but this time you have to structure this legal evidence into an argument and come to a conclusion.

Research

Read the relevant chapter in the textbook recommended for this particular module. Consider what you have learnt from this, together with your lecture and seminar material. Do you think that you understand this area of law and have some idea what the answer to the question should be? I often find that students read a large number of the standard textbooks as part of their research, but this can be a waste of time. Maybe read the appropriate chapter in, say, two textbooks to get different points of view, but after that all you will be reading is the same basic information explained in slightly different ways. Focus on the question that you have been asked. What do you not understand or need more information on? Concentrate on looking for the answers to those questions. Problem questions often revolve around the meaning of conflicting case law. See what people have written in books and academic articles about those cases and what was said in seminar discussions on those cases. Maybe you will need to read the case for yourself to get a full understanding of it. The same kind of research is relevant to essay questions too, but you may need to look at more academic opinion for those, as the questions tend to require more discussion of the legal issues.

Students sometimes ask me, 'How many academic articles do I need to refer to in this answer?' That is rather a silly question; an essay that refers to ten articles is not automatically better than one that references five. As stated earlier, it all depends on *relevance*. Does the article actually give a solution to, say, two conflicting cases and suggest which one should be followed and why? Does the article support a really useful argument that you want to make in order to answer your essay?

Public law is generally studied in the first year and you may not have much experience of legal research. Some training on this is generally given during Induction, and most law libraries have follow-up sessions in actual classes and online. Use proper law reports and recognized legal journals. A good journal for public law is called *Public Law*, but you will see others mentioned in the further reading in the 'Taking Things Further' section at the end of each chapter of this book. Beware of using the first thing that Google or some other search engine comes up with. The United States dominates the internet, and the law of the United States is similar to that of the UK. So if, say, you looked up 'Separation of powers', you would probably come up with the US version of this constitutional doctrine first, rather than the UK version. Practising lawyers often run their own websites where they update their clients on the latest legal changes. Beware of these sites, as they can have very individualistic views of the law. The same goes for sources like Wikipedia: the article might have been written by a law professor, but it could have been written by someone with their own, odd, opinions on the law. Stick to the established law journals that you see footnoted in your textbooks.

Writing Your Answer

Write as clearly and simply as you can in English that you can understand. There is no need to try to sound like a judge, just because you are writing a law coursework. Avoid words and phrases that seem to sound impressive, if you do not actually understand what they mean. An experienced marker will soon realize that you do not actually know what you are talking about, because the conclusions will not follow from what you have stated previously.

In an examination it is difficult to use quotations, unless you have a very good memory, but it is easy to do in a coursework. Do not overdo it, though. Choose your quotations well. Make sure that they are making an important point in your answer and say it in a way that is better than you could explain it. Lecturers dislike answers that are just a string of quotations linked together by a few of your own words, even in an essay. We want to see what you think and what you understand.

It is easy to make spelling and grammatical mistakes when typing on a computer. Read your work carefully, or get a friend to do so, before submitting. Use computer features like spellcheck. I am always amazed that many students appear not to do this.

When the coursework is set, there will usually be a standard set of instructions. Read them carefully and abide by them. The rules are different in different universities and are not always the same within the same university, for different faculties and departments. Most law departments require you to use a particular referencing system, which is usually OSCOLA, the Oxford Standard for the Citation of Legal Authorities. Do not use another system, because that might lose you marks. If you are unfamiliar with it, your law library will probably make training available, or you can easily find out how this system works online.

You will usually also be required to put a bibliography at the end of your work. This is a list of the sources that you have consulted and used to produce your answer. Follow the instructions on how to compile it closely. For example, you would probably have separate lists for books, academic articles, cases, and statutes.

Coursework instructions usually have a maximum number of words in which you must complete you answer, and there is usually some sort of penalty for exceeding it. Check what the rule is in your own institution and make sure you abide by it. Similarly, there may also be requirements as to the font that you use, for example Times New Roman, double spacing, and the computer format. For instance, at my university, we use online submission and online marking, where the system only accepts Microsoft Word. If the student uses something else they are risking failure, or at least annoying the marker, who has to waste valuable time in converting the file into a readable form.

Usually, your university or college will publish the criteria under which your work will be marked. To give you a typical example, at my own university we look at five aspects of the students' work. First we look for *subject knowledge*—that you know what the law is on the subject that you have been asked about. Then we look at your powers of *analysis*. It is not enough just to write the relevant law down; you must show that you understand it. This is done by applying the law to the facts of a problem and coming up with a reasoned conclusion in a problem, or using the law to support your argument in an essay. If the case law seems to conflict, you will need to decide which case to follow. Next we look at *organization.* Does the student's answer have a logical structure that is easy for the marker to read and follow their argument? We particularly dislike answers that dodge about all over the place; for example, you start talking about the separation of powers, break off to discuss the rule of law, then suddenly return to the separation of powers with no explanation of why you are doing this. *Research* is also important. Has the student gone beyond what they were told in lectures or could be found in the standard textbook and found out things for themselves? As noted earlier, this research has to be relevant to the question asked. Finally, we consider *communication*, which is not just that your English is grammatical and correctly spelt, but more importantly that you can explain what you mean to the reader.

Plagiarism

Different universities have different rules on plagiarism and assessment offences, but the basic idea is the same: when you write your coursework, do not claim someone else's words as your own. I am sure that you would know that it is not permissible to copy the work of another student, but many students commit an assessment offence inadvertently. While doing your research you might find a really good source that helps you answer the question. Obviously, you are not allowed to just cut and paste it, but should make your own notes. Make sure that your words are not too close to the original. If it turns out that you just cannot turn the original source into your own words, then you must credit the source in your footnotes. If the words are the same, then you must put inverted commas around them and treat them as quotation, clearly referenced in the footnotes. It is quite likely that your college or university will have a system, such as Turnitin, where you can check your own work for originality before you hand it in.

Coursework Example

Constitutions are never written down in *their entirety*,[1] so the fact that Britain lacks a *capital-C*[2] Constitution is *far less important*[3] than is often made out.

(A. King, *The British Constitution* (OUP, Oxford 2007))

Discuss this statement in light of the *UK's constitution*[4] and evaluate whether a codified constitution[5] is the best option for constitutional reform in the UK.

1. Most countries have written constitutions and they can be short or lengthy. Some are contained in one document and others in several documents, but none of these written constitutions would tell you everything that you need to know about how that country is governed. There would be details that would only become apparent if you studied the case law and political practices (in the UK we call them conventions) of that country as well.

2. Of course, the United Kingdom has a constitution. It has a well-established and well-organized system of government that has endured for centuries. There are rules, but they are not written down in one formal legal document, that is called The Constitution, with a capital C.

3. King is arguing that, in reality, it does not make much difference whether a constitution is contained in a written document or in multiple sources as in the UK. There are still rules and they are generally obeyed.

4. The question is about the constitution of the UK. Do not get sidetracked into a lengthy explanation of a well-known written system, like the United States. The question is about British arrangements. A brief comparison is all that would be needed.

5. A codified constitution would mean reducing the UK's arrangements to one formal, legal document. Could this be done? Would it be desirable? Who would do it? Would the public accept it?

The question is not just asking you to evaluate the advantages and disadvantages of a written constitution, as against the UK system. It is not just about rigidity against flexibility. You are being to explain how the UK constitution works at present and then you would go on to consider whether a written constitution would be an improvement. A brief comparison can be made between a typical written constitution and UK arrangements.

Many written constitutions start with a statement of the values that are important to that country. The UK has no equivalent, because maybe it is thought that values such as the rule of law and the independence of the judiciary are accepted anyway. Nevertheless, both these core values were given statutory force by the **Constitutional Reform Act 2005**.

Federal constitutions set out how power is shared between central government and the regions. The UK does not have that, but instead has Acts of Parliament such as the **Scotland Act 1989**, the **Government of Wales Act 1998**, and the **Government of Ireland Act 1998**, which go into detail about how the countries of the UK are governed and the powers of the Westminster Parliament over them.

It is common for a country to have basic human rights protected in the constitution. The UK does not have that, but it does have the same kind of protection in the **Human Rights Act 1998**.

Most constitutions contain a defined procedure under which the constitution can be changed. The UK, notoriously, does not have that. Instead, an Act of Parliament can change anything and nothing is permanent. The UK can join the European Community under the **European Communities Act 1972** and leave it using exactly the same procedure, under what will be the European Union (Withdrawal) Act. This flexibility is both a strength and a weakness, meaning the UK can adapt to changing circumstances and changes in public opinion, but also a weakness. Some fear that there is nothing to protect our rights against a determined and ruthless government that controls a majority in Parliament.

Case law is an important source of the UK constitution. The important question of parliamentary supremacy is not enshrined in any constitutional document, but has been decided by the courts in *Pickin v BRB* [1974] AC 765 and *R v Secretary of State for Transport ex parte Factortame* [1991] 1 AC 603. Even in countries with a written constitution, the courts have, ultimately, to decide what that document means, and the UK itself now has a Supreme Court since the **Constitutional Reform Act 2005**.

The glaring omission in the UK constitution is any laws that lay down who is to become Prime Minister, how he or she chooses a government, and exactly what the powers of the government are. It is all governed by convention (custom and practice). These conventions are written down, in various manuals drawn up by civil servants, but still lack any legal force. Could these conventions be codified into law or is it just too political and too complex?

One last little point on research. If you just make an internet search for, say, 'written constitution' you are likely to come up with a lot of US material, which is not directly relevant to this question. Even if you locate UK material, it is most likely to be aimed at students taking a Politics A level. Lawyers see the world a little differently to political scientists and such a source would lack the legal detail that you need. Look up research material through your university library website and make sure that what you find and use is legal material, from recognized books and authors. If in doubt, library staff and the people that teach you can give advice.

Check List

● Read the question carefully.

● Check your lecture and seminar notes.

● Focus your research on the issues raised in the question.

● Use reputable sources.

● Read your work carefully before submission.

● Read the coursework instructions carefully and follow them.

Make sure that you do not plagiarize.

Index

D